ELEMENTS

THE

TEACHER'S ASSISTANT,

OR

Hints and Methods

IN SCHOOL DISCIPLINE AND INSTRUCTION;

BEING

A SERIES OF FAMILIAR LETTERS TO ONE ENTERING UPON THE TEACHER'S WORK.

By CHARLES NORTHEND, A. M.,
AUTHOR OF "THE TEACHER AND PARENT," ETC.

CHICAGO:
GEO. & C. W. SHERWOOD.
1865.

TO THE

HON. JOHN D. PHILBRICK,

LATE SUPERINTENDENT OF COMMON SCHOOLS IN CONNECTICUT,
NOW SUPERINTENDENT OF THE PUBLIC SCHOOLS OF BOSTON,

THIS VOLUME

IS AFFECTIONATELY DEDICATED,

AS A MEMENTO OF MANY FRIENDLY HINTS AND KINDLY AIDS,
RECEIVED DURING NEARLY A SCORE OF YEARS,

BY HIS FELLOW-LABORER AND FRIEND,

The Author.

PREFACE.

THIS volume owes its existence, in part at least, to a request from a friend of the author to furnish advice and hints on one or two points connected with teaching. In complying with the request, it occurred to the writer that a series of familiar letters in reference to school duties and school exercises might prove beneficial to many. The idea has resulted in the preparation of this book, which is presented to the public, and particularly to teachers, with the hope that it may prove both acceptable and useful. The several letters have been written with special regard to the wants and wishes of those whose experience has been quite limited and brief. They embody such views and contain such suggestions as a long and varied experience in teaching has commended to the author as valuable.

It is not offered as a perfect guide to teaching, — nor as a work whose hints and methods may be adopted under all circumstances, — for no teacher should be a servile imitator or an exact copyist. It is hoped, however, that as a suggestive work it may accomplish somewhat for the class for whom it is prepared; and if it shall tend to awaken in the mind of any teacher more exalted views of his calling, or impart more correct ideas of school management and school instruction, it will not have been written in vain.

Such as it is, the author commends it to the kindly consideration of teachers, assuring them that his heart is in full sympathy with them in their efforts to discipline and instruct the youth intrusted to their charge. Engaged in a noble work, may they earnestly and constantly seek for higher and better qualifications, so that they may prove honorable and honored members of a profession of no mean importance.

NEW BRITAIN, CT., June, 1859.

CONTENTS.

LETTER XIII.

LETTER XIV.

LETTER XV.

LETTER XVI.

LETTER XVII.

LETTER XVIII.

LETTER XIX.

LETTER XX.

LETTER XXI.

LETTER XXII.

APPENDIX.

LETTER I.

THE TEACHER'S VOCATION.

My dear Friend: —

I am glad to learn that you have decided to devote yourself to the business of teaching; — glad because it is a noble work, and still more glad because I feel that you possess many traits which tend to fit you for your chosen calling. You ask me for advice on several points, — assuring me that you wish, in every possible way, to increase your qualifications. The very fact that you are desirous of learning what you can in relation to your duties, is one of the surest indications that you will succeed in their performance. It is a lamentable fact, that many persons engage in teaching without any just sense of its importance, — without any natural or acquired fitness for the duties to be performed, and without the least desire to become more enlightened. It has been from such persons that the teacher's profession, and the community, have long and greatly suffered.

It will afford me sincere pleasure if I can be in any degree instrumental in awakening any new ideas in your own mind, or in suggesting, as the result of my own experience and observation, any hints or plans that may be serviceable to you. In my own plain way, I will endeavor to comply with your wishes.

At the very outset, let me urge you well to consider the nature and importance of your contemplated mission. Without a true understanding of the work to be performed, it would be in vain to expect any very favorable results. Some seem to imagine that to "teach school" is merely to spend six hours daily, for six days in the week, in asking questions, hearing answers, and preserving a tolerable degree of stillness in the school-room. No very special results are thought of, no very desirable ones are realized. A certain formal round of daily duties is performed in a very formal and heartless manner. But with you, I am quite sure, it will be different. I am confident that you wish to know your duty, and also to perform it. The faithful teacher's work is a glorious one, both in its nature and in its results. We admire the skill of the artist, who causes the inanimate canvas to exhibit life-like expressions; — and the sculptor who, from the shapeless and lifeless stone, succeeds in producing the image and semblance of the human form and features, is deemed worthy of high honors and rewards. And this is well: we would not have it otherwise. But while we are ready and willing to accord to these the rich meeds of praise, we would not be unmindful of him who moulds and develops the living mind, — and to the faithful and successful teacher we would give the highest rank and the truest and most lasting honors.

To the instructor is committed the tender and impressible mind of childhood. It is his to mould and instruct; to fill with true and useful knowledge; to illumine with the light of science; to purify and ennoble with the full rays of moral truth; to fortify against the errors and the evils which will assail it; to fashion and discipline for wise, virtuous, and useful action, so that he may be made to "honor and glorify" his Creator. To take the child of to-day, in all his ignorance, weakness, and dependence, exposed to evil influences and temptations on every hand, and lead him on through the devious and dangerous paths of childhood and youth, and finally place him upon the battle-field of life a true-hearted and intelligent being, richly furnished with those traits and qualities which will nerve and strengthen him to "act well his part in life," — to do all this is the high privilege and duty of the teacher; and is it not a noble and godlike work?

The lamented Dr. Channing thus expressed his views of the teacher's work: "There is no office higher than that of a teacher of youth, for there is nothing on earth so precious as the mind, soul, and character of the child. No office should be regarded with greater respect. The first minds in a community should be encouraged to assume it. Parents should do all but impoverish themselves to induce such to become the guardians of their children.

They should never have the least anxiety to accumulate property for their children, provided they can place them under influences which will awaken their faculties, inspire them with higher principles, and fit them to bear a manly, useful, and honorable part in the world. No language can express the folly of that economy, which, to leave a fortune to a child, starves his intellect and impoverishes his heart."

It is said that, when "Jupiter offered the prize of immortality to him who was most useful to mankind, the court of Olympus was crowded with competitors. The warrior boasted of his patriotism, but Jupiter thundered; the rich man boasted of his munificence, and Jupiter showed him a widow's mite; the pontiff held up the keys of heaven, and Jupiter pushed the doors wide open; the painter boasted of his power to give life to inanimate canvas, and Jupiter breathed aloud in derision; the orator boasted of his power to sway a nation with his voice, and Jupiter marshalled the obedient hosts of heaven with a nod; the poet spoke of his power to move even the gods by praise, Jupiter blushed; the musician claimed to practice the only human science that had been transported to heaven, Jupiter hesitated; when, seeing a venerable man looking with intense interest upon the group of competitors, but presenting no claim, — 'What art thou?' said the benignant monarch. 'Only a spectator,' said the gray-headed sage; — 'all these were once my pupils.' '*Crown* him! *crown* him!' said Jupiter; 'crown the faithful *Teacher* with immortality, and make room for him at my right hand.'"

Some one has well said, "The real object of education is to give children resources that will endure as long as life endures; habits that time will ameliorate, not destroy; occupations that will render sickness tolerable, solitude pleasant, age venerable, life more dignified and useful, and death less terrible." Let this not be forgotten, but let it be your daily aim and effort to impress upon the minds of your pupils a true appreciation of the object of life. Teach them by precept and by example how to live, so that they may wisely act their parts in this life, and by a timely and faithful performance of present duties, be constantly and surely ripening for a higher and nobler existence when time shall be no more.

I might enlarge upon the magnitude and importance of the teacher's mission, but it may not be necessary. You have, I doubt not, well considered the subject; or if you have not already done so, I beg that you will, for unskilled or rude hands should never touch "the strings of that harp whose vibrations are felt in eternity."

In my next letter I will call your attention to some of the more prominent characteristics essential to the truly successful teacher, without which the highest literary talent and culture will prove of but little worth. With the earnest and sincere hope that you will prayerfully ponder the nature of the responsibilities you are about to assume, I remain, as ever,

Your sincere friend,

C.

LETTER II.

PATIENCE. — EXEMPLARY CHARACTER AND DEPORTMENT.

My dear Friend: —

In my last I promised to write in relation to some of the characteristics essential to insure success on the part of the teacher. You evidently wish to know what you shall *be*, as well as *what* and *how* you shall *do*, in your chosen work. I need not speak of the necessity of accurate and varied literary attainments. It would be absurd for any one to undertake to teach that which he does not himself understand. A thorough and exact comprehension of all the branches to be taught is of the utmost importance; and if an extensive stock of miscellaneous knowledge can be added to this, so much the better. As is the fountain, so will be the streams flowing therefrom. Without dwelling upon this point, I will proceed to designate some of the traits which you should carefully and earnestly cultivate.

Patience. — If there is any work that calls loudly and constantly for the exercise of patience, it is that of the teacher. His labors are arduous under the most favoring and favorable circumstances. The good seed sown in the school-room during the day may be rooted up by other hands in the evening, and, more than this, tares may be sown instead. Day after day will you, my friend, be called upon to *undo* and do over; and at times your very soul will almost sink within you, and exhausted Patience be ready to take her flight. But let her depart not. In the expressive words of another,* "Lift up your eyes to the fields; they are white already to harvest. With the blessing of Providence go to the field of your slow, patient work. That slowness of the result may be the bitterest element in the discipline.

> 'To-morrow! and to-morrow! and to-morrow!
> Creeps in this petty pace from day to day,
> To the last syllable of recorded time.'

Be content to wait for Him with whom *ages* are *days*, and in due season ye shall reap if ye faint not. Go out with faith, with supplication. Ye shall come again in the jubilee and sabbath of the resurrection, rejoicing."

You have an earnest desire to improve, to become a successful and accomplished teacher. This is well. Without such desire you would be an unworthy member of your chosen profession. The great thing is to have your desire controlled and modified by existing circumstances. You wish to have your pupils advance rapidly, — to excel. In your haste to have them do so, be not guilty of

* Professor Huntington.

overtasking them, or of losing your patience. Do not forget that children often arrive at results by slow and tedious processes. Refer to your own experience. It has been only by many long years of patient effort that you have gained a mastery of the subjects you undertake to teach. To you they are now perfectly familiar, but remember that this familiarity was not gained in a day. It was only by long-continued effort that you acquired your present stock of knowledge. As you consider this, you will learn to be patient with the little ones, even when they seem to be intolerably dull and stupid. Be very careful to discriminate between what may be called dulness and that which is really nothing but heedlessness. Never censure a pupil for failing, for the fiftieth time, to comprehend a principle, if you are sure he is doing as well as he can. Some minds are exceedingly sluggish in their movements, — some naturally so, and others by mere habit. The former should be dealt with in the most kindly and alluring manner, while a degree of sharpness may not only be allowable, but desirable, towards the latter. I have somewhere seen an anecdote illustrating my point in part. A certain teacher had among her pupils a little Irish lad. She was endeavoring to teach him the letters of the alphabet; but, though an honest boy, he seemed to learn very slowly. After much patient effort, she succeeded in making him acquainted with all the letters but *p* and *q*. The little fellow could not comprehend these, and, time and again, confounded the two. In an unguarded moment, after he had repeatedly miscalled the letters, the teacher shook him, somewhat passionately, and said, in tones of censure, "Patrick, will you *never* learn your letters?" With most imploring looks and words, — such as that teacher will never forget, — he said, "*Plase, ma'am, if you will say them a little asier I'll thry.*" Can you not learn a lesson from this? For wilful or heedless inattention, it may be right to reprove severely; but never for natural dulness.

Every hour of almost every day will your patience be taxed, and sometimes, seemingly, beyond the power of endurance. But be not overcome. Let patience have her perfect work, and be not guilty of word, feeling, or act that will need to be repented of. Recollect that young minds develop slowly, and ever be willing to follow nature's teachings, — "First the blade, then the ear, after that the full corn in the ear."

EXEMPLARY CHARACTER AND DEPORTMENT. — To one whose demeanor and habits are so correct as I know yours to be, it may seem out of place to say a word under this head. And yet, if possible, I would have you feel still more strongly the extent and force of *example* in teaching. No one can exist in and for himself alone. Parts of a mighty whole, each individual contributes to its general character and condition, and no individual part can deviate or become remiss without causing the whole to suffer.

You know how prone the young are to be affected

by the habits and views of their parents; and though the effect of good and faithful parental instruction and example may, for a time, appear lost or inefficacious, yet it is as sure to become visible and forceful, at some future time, as good seed, seasonably and properly sown, is sure to germinate and bear fruit, it may be an hundred-fold. And if a parent's influence is so great, it must be admitted that the teacher, who for so large a portion of time stands "in the place of parents" for a whole neighborhood, must exert a power, for good or ill, which is truly immense. Do not, my dear friend, forget that you are daily surrounded by young and tender minds, whose very being is intimately connected with yours. A hasty word or act, an unkind look, a slight deviation from the true path of duty, an improper or careless expression, or any kind or degree of unfaithfulness, on your part, may be instrumental of never-ending consequences, even

> "As a pebble in the streamlet scant
> Has turned the course of many a river, —
> A dew-drop on the infant plant
> Has warped the giant oak for ever."

As you enter the school-room, ever bear in mind that the eyes of your pupils are upon you to notice every movement, — their ears open to catch every tone of your voice. They spend more of their time, daily, under your immediate influence and discipline, than they do under the immediate care and observation of their parents. To a great extent you will be their exemplar. Earnestly strive to be a worthy one. Let all your movements, expressions of countenance, tones of voice, your entire bearing, be such as they may safely imitate. What you are, such, in a good degree, they will become. If you are fretful, unkind, impatient, they will partake of the same spirit. Said a little girl, "Mother, I try to love my teacher, but she gets angry in school and speaks unpleasantly, and then I find it very hard to love her. Is it right to get angry, mother?" How natural, and yet how significant. If teachers could only be unseen listeners to the conversation of a group of their young pupils, how many useful lessons might they learn!

As your pupils return to their several homes at night, you will not be forgotten. At the tea-table or by the fireside, (must I say *stove*-side?) your sayings and doings will form prominent topics for discussion; and the happiness of the little ones will be increased or diminished just in proportion to your fidelity and kindness, or to your deficiencies. "I love to go to school, now," said little Genevra, "for my new teacher is so kind and so pleasant that she makes me feel happy. She is not cross, as my other teacher was, but she always tries to help me. I love her dearly, and I mean to do all I can to please her." These words were uttered to Mary, who attended another school having a very different teacher. As she heard the remarks, she looked sad, and said, "I wish I could go to your school, for my teacher is hardly ever pleasant to us, and she never speaks kind words, and there 's no use in trying to please her."

Do not forget, my friend, that your pupils are but children. Some of them may possess many unlovely and unlovable traits, but most of them possess loving and confiding hearts. They may have been mismanaged, neglected, or even abused, at home, and their uninviting traits may result from such wrong treatment. Win them to you by kindly words; bind them to you by kindly acts, and then you may control and guide them at will. You will often find generous hearts and noble impulses in the breasts of those whose exterior is coarse and unattractive. Let your own example be correct, and it will be potent for good. I would thus sum up my advice under this head: *Speak as you would have your pupils speak; appear as you would have them appear; act as you would have them act; be what you would have them be.*

Your sincere friend,

C.

LETTER III.

CHEERFULNESS. — LOVE FOR THE WORK. — INDIVIDUALITY. — ACCOUNTABILITY.

My dear Friend: —

I do not propose to write at length of the several characteristics essential to give success to the teacher. The model teacher should possess, in an eminent degree, every good trait, and exercise every virtue. You say you cannot hope to become a *model* teacher; but you certainly must hope to become a successful one. You should, then, aim to become just what we claim for the model teacher. Place your mark high, have it right, and constantly strive to reach it. I shall in this letter speak of other qualities, which I consider as peculiarly important, on account of their direct bearing upon your pupils; though they are all implied in the "summing up" of my last letter.

Cheerfulness. — This is all-important. Your school is a miniature world; you are the controlling power, and your pupils are the subjects. Let them see that you desire nothing so much as to do them good, and if you really possess this desire, it will make you happy and cheerful. As your pupils assemble in the school-room, greet them with the light of a cheerful countenance. You are really the sun of the little community, and you should let no clouds come between you and them, unless such as may be caused by their follies or indiscretions. It was my lot for a short time to be a pupil in a school whose teacher was one of those morose, uncongenial, capricious spirits, which cast a shadow on all around them. Nothing pleased her; nothing that we, her pupils, could do would cause her to assume a cheerful look; she never smiled, but often scowled; she never spoke pleasantly to us, but always in tones of censure and petulance. We lost all respect for her; or, rather, we never gained any; and our chief delight was in annoying her, that we might see the clouds thicken upon her brow. Our associations connected with that school are all sad and unpleasant. My next experience was under a teacher whose cheerfulness was prominent and constant. She loved her pupils, and they loved her, and it was their highest wish to merit her approval, to gain her smiles. To me the school-room was pleasant, and to this day all my memories of the school and teacher are pleasant, and ever will be. As you hope to succeed, let me urge you studiously and constantly to cultivate a spirit of genial cheerfulness. It will be promotive both of health and happiness; it will also greatly increase your influence and usefulness. "*As is the teacher, so will be the school.*"

LOVE FOR THE WORK. — I should have placed this as the very first requisite for a successful teacher. One may saw wood, and do it well, and yet have no love for the work. The same may be true of many kinds of labor; but it is not true of teaching. A person cannot, in the highest, best, and broadest sense, become a successful teacher, unless he possesses a love for the business, and feels a true and lively interest in the welfare of those under his care. He may perform a certain daily routine of duties, but they will lack vigor and efficiency, and the results will not be what they should be. I would say to you, my friend, at the very outset, that, if you have no taste for the work before you, do not engage in it; it will prove anything but pleasant work. I have sometimes heard teachers say that they *hated* the very name of school; and I have always thought that such must prove *hateful* teachers. I know you too well to anticipate any such feelings on your part. I know you view the whole subject in a true light, and that you have a heart alive to the business in which you are to engage. You may, and doubtless you will, have days when school, and all its exercises, will appear burdensome; and at times you may almost despond. Ill-health, impure atmosphere, or over-work, may so affect your nervous system as to cause you to be unfit for any work. But this will only be an exception to your general feeling; and whenever you do thus feel, study carefully to repress sadness, and still wear the genial countenance. If possible, never yield to feelings of despondency.

A true and sincere love for your vocation will enkindle within you that spirit of earnest and well-directed enthusiasm which will tend to give point and success to your efforts. By *enthusiasm* I would not be misunderstood. I do not mean that reckless zeal which is not according to knowledge, nor that over-active feeling which leads to *over*-doing a work, and *un*-doing the workman; but by it I mean an earnest and devoted application to the accomplishment of a work, — the combined result of a just appreciation of its importance, and a determined will to perform it in the most prompt and efficient manner, — a zeal tempered by prudence and modified by knowledge. With such an enthusiasm you will not only be sure to succeed in your own efforts, but you will also awaken an interest and secure a cheerful co-operation on the part of your pupils and their parents; and without such interest and aid, you will fail to accomplish all that you may desire, and all that you ought to accomplish.

INDIVIDUALITY. — No two persons are precisely alike in their views or actions. There may be many points of close resemblance, but there will be shades of difference more or less striking. While you should ever be watchful to learn from others, you should never seek to attain results in precisely the same way that you have seen them secured by others. The first point with you should be to know fully and clearly what you wish to gain; and the second is to use all suitable appliances for the accomplishment of the end in view, — only using them in your own way. You may receive hints and suggestions which you may safely and profitably incorporate into your own stock of knowledge, and modify by your own peculiar views. Have a way of your own, only be sure that it is a good way. Study to improve upon others, and be sure to improve upon yourself day by day. Some teachers are perfectly content to walk in a beaten track. For them it is sufficient to know that *their* teacher "did or said so and so." They are willing to follow in the old paths, without even admitting that better ones may be found, or old ones improved. They resemble the man who could not be induced to do anything differently from what he had seen his father do it before him. The father had uniformly been to the mill over a very hilly and circuitous road; simply, perhaps, because it was the only one open. After his death a new road was made, whereby half the distance was saved, and the hills were avoided. But the son could never be induced to travel the new road, and when urged for a reason, he said, "My father always went the old road, and I shall do the same, for I know it is the best." This was an excess of regard for parental example; and even the old sire, if he could return to earth, would probably laugh at the son's stupidity. But no less blind and stupid are some teachers. They tread in beaten tracks, without seeking for better ones, or without walking in them if they see them. Be not, my friend, a stereotyped teacher.

Old methods may be greatly improved; new and better ones may be devised. If you would make your school interesting, be constantly seeking for new modes for illustrating principles and interesting your pupils, and be sure that they bear the impress of your own mind and thoughts.

ACCOUNTABILITY. — Do not for a single day forget that you are but an agent of the Great Teacher, and that he will call you to give a strict account of your stewardship. Daily go to Him for the instruction you daily need. He can teach you how to teach; he can aid you in all your efforts. Confide in him, and he will not disappoint you. You need much of his spirit to guide and sustain you; much of his wisdom to assist you in your important work. Let your whole life, and all your words and deeds, be strongly marked by a truly religious spirit, — and in every way do what you can to induce your pupils to feel that they are accountable to their Creator for all their deportment, and for the manner in which they attend to all their duties. By your own pure and Christian character, lure them to love and practise all that is "lovely and of good report," — and in blessing them you will be doubly blessed.

I might proceed to name other traits and characteristics which should be cultivated by every good teacher, but it will not be necessary. I shall have occasion to allude to some of them in connection with the exercises of the school-room. You already feel, I dare say, that I have set a very high mark for your attainment. But, my friend, is it too high? Your chosen work is one of the most important and ennobling ever intrusted to mortal, and it calls for high qualifications, for excellent and lovely traits, for hearts and intellects well disciplined and ready for every good effort. Unless you *are* what you would have your pupils *become*, you can hardly hope to make them what you *ought* to be, but *are* not. In your daily walk and conversation you must ever exemplify the correctness and the value of the views and principles you would inculcate in the hearts of your pupils. Strive, therefore, to be unto them as a "living epistle," plain and full of instruction.

I have somewhere read that Napoleon, on his departure for Belgium, thought it prudent to guard with extra care against the dangers which threatened, having all Europe leagued against him. He therefore sent for a skilful and accomplished workman, between whom and himself the following conversation was held.

Napoleon. "Do you consider yourself competent to make a coat of mail of such texture and strength that no weapon whatever can penetrate it?"

Workman. "I think I am."

Napoleon. "I wish you to make one with as little delay as possible, and for the same you shall receive eighteen thousand francs."

Workman. "The article shall be ready in the shortest possible time, — and the compensation you offer will well reward me for doing the work thoroughly."

The work was speedily performed, and on an appointed day the artificer took it to the palace. Bonaparte examined it with much care, and then requested the maker to put the armor on. The man obeyed, when the Emperor, taking a pistol, said, "We shall now see if this work is of the texture and strength you promised." He then fired at his breast and at his back, time and again; but the armor proved sure proof against such attacks. Next a long fowling-piece was used, but still the armor proved effectual, and its maker stood unmoved, full of confidence in the completeness of his work.

The delighted Emperor, instead of paying the stipulated price, presented the man with a check for thirty-six thousand francs, saying, "You are one of the few men whose *works* verify their *words*."

And so let teachers go forth to their daily labors with armor bright, and sure proof against the attacks of the ignorant and self-conceited, — ever bearing clear proof that they are thoroughly furnished for the great work before them, — and they will not only receive their stipulated reward, but a twofold greater, from the consciousness of having labored faithfully and successfully; and ever will their well-rendered efforts be held in grateful remembrance in the hearts of those whom they have led to right thought and action.

I know full well, my friend, under what discouraging circumstances you, and other teachers, may be called to labor; — opposed, perhaps, by the parents for whose children you toil; unencouraged by the wealthy, uncheered by the community; scantily remunerated; your best acts and motives, it may be, grossly perverted and misrepresented; and others, perchance, reaping where you have sown, — so far as the eye of the world is concerned. But be of good cheer. "In due season ye shall reap, if ye faint not." Though clouds and darkness do sometimes gather around you, and others appear to enter in upon, and, as it were, eat the fruits of your patient and skilful culture, yet despair not, despond not; in due time all will come right, and justice will be done.

It is recorded of an ancient king of Egypt, — one of the Ptolemies, — that he employed a celebrated architect to construct a magnificent light-house for the safety of shipping, and ordered an inscription in favor of himself to be engraved on a conspicuous part. The architect, though inwardly coveting the honor of such a record for himself, felt obliged to comply with the king's order; but he made the inscription on a plaster resembling stone, but of a perishable substance. After the lapse of years this crumbled away, and the next generation saw another inscription, recording the name, not of the king, but of the architect, which had been secretly engraved on the durable stone, beneath the perishable covering, — a lasting memorial of the skill of him who planned and reared the colossal structure.

And thus, my friend, will it be with you, if you are faithful to your high trust. The lines which you are daily writing, and the impressions which you are hourly making, upon the young and susceptible minds and hearts of those under your training, will grow broader and deeper and brighter through all coming time, and the impress of your heart and moulding hand will become distinctly visible, and stand as an ineffaceable honor to your fidelity and skill. Then go patiently and hopefully to your noble work, and in the time of the true harvest you shall come again rejoicing, "bringing your sheaves with you."

Having said thus much of the greatness of the work before you, — having spoken of some of the requisites for success, and hinted at the rich rewards which will crown well-rendered efforts, — I shall in my next go with you to the field of your labors, and endeavor to give you such advice, and offer such hints, as may seem pertinent. For a more detailed enumeration and consideration of the qualities essential in a successful teacher, you are referred to "The Teacher and Parent," and Page's "Theory and Practice of Teaching," two educational works published by A. S. Barnes and Company, New York.

Your sincere friend,

C.

LETTER IV.

MEANS OF PROFESSIONAL IMPROVEMENT.

My dear Friend:—

You ask me what you shall do in order to keep alive your interest in your chosen work, and at the same time better qualify yourself for your highly important and responsible duties. The mere fact of your asking for this information greatly raises you in my estimation, and confirms me in the belief that you will prove an honor and an ornament to your profession. Most cheerfully will I advise you on this subject; and though I may not say all that might be said, I hope I may offer a few hints that will prove beneficial.

We need no arguments to prove that "knowledge is power"; it is an admitted fact in all departments. To know how to do a work just as it should be done, is worth far more than to know how to do it in a way barely passable. They who really excel in ability to communicate information, or perform a work, will have an influence that will be truly valuable. Knowledge is wealth,— it is capital. An eminent lawyer was once consulted by a farmer in relation to a question of great importance to the latter. The question was promptly and correctly answered by the simple monosyllable, "No." "How much am I to pay you for your opinion?" said the farmer. "Ten dollars," said the counsellor. "What! ten dollars for just saying *No?*" "Ah, but you must consider that I spent much time and money, and studied many books, that I might know when to say *No.*"

The negro, who prided himself on his peculiar skill as a butcher, realized that knowledge was wealth. Pompey was employed to dress a calf, — a work which he performed with remarkable skill and despatch, and for which he demanded two dollars, — just double the common price. His employer remonstrated, saying that one dollar was the usual price. "But," said Pompey, "I charge one dollar for the work, and one dollar for *the know how!*" True knowledge and practical skill will prove a mine of power and wealth to the teacher; and truly wise is every one who seeks for and improves all means for professional knowledge and growth. I will name a few of the more prominent.

Read Works on Education. — The number of works bearing directly upon the teacher's mission is, I am sorry to say, very small, and most of them of very recent origin. I would recommend that you get access to as many as possible, and from time to time, as opportunity offers and means allow, add such works to your own professional library. It may seem novel to you to have me speak of the teacher's "professional library"; and I am very sure that the idea would seem quite marvellous to many who have devoted years to the business of instruction. But can you see any good reason why a teacher should not have a library? Can you not, indeed, think of many reasons why he should have one? What would be thought of a clergyman, physician, or lawyer, who should enter upon his professional career without first securing a collection of books for general reference as bearing upon the interests of his peculiar calling? Would such a one be likely to succeed, or would he long possess any of that *esprit de corps* which ought to characterize him? The man who wishes to excel as a sculptor will make any sacrifice to learn what has been said and written in relation to his favorite work. The artist who would prove a workman of no mean repute will practise any amount of self-denial in order to become the possessor of volumes treating upon his employment. And if they who work on inanimate material are thus interested to increase their knowledge and skill, should they not be equally so who are called upon to fashion and develop that living material which will exist throughout the endless ages of eternity? It is sad, indeed, to reflect that so many engage in teaching who never manifest the least interest in reading. My mind now recurs to the case of two young ladies who engaged in school-keeping under very favorable circumstances. They possessed many desirable qualifications, and, at first, manifested an active interest in their work. But it was only ephemeral. Though they had access to numerous books, they were never known to peruse them. As a consequence, and a very natural one, their interest soon waned. Their first term was quite successful, because the novelty of the work enlisted their interest and efforts. They soon, however, fell into a lifeless, formal routine, and became inefficient teachers, and were obliged to abandon the work. Had they devoted a small portion of their leisure time to the perusal of educational works, their interest would have been kept alive, their zeal increased, and their minds enlarged and improved.

I rejoice that with you it is otherwise. I have long known the interest with which you have perused all works calculated to increase your general and professional knowledge. You, I know, need no urging on this point, and I will simply offer one or two hints in relation to your reading, for it is quite as important *how* you read as it is *what* you read. One person will read a valuable and instructive volume, and be none the wiser, — gaining no new ideas, receiving no impressions or hints tending to confirm or modify his former views. He reads carelessly, — without reflection and without profit. Another person will arise from the perusal of the same book with enlarged views, better plans, nobler aspirations, stronger purposes.

In reading, therefore, endeavor to obtain something from every work which will make you wiser, stronger, better. To this end, read with a discriminating, reflecting mind. So far as the book you read is sound and valuable, aim to make its general spirit and views your own; but do not often adopt as your own a *specific* plan or course, until you have adjusted it to existing circumstances, and proved its general adaptedness to your situation and wants. A course that may have been entirely successful with another, under peculiar circumstances, may result quite differently with you, under circumstances varying but slightly. In order that any scheme may produce precisely the same results, in different times and places, it is not only essential that its operation be under circumstances exactly similar, but also that the moving or operating power be precisely the same; — and such a combination seldom occurs. One man, for example, may use some improved machine with entire satisfaction, and delight in its operation and success, while another may use the same machine and pronounce it worthless, — simply because in the manner of using, or of some unusual or peculiar circumstances in relation to his work, he did not understand the principles of the machine sufficiently to adjust it to existing peculiarities. Some slight change in the adjustment of some part of the machine, or in its mode of operation, might have insured its entire success. In all your reading, aim to grasp general views and principles, rather than to adopt some precise and undeviating plan; for your success as a teacher will depend much upon your own efforts, and upon your power to impart a degree of individuality to whatever plans you may introduce.

I would not be understood to advise that all your reading be exclusively of a professional bearing. Far otherwise. Let it partake of variety, but never of that trashy and ephemeral literature which is scattered broadcast over the land. Read well-written books, that you may increase your knowledge and discipline your mind. A well-conducted newspaper may be the medium of much valuable information. I would recommend that you habitually read some good newspaper, with a view to keeping enlightened in regard to the prominent and important events and movements of the day. Read, that you may learn; and learn, that you may teach. Every new attainment, every wise acquisition, every practical idea gained by you, will give you influence over those under your care. Therefore read, that you may increase your ability to instruct and discipline others. Knowledge is power, — and a power that every teacher should gain in the highest possible degree.

Be sure to subscribe for, and read, at least one educational periodical. Teachers' Journals are a modern aid. All the monthlies, now in existence, supported by teachers, and devoted to the great interests of popular education, have been established within twelve years, and most of them within five or six years. It is one of the most hopeful signs of the times, that teachers themselves are assuming the editorial charge of these journals, thus insuring a practical character. The monthly receipt and perusal of a well-conducted work of this nature will prove beneficial to you. It will bind you to your profession; it will enlighten your mind; it will cheer your heart; it will prove a valuable medium of intercommunication; and in various ways it will be of service. If you have not sufficient interest in your work to induce you to become a subscriber to one of these works, the sooner you abandon the business of teaching, the better it will be for the community. And what I say to you, I would say to all others. *No person should assume the employment of teaching, who does not possess enough of professional interest to cause him to aid in the support of a periodical devoted to the great interests of his profession.*

Be a Contributor to some Educational Journal.— Do this for your own good, and for the good of your profession, ever bearing in mind, that whatever you do for your own improvement will result in the good of your profession, and also that whatever you do for the elevation of your chosen calling will result in your personal benefit. The whole is made up of parts, and the several parts are affected by the general tone and condition of the whole. Do you say you cannot write,—that you have not accustomed yourself to it? Then I say you should commence and ascertain whether your inability is *real* or only *imaginary*. My impression is, that you will find no difficulties that you will be unable to overcome,—no obstacles that will prove insurmountable to a determined spirit. It will do you good to cope with difficulties,—strengthen you to conquer them. You owe it to yourself, no less than to your profession, to contribute something from your own mind and experience for the benefit of those laboring in the same cause.

Visit the Schools of Others. — If you will do this with the right spirit, with a desire to learn, it will prove highly beneficial. The watchful and discriminating teacher will gain some useful information, or receive some valuable hint, from every school he may visit. He will profit not only from the excellences, but also from the errors, of others. It may be that errors exist in your school which have been formed so gradually as to have escaped your notice. Your attention is so constantly directed to two particulars, — governing and instructing, — that it would not be strange if some deviations should escape your watchful eye. When you visit the school of another, circumstances are different; you go as a spectator; you feel that you have no direct interest in the exercises; you have nothing to do but to listen and observe. You will, very naturally, look for excellences and for defects; and from both you may derive profit, — only do not be captious. It may be that you will, on your return, see your own school in a different light, and learn that you are not above criticism. Perhaps I may be better understood by relating an instance in my own experience; for I have visited many schools, and always with profit. I once visited the school of a friend, who enjoyed a good reputation as a successful teacher. The school was, in the main, a good one, but I noticed one habit in the spelling exercise which I considered a bad one. As the pupils spelled, they neither pronounced the syllables as they spelled them, nor the words when finished. It appeared to me a little singular, that so good a teacher should allow so bad a habit to prevail; and I rather congratulated myself that I was more careful in my own practice. To my surprise, when I next conducted a spelling exercise in my own school, I found that precisely the same error, in kind, if not in degree, existed somewhat on the part of my pupils. From it I learned a useful lesson. Visits to the schools of others may impart many such lessons.

Teachers' Meetings and Teachers' Institutes.— You will find it much for your interest and professional improvement to attend teachers' meetings as often as opportunity offers. It will do you good to meet with those who are engaged in a similar employment,—with those who can sympathize with you. Such meetings, whether large or small, may be productive of much good. Two or three farmers, mechanics, ministers, or physicians would probably derive mutual benefit from an hour's interview and familiar talk. So, particularly, will it be with teachers; they will either obtain new information, or become more fully confirmed in some old plan or method. But, if you would be truly benefited by teachers' conventions, you must exercise the right spirit; and while you aim to receive some benefit and some new information from every such gathering, do not expect that everything you may hear will be new to you, or precisely adapted to your individual circumstances or wants. Remember, it is only "little by little" that we make advancement or growth in knowledge, whether of a general or professional nature. Strive constantly and in every suitable way to honor and elevate your chosen profession, by adding to your own personal qualifications, and thus proving yourself an intelligent, earnest, and active member. Seek to honor your calling, and not live and act as though you expected that to honor and exalt you.

Be Diligent in Professional Labors.—If it is ever true in the material world, that "the hand of the diligent maketh rich," it is emphatically true that the mind is enriched and expanded by diligent application and wholesome exercise. As bodily sloth and idleness lead to destitution, want, and misery, so mental inactivity will lead to mental imbecility and unproductiveness. Persevering diligence in any work will overcome obstacles apparently insurmountable, and secure the accomplishment of the most important and surprising results. It is this that has subdued the wilderness, and caused it to be a fruitful garden. It is this that has furrowed our country with railroads, and made a safe track for the iron horse from the ocean to the mountains and the valleys beyond. It is this that has sprinkled all over the surface of our country beautiful and thriving villages. It is this that has brought the luxuries of distant lands and the wealth of the ocean to contribute to our comfort and welfare. The sails that whiten our oceans; the steamers that plough our waters; the locomotives that sweep through our towns and villages, rushing through mountains, over plains, and across rivers and ravines; the wires that extend through the land and under the ocean,—all declare the power of well-directed diligence. Be ever active in all the operations and concerns pertaining to your profession, ever laboring to improve yourself, to aid others, to promote the great interests of education, and the fruits of your efforts will be neither few nor small.

Your sincere friend,

C.

LETTER V.

SCHOOL DISCIPLINE AND SCHOOL MANAGEMENT.

MY DEAR FRIEND: —

WITH your permission, I will now accompany you to the school-room, the scene of your labors, and speak with you freely and plainly of some of the duties to be performed. I shall endeavor to tell you *what* to do, and *how* to do; or, in other words, I will aim to give you such hints as the results of my own experience and observation have impressed upon my own mind as important and pertinent.

I know full well the anxiety with which you anticipate your labors. I know the feelings which will fill your breast, as for the first time you occupy the teacher's desk and assume the teacher's duties. *What shall I do? How shall I do? When shall I do?* are questions that will often arise in your mind; and you must be prepared to answer them, and that, often, without much opportunity for reflection, with none for consultation. But if you have duly considered the nature of your office, and studiously cultivated the qualities I have named, you have done much to prepare yourself for the efficient discharge of incumbent duties. Give the first moments of every morning to devotional exercises, and thus let your pupils see that you and they have one common friend and counsellor in "Our Father who art in heaven."

Discipline is the first item that will claim your attention, and it is an all-important item. It lies at the very foundation of your labors; and unless you have right views and adopt right measures on this point, it will be useless for you to hope for success in teaching, — for without good discipline, there can be no truly successful teaching. One may be able to *govern* a school, and yet not competent to *teach* the same; but he cannot, in the highest and truest sense, teach a school, unless he can also govern it. True teaching implies correct discipline. But I will proceed to give a few hints, which, I hope, may be of some service to you.

Try to cause your Pupils to feel that you are their Friend. — Let all your plans and arrangements be made with reference to their good. As, for the first time, you enter the school-room, do it with a cheerful look, which shall indicate that your heart is in your work. Let your words be but the kindly expression of friendly feelings and good intentions; let no frowns cloud your brow, even though all may not, at the outset, be just as you might wish. Perfect discipline cannot be established in a day; yet you must aim to secure it gradually and surely. But you may ask what I mean by *perfect* discipline. I say, negatively, that

I do not consider it to consist in rigid and upright positions, in exact and undeviating movements, nor in constrained looks. I say, positively, that I consider that school in a good state of discipline, in which the pupils attend to all their duties, perform all their movements, and regard all the requirements of the school with cheerful alacrity, and with an evident and constant desire to co-operate with the teacher, — studiously and pleasantly refraining from every act, which may tend to disturb the teacher or the school. "I consider a school judiciously governed, where order prevails; where the strictest sense of propriety is manifested by the pupils towards the teacher, and towards each other; where they are all busily employed in the appropriate duties of the school-room, and where they seem to be under the influence of the teacher as a leader, but not as a driver. There is some difference of opinion as to the degree of stillness possible or desirable in a school. We all agree, however, that, for a still school, all *unnecessary* noise must be excluded." * The best governed are they who seem to be ungoverned, save by the inward desire to do right; and the best disciplinarians are they who govern without seeming to govern. If you would succeed, do not attempt to govern too much. Lure your pupils into the right path by kindly words and friendly acts, and thus gain that perfect control over them which you should possess, and at the

* Admiral Stone.

same time have their obedience cheerful and prompt. In this way you will govern them, and at the same time they will not feel that they are governed.

Govern Yourself. — Unless you can exercise a good degree of self-government, you can hardly expect to govern others. It will not always be an easy matter for you to exhibit perfect self-control, but you must aim to do so; and if you can succeed in so governing your own feelings as never to appear angry or annoyed, you will find no difficulty in governing your pupils. I do not mean that you should be entirely regardless of the conduct of your pupils, but merely that you should not allow their errors to cause you to lose your patience, by exhibiting some sudden ebullition of passion. You know how ready some people are to take offence and show anger. A faithful servant, who had long borne the abusive words of a petulant master, finally said to him that he could no longer tolerate his captiousness, and that he was determined to leave his service. "But, Peter," said the relenting master, — "Peter, you know I mean no harm, and that I am no sooner mad than pleased again." "Very true, master," replied Peter; "but I also know that you are no sooner pleased than mad again." So it is with some teachers, — they allow feelings and expressions of anger and pleasantness to follow each other in such ludicrously rapid succession, as entirely to impair their influence.

Let Circumstances modify your Views of Order and your Plans to secure it. — Some teachers form a certain view of discipline, and certain undeviating plans for securing it. With them, attending circumstances have no influence. The act is judged in and of itself, entirely independent of the motives which led to it. This, of course, is wrong. If you would govern successfully and justly, study all the particulars bearing upon a transgression. Sometimes an act, in itself wrong, may be divested of all actual wrong when the circumstances are duly considered. In a certain school, for example, a boy of very orderly deportment and studious habits, suddenly whistled, — no less to his own astonishment than that of his teacher. He was called out by his teacher and asked if he had whistled, when the frightened lad exclaimed, with all honesty of heart, "*No, Sir, I did n't whistle, — it whistled itself!*" The little fellow had been so intent on his lessons, and perhaps so delighted at overcoming some difficulty, that, forgetful alike of time, place, or circumstances, he expressed his joy by an unpremeditated whistle. That the school was interrupted was obvious, but no sensible teacher would deal with such a lad as he would with a culprit. Precisely such an interruption would seldom occur; and yet pupils will often be guilty of deviations in *act*, when the *motives* are entirely correct. Study, therefore, very carefully to discriminate between a wilful wrong and an unintentional error. Only a bad pupil can be guilty of the former, while a very good one may be of the latter.

Then there are other circumstances which you must always take into consideration. There are certain days in the experience of every teacher which are hard days; there is something in the atmosphere, in the state of the teacher's health, or some incidental circumstances, which have an unfavorable influence upon the state of feeling, and consequently upon the apparent order of the school. You will, undoubtedly, sometimes enter your school-room in a depressed state of mind, and everything may seem to you "out of place," — nothing meeting your expectations, — and yet you may not be able to tell precisely *what* or *where* the trouble is. Under such circumstances, do not make a bad matter worse, by manifesting an unduly sensitive spirit. The Rev. Dr. Huntington, of Harvard College, gives the following excellent advice in relation to such days: —

"It is in the experience of most teachers, I presume, that on certain days, as if, through some subtle and untraceable malignity in the air, the school-room seems to have fallen under the control of a secret fiend of disorder. There is nothing apparent to account for this epidemic perversity; all the ordinary rules of the place are in full recognition; the exercises tramp on in the accustomed succession; the parties are arranged as usual. There are the pupils coming from their several breakfasts, bringing both their identity and individuality; no apostasy nor special accession to depravity over night has revolutionized their natures; no comparing out of doors has banded them into a league of rebellion. Yet the demoniacal possession of irritability has somehow crept into the room, and taken unconditional lease of the premises. You would think it was there before the first visible arrival. The ordinary laws of unity have been suddenly bewitched; the whole school is one organized obstruction; the scholars are half-unconscious incarnations of disintegration and contraposition, — inverted divisors engaged in universal self-multiplication.

"How is such a state of things to be met? not, I think you will agree, by direct issue; not *point blank.* You may tighten your discipline, but that will not blind the volatile essence of confusion. You may ply the usual energies of your administration, but resistance is abnormal. You may flog, but every blow uncovers the needle-points of fresh stings. You may protest and supplicate, and scold and argue, inveigh and insist; the demon is not exorcised, nor even hit, but is only distributed through fifty fretty and fidgety forms. You will encounter the mischief successfully when you encounter it indirectly. What is wanted is, not a stricter sovereignty, but a new spirit. The enemy is not to be confronted, but diverted. That audible rustle through the room comes of a moral snarl, and no harder study, no closer physical confinement, no intellectual dexterity, will disentangle it. Half your purpose is defeated if the scholars even find out that you are worried. The angel of peace must descend so softly, that his coming shall not be known, save as the benediction of his presence spreads order, like a smile of light, through the place.

"If a sudden, skilful change of the ordinary arrangements and exercises of the day takes the scholars, as it were, off their feet; if an unexpected narrative, or a fresh lecture on an unfamiliar theme, kept ready for such an emergency, is sprung upon their good-will; if a sudden resolving of the body into a volunteer corps of huntsmen on the search of some etymological research, the genealogy of a custom, or the pedigree of an epithet, surprises them into an involuntary interest; or, in a younger company, if music is made the Orphean minister of taming savage dispositions again, — then your oblique and unconscious tuition has wrought the very charm that was wanted; the room is ventilated of its restless contagion, and the furies are fled.

"Or if, as is more than probable, the disorder was in the teacher himself; if the petulance of the school all took its origin in the disobedience of some morbid mood in the master's own mind or body, and only ran over, by sympathetic transmission, upon the benches, so that he saw it first in its reflection there, — of what use to assail the insubordination by a second charge out of the same temper? His only remedy is to fall back on the settled spiritual laws of his own being. He must try to escape out of the special disturbance into the general harmony; he must retreat, in this emergency of temptation, into those resources of character, principle, affection, provided by the previous and normal disposition of his soul. This he will achieve by some such process as that just specified, displacing the ground of a direct and annoying conflict by new scenery, and rather leaping up out of the battle with foes so mean, than staying to fight it out on their level."

Talk not Much nor Loud.—It is a very common error with young teachers, that they talk too much and too loud;—and wherever you meet with one of these garrulous and noisy teachers, you will be sure to find a disorderly school. Let us call at two schools and notice the difference. Here is a school of fifty pupils, kept by Miss Matilda Captious Fussy. The pupils are nearly all untidy in appearance, inattentive to lessons, disorderly, and noisy,—whispering, and constantly asking unimportant questions of the teacher. It is a sort of "Bedlam let loose." But the children are not the only actors. Listen to the teacher, who, in loud and petulant tones, and in rapid succession, thus speaks:—"We must have less noise, scholars." "You are the worst set of children I ever saw." "Sit down, Mary." "John, did n't I tell you not to whisper?" "Susan, what are you doing?" "Sarah, I 've told you twenty times that you must n't look out of the window, and you don't mind one word I say." "Peter, did n't I tell you I should punish you if you did that again? You 'll get it by and by."

"Thomas, what are you out of your seat for? If you don't mind better, I shall punish you." And thus it continues through the livelong day,—the teacher noisily issuing meaningless orders and threats, the pupils hearing them as they would the whistling winds. The room is unswept and in disorder; the teacher, slovenly in her personal appearance, and unlovely and forbidding in look and manner. All is discord,—no discipline, no true teaching, no good habits. The classes are called upon to recite without any seeming regard to time or manner; they move noisily and dilatorily to the recitation seat; their answers are indistinct, and mostly imperfect; there is an entire heartlessness and heedlessness about every exercise and every effort.

We have stopped long enough,—let us pass along. Here we come to another school, of the same size, kept by Miss Mary Cheerful Method. We enter, and are greeted by the teacher's pleasant smile, welcoming us to her school. She looks pleasant and happy; the room is a model of neatness and order; the pupils look cheerful and industrious, each earnestly attending to his lessons. There is no whispering, no useless questioning, no confusion; cheerful quietness and well-ordered industry meet the eye on every hand. The teacher says but little, and every remark is made in that pleasant and subdued tone which is sure to be heard and regarded. "The still, small voice" is readily heard, and promptly obeyed. When the classes are called to recite, they take their places with alacrity, and without noise; and, as we might expect, the lessons are well committed and distinctly recited. It is in all respects a pleasant and well-managed school. And do you not see that, in each school, as was the teacher, so were the pupils? I trust you have learned a useful lesson from these visits, and that you will not hesitate which of the two to take as your model.

Insist on Prompt and Exact Obedience. — Be sure that your requirements are reasonable and right, and be satisfied with nothing short of an implicit, exact, and prompt obedience to them. There is an unwilling, hesitating compliance with requisitions, which is little better than downright disobedience. Indeed, it is often more annoying, from the difficulty of meeting it. Positive and direct refusal to obey orders you know how to deal with; but a half-way obedience, a sort of attempt on the part of the pupil to compromise by meeting you half-way, may sometimes seem to lack definiteness. But really it has point, and must be met without hesitation. Early, then, impress upon the minds of your pupils that you make no difference between a direct act of disobedience and obedience reluctantly and sullenly rendered. In some instances the latter may be the worse.

Never promise what you cannot perform, nor that which it would be Wrong or Unreasonable to perform. — Very young pupils will readily discover if you err in this particular. My earliest school recollections are of a "schoolma'am" who often threatened to cut off the ears of her pupils if they did not sit still. Child as I was, I thought she meant what she said, and with almost breathless stillness I kept my eye for the entire first day upon a pair of scissors which were attached to her person. I regarded them as the ear-shortening implements; but after having heard the threat many times repeated, and finding my own ears were uninjured, I concluded that the teacher was uttering idle threats, and I lost the little respect for her that I first had. It was soon ascertained that she said what she did not mean, and then her words fell upon our ears as the idle wind. Ever, my friend, study to verify your words by your acts; but also study to have both words and acts consistent and right.

Never threaten to inflict a certain Mode or Kind of Punishment for certain anticipated Offences.— Different pupils require different inducements and different methods of discipline. As no two cases of transgression will be precisely similar in all their bearings and particulars, so it will not be wise to have a uniform and undeviating kind of punishment for all offenders. Aim always to deal justly and impartially; and in order that you may so deal, you must carefully weigh all circumstances, and studiously adapt your discipline, both in kind and in degree, to the peculiar temperament and disposition of each offender. Let the motives and circumstances attending the error always be duly considered. The following incident, which I find in the Canada Journal of Education, will illustrate my position, and, I hope, convey a good lesson: —

"My third attempt at teaching was in the parish of St. A——. I had been engaged in the ordinary duties of a common school for three or four weeks, when, on a very cold, bright day in January, a group of children arrived rather earlier than the usual hour. They were all new pupils, except one. This was pleasing to me. As the children approached, I heard sobbing, and, upon opening the door, the lad, who had previously attended the school, entered, leading by the hand a little girl about seven years of age. Her eyes were large and blue; her hair, which was too fair to be golden, hung around her neck in little ringlets; her cheeks were red, though partly concealed by frozen tears. Her complexion was very fair, and her features of an exquisite mould. Her cousin Charley was about twelve years of age, tall, and well formed; his eyes were black, and his hair was of the same color; his features were regular, and indicative of intellect as well as benevolence. As Charley entered, he said, 'This is Cousin Polly; she 's coming to school, please, Sir, and I told her you would n't whip her if she is a good girl; she 's crying with the cold.' With a little chafing of the cold hands and the aid of a good fire, Polly soon became comfortable. After this introduction, Polly, Charley, and myself were very good friends. Time glided pleasantly away, for we had a most agreeable assemblage of youth, and, with one exception, a pleasant school-room. The exception was, that two of our windows overlooked the highway, and thus presented a temptation to violate the rules of discipline, by looking at passers-by in the time of study. The winter was nearly over, and I had become strongly attached to Charley and his Cousin Polly, for they were docile and obedient,—seemingly full of affection for me, as well as for each other. I had never had occasion to chastise either of them during the term. Indeed, I had to be cautious about addressing them in a hasty or excited manner, else they would have burst into tears immediately; and to *speak harshly* to them would be worse than *whipping* some children. One day, near the close of the term, I had been disturbed several times, while attending to classes, by the scholars seated near the windows already mentioned. They would rise from their seats to look at any vehicle which might be passing. After having been interrupted three times while engaged with a class, and as often remonstrating, I lost patience, and said that I should ferule the first one who arose again to look out of the windows. After this announcement all were very quiet for some time; but before I had concluded the exercises of my class, I heard a noise, and, looking around, I saw Polly standing upon a desk and stretching past two girls to look out of the window. Here was a case. All eyes were upon me. I had described a certain kind of punishment, and pledged my word to inflict it upon the one who should violate the rule. Polly was the last one I deemed likely to be guilty, and the last person in the school whom I wished to punish in such a manner; but now my only alternative was to break my word or to punish Polly. I called her to me; she came, with tears in her eyes. I asked her why she wept? She said she was sorry she had forgotten the rule; that she had been told, by Fanny Conly, that her papa and mamma were coming for her in the sleigh, and she got up to look out without thinking. I replied, 'If I should not punish you as I said, I should be guilty of an untruth, which is sinful, and I should lose your respect and esteem, as well as that of your schoolmates.' 'O dear! yes, you must punish me,' said Polly, with a gush of tears; 'but I feel so bad *because I cannot help it now!*' and she held out her hand. I stood up as though I was about to inflict the expected blows, when Charley approached, and, holding out his hand, said, 'Please, master, whip me, and don't whip Polly.' From this little incident I learned two things about discipline; — first, never to pledge myself to any particular kind of punishment beforehand; and second, that children often shed tears because their error is past recall, or, in the words of Polly, 'because they cannot help it,' when their teachers suppose they are crying for fear of the punishment."

A particular Offence does not necessarily call for the Infliction of a Specific Punishment. — All attendant and palliating circumstances should always be taken into account in deciding upon disciplinary measures. A course that would be highly salutary in one case, under one set of circumstances, would prove far otherwise in another case, and under other circumstances. A certain physician once had as a patient an Englishman. The disease was fever. He allowed the patient to partake frequently of chicken-broth. The sick man was restored to health; and the doctor wrote in his note-book, "Chicken-broth is good in case of fever." His next patient was a Frenchman, and the disease fever. He was allowed to partake of chicken-broth, and died. The next memorandum in the note-book was, "Though chicken-broth is good for an Englishman in case of fever, it will kill a Frenchman." From this learn a lesson in school discipline, and study to adapt the mode of discipline to existing circumstances and peculiarities, and never feel that the same means will always produce the same results.

Be Calm and Self-possessed.—Never give your pupils opportunity to feel that they can annoy you; for if they find you over-sensitive, they will ever be on the alert to do things which will vex you. But while you aim to let them see that you control yourself, be sure also to have them feel that you shall control them; and that any degree of impropriety on their part will be duly considered, even though it may not receive immediate notice. It is well, occasionally, to let certain errors and deviations pass, apparently unnoticed, during the day, and be taken into consideration at a quiet hour after school. In a calm but firm manner, call the offenders to an account, administering such punishment, or censure, as may seem necessary. Do not forget that there is a right time, place, and manner in which to say things, and never administer reproof or punishment, when either the erring or yourself are in a state of undue excitement.

Cultivate Habits of Neatness and Courtesy as Helps to Discipline. — If you can so inspire a boy with feelings of self-respect, that he will always enter the school-room with his person and apparel in a neat and cleanly condition, you will at the same time create within him a desire to regard the rules of the school. If, in addition to this, you can induce him to regard the rules of propriety and courtesy in his manner and conversation with others, you may be quite sure all else will be right. A courteous pupil will, almost as a matter of course, be an obedient and attentive pupil.

You ask, if you must ever resort to corporal punishment. In answer to this, I wish I might feel warranted in saying that it is never necessary. I hope the time may come when it will be wholly unnecessary; but I do not believe that time has yet arrived. I will advise, however, that you inflict corporal punishment as seldom as possible. Make it your "strange work"; and when you resort to it, do it in such manner and in such spirit as will make the right impression. In most cases, I would recommend that corporal punishment be inflicted in private; and yet there will be cases, in which the greatest good of all concerned will require that the punishment be inflicted in the presence of the whole school. If a boy wilfully sets at defiance all wholesome authority, and says or does things, in the presence of the whole school, for the purpose of showing that "he will do as he pleases," the better way will be to administer to him the well-deserved punishment in the presence of all who have witnessed the transgression. If, however, you can secure the entire co-operation of the parents, you will not often have any trouble of a disciplinary nature. I do not hesitate to express the belief, that, when all teachers shall be thoroughly qualified for their high duties, and enter upon their discharge with an earnest fidelity, and when all parents shall be faithful in training their children in "the way in which they should go," we shall hear no complaints touching school discipline. But until that good time shall come, the best of teachers may sometimes find it necessary to resort to corporal punishment; but ordinarily, the higher the qualifications of the instructor, the less frequently will such occasions occur.

Never scold.—If whipping is objectionable, scolding is much more so. If you speak in fretful and fault-finding tones, your pupils will soon lose all respect for you, and they will, to a great extent, partake of your spirit. In such things "like produces like." Mild and pleasant tones, combined with a firm and determined manner, will, in most cases, secure the desired result. I once visited a school, kept by an accomplished lady, who ever exercised the most perfect control over her feelings and actions. A class was called upon to read. In it was one of those disagreeable things, — an obstinate, mulish girl. When her turn to read came, she paid no regard to it. The teacher very pleasantly, but firmly, said, "Read, Mary." But, in stubborn expression, Mary's countenance said, "I won't." The teacher, with the utmost composure, said, "You may continue standing, and the next may read." Wishing to know the teacher's plan in such cases, I asked what she intended to do in this instance. Her reply was, "I shall let my patience have its perfect work, and Miss Obstinate will not be allowed to leave her place, until she has performed her part; and as the regular time has passed, she must await my time, — which will not be until every other lesson has received attention, and the faithful pupils have been dismissed." Throughout the whole, the teacher was as calm as a summer's day; and I doubt not that the plan adopted was entirely effectual.

Never attempt to frighten a Pupil into Obedience. — Temporary subjection may be secured by terror, but it will not be a true submission. The motive is a wrong one, and the result will have no permanency. Let it be ever your aim to exercise that influence over your pupils, which will lead them to respect authority, and to do right, from high and honorable motives. So far as possible, train them to habits of self-control and self-discipline. Be to the little ones under your care an example of all that is "lovely and of good report," ever manifesting on your part a willing and prompt obedience to the higher powers. Remember always that

> "The mind, impressible and soft, with ease
> Imbibes and copies that she hears and sees,
> And through life's labyrinth holds fast the clew
> That first instruction gives her, false or true."

How important is it, then, not only that right impressions be made on tender minds, but also that they be made in the right way and in the true spirit. It is unquestionably true, that parents and teachers do wrong by being over-exacting and over-rigid in their treatment of the young, not making sufficient allowance for youthful feelings and buoyancy of spirit. Is there not a lesson prettily expressed in the following lines?

> "He who checks a child with terror,
> Stops its play, and stills its song,
> Not alone commits an error,
> But a great and moral wrong.
>
> "Give it play, and never fear it, —
> Active life is no defect;
> Never, never *break* its spirit, —
> *Curb* it only to direct.
>
> "Would you stop the flowing river,
> Thinking it would cease to flow?
> Onward it must flow for ever, —
> Better teach it *where* to go."

Have System in Relation to all your Exercises.— This will be of great service to you in the discipline of your school. Have a time for every recitation, and have every recitation at its proper time. See that every pupil has work enough to occupy his time, and do all you can to make every lesson interesting by illustrations of your own. Pupils love order and system; and, if they are kept properly employed, they will not be tempted to wrong action. Nothing is more true, than that a certain noted "busybody" has always some mischief for idle hands to do; and if you fail to give your pupils useful work, he will give them that which will greatly increase your labors and trials.

Aim earnestly and constantly to make all the Exercises of the School-room pleasant and attractive. — Many a child has acquired an unconquerable dislike of school, and all that pertains to it, on account of the forbidding manner or injudicious chiding of unwise teachers; — even as some children, from ill-treatment at home, have been brought to regard any place as more attractive than home. On this point let me quote from the quaint language of Roger Ascham, in "The Schoolmaster," published in London, in 1571.

"Yet some will say that children of nature love pastime, and mislike learning, because in their kind one is easy and pleasant, the other hard and wearisome. Which is an opinion not so true as some men ween. For the matter lieth not so much in the disposition of them that be young, as in the order and manner of bringing up by them that be old; nor yet in the difference of learning and pastime. For beat a child if he dance not well, and cherish him though he learn not well, ye shall have him unwilling to go to dance, and glad to go to his book; knock him always when he draweth his shaft ill, and favor him again though he fault at his book, ye shall have him very loth to be in the field, and very willing to go to school. . . . . . And one example, whether love or fear doth work more in a child for virtue and learning, I will gladly report, which may be heard with some pleasure, and followed with more profit.

"Before I went into Germany, I came to Brodegate in Leicestershire, to take my leave of that noble Lady Jane Grey, to whom I was exceeding much beholden. Her parents, the Duke and Duchess, with all the household, gentlemen and gentlewomen, were hunting in the park. I found her in her room, reading 'Phædo Platonis,' in Greek, and that with as much delight as some gentlemen would read a merry tale in Boccace. After salutation and duty done, with some other talk, I asked her why she would lose such pastime in the park? Smiling, she answered me: 'I wist, all their sport in the park is but a shadow to that pleasure that I find in Plato. Alas! good folk, they never felt what true pleasure meant.' 'And how came you, madam,' quoth I, 'to this deep knowledge of pleasure? And what did chiefly allure you unto it, seeing not many women, but very few men, have attained thereunto?' 'I will tell you,' quoth she, 'and tell you a truth which perchance ye will marvel at. One of the greatest benefits that God ever gave me is, that he sent me so sharp and severe parents, and so gentle a schoolmaster. For when I am in presence of either father or mother, whether I speak, keep silence, sit, stand or go, eat, drink, be merry or sad, be playing, sewing, dancing, or doing anything else, I must do it, as it were, in such weight, measure, and number, even so perfectly as God made the world; or else I am so sharply taunted, so cruelly threatened, yea presently sometimes with pinches, nips, and bobs, and other ways (which I will not name for the honor I bear them) so without measure misordered, that I think myself in hell, till time come that I must go to Mr. Elmer, who teacheth me so gently, so pleasantly, with such fair allurements to learning, that I think all the time nothing while I am with him. And when I am called from him, I fall on weeping, because whatsoever I do else but learning is full of grief, trouble, fear, and whole misliking unto me. And thus my book hath been so much my pleasure, and bringeth daily to me more pleasure and more, that in respect of it all other pleasures, in very deed, be but trifles and troubles unto me.'"

May not parents and teachers draw a lesson from this? Some poet thus happily portrays the power of gentleness and kindness:—

"Wouldst thou a wanderer reclaim,
A wild and restless spirit tame,—

Check the warm flow of youthful blood,
And lead an erring one to God?
Pause; — if thy spirit's wrath be stirred,
Speak not to him a bitter word; —
Speak not, — that bitter word may be
The stamp that seals his destiny.

"If widely he hath gone astray,
And dark excess has marked his way,
'T is pitiful, but yet beware; —
Reform must come from kindly care.
Forbid thy parting lips to move
But in the gentle tones of love.
Though sadly his young heart hath erred,
Speak not to him a bitter word.

"The lowering frown he will not bear;
The venomed chiding will not hear;
The ardent spirit will not brook
The stinging tooth of sharp rebuke.
Thou wouldst not goad the restless steed,
To calm his fire or check his speed;
Then let no angry tones be heard, —
Speak not to him a bitter word.

"Deal kindly with him; make him feel
Your heart yearns deeply for his weal;
Tell him the perils of the way
Wherein his devious footsteps stray:
So shalt thou win him, — call him back
From pleasure's smooth, seductive track;
And warnings, thou hast mildly given,
May guide the wanderer to Heaven."

I have written you a long letter on the subject of discipline. The great importance which I attach to the subject must be my apology, and if you can gain a single new and correct view of this part of your duty, I shall not have written in vain, nor will you have read in vain. I have given you some specific directions, which I trust may be of service to you. In closing, let me urge upon your attention, briefly, the importance of making your school pleasant and attractive, by doing all you can to make its lessons clear and interesting. Let the pupils see that they have in you a sincere friend, — one who loves them, and wishes to do them good. Study carefully their natures, dispositions, temperaments, peculiarities. Learn what you can of their home-training and "out-of-school" influences. Gain their confidence and secure their affection, and you may guide and control them at will. So far as circumstances will allow, cultivate the acquaintance of the parents of your pupils, and strive to inspire them with the feeling that you are but a co-worker in the business of educating their children. If possible, cause them to feel that they can aid you, and that you have a just claim upon their cheerful and constant support and co-operation. With the good-will and kindly feelings of your pupils, and with the approving efforts of their parents, you will be strong for any work; without these, you will labor at great disadvantage, and your best intentions and plans will fail of accomplishing what you may desire to accomplish. As parental co-operation is so essential to your highest success in disciplining and instructing your pupils, I shall in my next give you a few hints in relation to your intercourse and duties with the parents of your pupils.

Your sincere friend,

C.

LETTER VI.

PARENTAL CO-OPERATION.

MY DEAR FRIEND: —

THE highest success of a school demands the united and harmonious efforts of three parties, — teachers, parents, and pupils. If you would hope to be truly successful in your labors, you must not only have your own efforts earnest and judicious, but you must also be able to devise means and adopt plans that will awaken and keep alive an interest on the part of your pupils and their parents. It will be my purpose in this letter to offer a few hints in this direction.

You must manifest a deep Interest in your Daily Work. — If you possess true enthusiasm, and labor with a will and with efficiency, your pupils will not only imbibe of your spirit, but they will impart it to their parents. Let your scholars see that you feel a sincere interest in their studies, and that you take delight in their improvement; let them see that you are ever devising plans which will tend to make their lessons more intelligible, pleasant, and profitable, and they will be quickened in their efforts and cheered in their labors. "O mother!" said a little girl, "I never loved to go to school till this term, and now I don't wish to be absent a single hour." "But why," said the mother, "are you so much interested in your school now?" "Because, mother, our teacher is so pleasant and kind. She always helps us all she can, and then she makes our lessons so interesting! All the scholars love her, and mean to do all they can to please her."

Do not, however, imagine that you are to gain the good-will of your pupils by an easy discipline, or by making the lessons so simple as to excuse them from all mental effort. Pupils like order and study, if secured in the right way. Teach them how to study. Cause them to feel that they have a special interest in the prosperity of the school, and that they will be doing the most for themselves, when they are earnestly co-operating with you, by yielding an implicit, prompt, and cheerful compliance with your wishes and requirements. Make them realize that your success and theirs are identical. If they thus feel an interest in you and your efforts, they will not be slow in making their feelings known at the home fireside.

Visit the Homes of your Pupils.—Do this for your own good, and for the good of your pupils and their parents. These visits, made in the right spirit, will give you an influence that will be worth much to you, and prove valuable in all your labors.

Make them occasions for learning all you can in relation to the home influences, which conspire to aid you, or to counteract your efforts. It will tend to please both parents and children to see that you have an interest in them, that extends beyond the limits of the school-room. But that these visits may prove mutually pleasant and profitable, manifest a friendly and cheerful spirit. Exhibit no angular points of character or disposition, but strive to make your conversation both agreeable and beneficial. If questioned by the parents, in reference to the progress or deportment of their children, give prudent and truthful answers. Do not feel that you must utter words of commendation. If there has been a lack of interest in study, or a disregard of the rules of the school, or misconduct of any kind, say so in the spirit of kindness and courtesy, and ask for friendly sympathy and co-operation in your endeavors to secure better results. Unless you, and the parents for whom you labor, can have a singleness of purpose and union of action, you cannot reasonably expect to accomplish much that will be desirable. Diversity of opinion, alienation of feeling, or want of harmony in action, between teachers and parents, will in results prove like "a house divided against itself." In all your acts and words study for those things which make for peace, and be strictly careful not to utter words or perform acts that will "need to be repented of"; and be not over-sensitive in regard to what may be said *to* you, or *of* you. So live, so act, and so speak, that words of scandal or misrepresentation will fall powerless. If parents prefer charges, or utter complaints, listen in a spirit of candor, — answer in a spirit of frankness and conciliation. Many teachers prove their own worst enemies by uttering unguarded words, or doing imprudent or injudicious things. They should strive to be "as wise as serpents, but harmless as doves."

Invite the Parents to visit the School. — This is of the greatest importance. It will do them good, encourage you, and stimulate and cheer your pupils. But when such visits are made, put on no unusual airs, make no attempt at parade or show, neither strive to exhibit the proficiency of your best scholars. Go on with the regular exercises of the school, and if some pupils fail to answer, or make blunders, do not make a bad matter worse, by saying, — as I have often heard teachers say, — "I never knew my scholars do so badly before; they always do the worst when I have company!" You know that some of them will fall short of the true standard every time they recite, and there is no reason why you should be unwilling to have visitors see your school as it actually is. Let them see that you daily meet with difficulties, and that, with all your efforts, you cannot always get the results you may desire. If you attempt anything unusual when company is present, you will fail to meet your own expectations, or those of your visitors, and perhaps forfeit the confidence and respect of your pupils.

Special Occasions.

You will find some advantages in having special seasons for the visits of parents, in addition to those of an every-day nature. Exercises in declamation, composition, etc. possess more than ordinary interest for visitors. Let such exercises be given occasionally, not as evidence of proficiency in daily studies, but as an exhibition of what can be done in particular departments. Examinations and exhibitions are both important auxiliaries in school matters; but the latter should in no instance be made a substitute for the former.

I will not enlarge on the subject of this letter, but will merely urge that you make every suitable effort to awaken and increase parental interest in school matters, ever bearing in mind, that, "*As is the teacher, so will be the school*"; and, "*As are the parents, so will be both teacher and pupils.*"

Your sincere friend,

C.

LETTER VII.

MORAL INSTRUCTION.

MY DEAR FRIEND:—

YOU seem anxious to know what you can do for the moral culture of your pupils, and how you may influence them to act from pure and honorable motives. This is all-important, and I rejoice that your thoughts incline in this direction. It has too often been the case in our schools, that the intellect has been cared for, while the moral nature has been neglected. But if it is true that "out of the heart are the issues of life," how important is it that the source of these issues be made pure? It should be the constant and earnest endeavor of every teacher so to train his pupils that the finer and nobler feelings of the heart shall be developed and strengthened. A brilliant and cultivated intellect may dazzle and attract only to poison and destroy, unless chastened and controlled by right heart-training. True education implies the proper culture of all the faculties of the heart and intellect, and the right development of the physical powers. Of these, the first-named is the most essential, and any system of education which neglects to provide for this is sadly defective.

You are doubtless ready to assent to the truth of this, and are almost impatient to know how you shall do what you so strongly feel ought to be done. I can, of course, give you no specific and undeviating directions. I can merely give you a few hints. If your heart is alive to the true magnitude of the subject, these hints may be valuable; but if you have no deep and abiding interest in it, more full and definite directions would prove "like water spilled on the ground." In the first place I would say, avoid all set and formal lessons in moral science for young pupils. There is a fit time, and place, and manner in which to say and do things for the heart's good. Precisely when, where, and how these may occur, I cannot tell you; nor can any one. They must depend on circumstances, and these can be known only by yourself. It may be, at the opening of the school, during some recitation, on the play-ground, or after the close of the school. It may be, when God speaks in the thunder, smiles in the flowers, or blesses in the bounteous fruits. It may be in the school-room, by the wayside, or in the grove. At any time, in any place, and in many ways, there will be opportunities to reach the heart by the "still, small voice," uttered in tones of kindness and love. Seek every opportunity, and improve it.

But, if you would succeed in making any true and lasting impressions, you must yourself be a "living epistle," read and felt by your pupils. What you would have *them become*, *you* must *be*,— a bright and consistent example of all that is lovely and lovable. You must not only *point* to the right, but *lead* the way, and by your own cheering words and kindly acts lure the "little ones" to follow you. You cannot force them to be good; you cannot scold them into the true path.

Sometimes it will be well for you to labor with individual pupils; but you may, more frequently, perhaps, make general application of your efforts. Boys sometimes err and do wrong without any premeditation,—without realizing the nature of their doings. You may have several pupils guilty of the same fault in kind, if not in degree. In such case, some general remarks may best serve to accomplish the desired end. But at all times, and under all circumstances, you should strive to impress upon the hearts of your pupils a sense of their responsibility to a higher power. Lead them to feel, that, if they would be truly successful in eradicating their wrong habits, and resisting the temptations to sin, which will be sure to assail them, they must look to their Heavenly Father for guidance and support.

But let me suppose a case,—one which may occur. You learn that during recess, upon the playground, two boys have been guilty of quarrelling. Their names are Peter and James. You call them to an account at the proper time; but not until all anger has subsided, and the boys have had time for reflection. We will suppose that the following conversation takes place in presence of the school.

Teacher. "I am very sorry to know that you have been quarrelling. You have been guilty of a great wrong. You have not only wronged yourselves, but you have wronged me and the school; and, more than all, you have wronged your Maker, that good being who gives you all your blessings. I know not which commenced the wrong, but you are both guilty, and deserving of punishment."

Peter. "He struck me first."

James. "Well, he called me names."

Teacher. "I understand; you have both done wrong, and you give no good reason for so doing; indeed, you cannot give any. Peter says James struck him first, and James gives as a reason for his wrong-doing, that Peter called him names. Both these acts were wrong, and the only excuse you give is, that each of you did wrong because the other did. If one is more guilty than the other, it is he who commenced the difficulty. Peter did wrong in 'calling names,' but in this he injured himself much more than he did James. Remember, my young friends, that, if some one calls you 'fools,' it will not injure you, unless you make yourselves such by foolish acts. *Be* right and *act* right, and no one can injure you half so much as you can injure yourselves by one wrong or foolish act. No other person has half the power to injure you that you have to injure yourselves."

With a few such general remarks as these, the

subject may be left for the reflection of the offenders, who, at another hour, should receive a more private and particular direction. The main points in the general remarks should be to lead the pupils to see that it is no excuse for them to do wrong to others because others have done wrong to them; and also to cause them to feel that no one can injure them so much as they can injure themselves.

Within a year or two an excellent little book has been published, for the purpose of aiding the teacher in imparting moral instruction. It is entitled "Cowdery's Moral Lessons"; and I will give one or two of the stories, accompanying them with a few suggestive hints.

Let me suppose that you discover, on the part of some of your pupils, a wayward disposition, — an inclination to disregard the wishes of their parents, — a feeling that they will not be under the control of any one, — a sort of pride in showing that they will have their own way, regardless of the directions or wishes of their parents, — a sort of an impression that it is humiliating to submit to any authority, and particularly that of a mother. Read to them the following story, and accompany it by such remarks as will readily suggest themselves as pertinent.

"I was sitting by a window in the second story of one of the large boarding-houses at Saratoga Springs, thinking of absent friends, when I heard shouts of children from the piazza beneath me.

"'O yes! that 's capital! so we will! Come on,

now! there's William Hall! Come on, William! we're going to have a ride on the circular railway! Come with us!'

"'Yes, if my mother is willing. I will run and ask her,' replied William.

"'Oh! oh! so you must run and ask your ma! Great baby, run along to your ma! Are n't you ashamed? I did n't ask my mother.'

"'Nor I,' 'Nor I,' added half a dozen voices.

"'Be a man, William,' cried the first voice; 'come along with us, if you don't want to be called a coward as long as you live; — don't you see we're all waiting?'

"I leaned forward to catch a view of the children, and saw William standing with one foot advanced, and his hand firmly clenched, in the middle of the group. He was a fine subject for a painter at that moment. His flushed brow, flashing eye, compressed lip, and changing cheek, all told how the word 'coward' was rankling in his breast. 'Will he indeed prove himself one, by yielding to them?' thought I. It was with breathless interest I listened for his answer; for I feared that the evil principle in his heart would be stronger than the good. But no.

"'*I will not go* without asking my mother,' said the noble boy, his voice trembling with emotion. 'I am no coward, either. I promised her I would not leave the house without permission, and I *should* be a base coward, if I were to tell her a wicked lie!'"

If you have occasion to reprove a selfish disposition, and encourage kind and benevolent feelings and acts, read the following story, from the German: —

"WHO DID THE BEST WITH HIS PEACH.

"On returning from the city, one day, a gentleman took home with him five of the finest peaches he could procure. He divided them among his four children, retaining one for their mother. The children rejoiced over them exceedingly.

"In the evening, before the children retired to their chamber, the father questioned them by asking, 'How did you like the soft, rosy peaches?'

"'Very much indeed, dear father,' said the eldest boy; 'it is a beautiful fruit, — so soft and nice to the taste! I have preserved the stone, that I may cultivate a tree.'

"'Right, and bravely done,' said the father; 'that speaks well for regarding the future with care, and is becoming in a young husbandman.'

"'I have eaten mine and thrown the stone away,' said the youngest; 'besides, mother gave me half of hers. O, it tasted so sweet, and so melting in my mouth!'

"'Indeed,' answered the father; 'thou hast not been prudent. However, it was very natural and childlike, and displays wisdom enough for your years.'

"'I have picked up the stone,' said the second son, 'which my brother threw away, cracked it, and eaten the kernel; it was as sweet as a nut to the taste; but my peach I have sold for so much money, that, when I go to the city, I can buy twelve of them.'

"The parent shook his head reprovingly, saying, 'Beware, my boy, of avarice. Prudence is all very well, but such conduct as yours is unchildlike and unnatural. Heaven guard thee, my child, from the fate of a miser.'

"'And you, Edmund?' asked the father, turning to his third son, who frankly and openly replied, 'I have given my peach to the son of our neighbor, — the sick George, who has had the fever. He would not take it, so I left it on his bed, and I have just come away.'

"'Now,' said the father, 'who has done the best with his peach?'

"'Brother Edmund!' the three exclaimed aloud; 'Brother Edmund!'

"Edmund was still and silent, and the mother kissed him, with tears of joy in her eyes."

If you discover a disposition to evade the truth, to act the false part, read the following story, and lead your pupils to feel that they may be quite as guilty for acting lies, or withholding the truth, as in uttering the lie direct. In some cases it may even be more mean.

"'Why, Alfred, how could you tell mother that wrong story?' said Lucy Somers to her brother. 'You know you did eat one of the apples that was in the fruit-dish, yet you told mother you did not.'

"'Now, Lucy, I did n't tell any lie about it at all,' said Alfred. 'Mother asked me if I *took* one of the apples from the dish, and I said, No. And that was true, for the apple rolled off from the top of the dish, when I hit the table, and I picked it up from the floor. Mother did not ask me if I *ate* one, but if I *took* one from the dish. So you see I got along finely with it, and told nothing but the truth.'"

Can you not make such a story the medium of good moral impressions, and cause your pupils to feel that, if they would appear truthful to Him who knows the heart, they must live and act the truth, as well as speak it?

Sometimes boys do forbidden acts, relying on the kindness of their parents, or teachers, for overlooking the error. Read to them the following: —

"A boy was once tempted, by some of his companions, to pluck some ripe cherries from a tree, which his father had forbidden him to touch.

"'You need not be afraid,' said one of them, 'for if your father should find out that you had taken them, he is so kind that he would not punish you.'

"'*That is the very reason*,' replied the noble boy, 'why I will not touch them. It is true my father would not hurt me, but I know my disobedience would hurt my father, and that would punish me more than anything else.'"

In endeavoring to make correct moral impressions by repeating particular texts of Scripture, be sure that the spirit of the quotation is comprehended. The following will show how wide of the true meaning the young will sometimes strike.

"'A little boy, getting angry with his sister in their play, struck her. She cried out, 'Ma, ma, budder knock me! budder knock me!'

"'O well, my daughter,' said the mother, 'don't mind it! Just run up and kiss your little brother, and heap coals of fire upon his head.'

"The little girl ran up and kissed her brother, and then said, 'Where is the shovel, now? where is the shovel?'

"This, we apprehend, is by no means a peculiar perversion of the moral teachings of Christ."

If you can instil into the hearts of your pupils a true regard for truth, so that not only all their words, but all their acts, shall bear the impress of truthfulness and honesty, you will accomplish much in the right direction. I have sometimes thought teachers erred in being unduly suspicious of their pupils, exhibiting a lack of confidence in them. It is better, unless a pupil has really deceived you, and forfeited all claim to your respect, to confide in him, and cause him to feel that you consider him as incapable of doing a wrong or unworthy act. It is better to confide and occasionally be deceived, than never to confide.

Never tempt a child to tell an untruth, or to give a false reason for an act. This may be done in various ways, but more frequently through fear of threatened punishment. Cause a child to feel that deception and prevarication are always despicable, — and that any one guilty of them deserves punishment, — and, at the same time, lead him to feel that a full and candid confession of an error is alike right and manly. Children *do* and *say* many things for which they can give no good reason, and parents and teachers often tempt them to give a false reason by unduly insisting upon having some reason for an act performed, or an expression made. Wordsworth has thus beautifully expressed the same idea in the following

METRICAL LESSON.

"I have a boy of five years old;
His face is fair and fresh to see;
His limbs are cast in beauty's mould,
And dearly he loves me.

"One morn we strolled on our dry walk
Our quiet home all full in view,
And held such intermitted talk
As we are wont to do.

"My thoughts on former pleasures ran;
I thought of Kilve's delightful shore,
Our pleasant home when Spring began,
A long, long year before.

"A day, it was, when I could bear
Some fond regrets to entertain;
With so much happiness to spare,
I could not feel a pain.

"The green earth echoed to the feet
Of lambs, that bounded through the glade,
From shade to sunshine, and as fleet
From sunshine back to shade.

"Birds warbled round me, — every trace
Of inward sadness had its charm;
'Kilve,' said I, 'was a favored place,
And so is Liswyn farm.'

"My boy was by my side, so slim
And graceful in his rustic dress;
And, as we walked, I questioned him,
In very idleness.

"'Now, tell me, had you rather be,'
I said, and took him by the arm,
'On Kilve's smooth shore, by the green sea
Or here at Liswyn farm?'

"In careless mood he looked at me,
While still I held him by the arm,
And said, 'At Kilve I'd rather be
Than here at Liswyn farm.'

"'Now, little Edward, say why so;
My little Edward, tell me why.'
'I cannot tell, I do not know.'
'Why, this is strange,' said I;

"'For here are woods, and green hills warm;
There surely must some reason be
Why you would change sweet Liswyn farm
For Kilve by the green sea.'

"On this my boy hung down his head;
He blushed with shame, nor made reply;
And five times to the child I said,
'*Why*, Edward, tell me why.'

"His head he raised, — there was in sight —
It caught his eye, he saw it plain —
Upon the house-top, glittering bright,
A broad and gilded vane.

"Then did the boy his tongue unlock;
And thus to me he made reply:
'At Kilve there was no weathercock,
And that 's the reason why.'

"O dearest, dearest boy! my heart
For better lore would seldom yearn,
Could I but teach the hundredth part
Of what from thee I learn."

Be not regardless of the lesson contained in the above lines. It is an important one, — one that should be heeded by every teacher and parent. At all times do what you can to encourage an honest expression of views and feeling; but do not forget that young children may sometimes be unable to give a definite reason for preferences they may feel.

I will close this letter by enumerating several particulars in relation to which you should strive to cultivate correct moral impressions, and secure right moral action. At appropriate times, read stories or relate anecdotes which have a bearing upon these subjects, and do what you can to quicken and strengthen the better feelings of the heart, and call into action all those refined and moral susceptibilities which tend most to elevate and ennoble human nature. In doing this it will not be necessary that you should advance any ideas of a sectarian bearing. You may say and do all that may be essential, without manifesting any of those distinctive preferences which will be offensive to others. Moral and religious duties and obligations you may teach and enforce; but theological dogmas and discussions belong not to the school-room. Be judicious, and you may accomplish much on each of the following subjects: —

Obligations to our Creator.

Duties to parents; to teachers; to brothers and sisters; to friends and companions; to strangers; to the unfortunate.

Obedience to parents and teachers: should be prompt and cheerful, and not forced and reluctant.

Patience and perseverance.

Diligence.

Self-control, — both in cases of personal danger and in times of provocation.

Benevolence and selfishness, — contrasted.

Generosity and covetousness, — contrasted.

Anger, — government of passions.

Cruelty to animals.

Neatness in appearance and habits.

Punctuality.

Gentleness, — in word and deed.

Duty to obey the laws.

The golden rule.

Doing good to all, — even to those who injure us.

Speaking evil of others.

Make promises with caution, — fulfil with promptness.

True courage is daring to do right.

Think the truth, — speak the truth, — act the truth.

Honesty in word and deed.

Subjects. — Continued.

Bad habits.

School duties.

Courtesy, — politeness.

Forgiveness of injuries.

On use of profane or improper language.

Fidelity to every trust.

Labor conquers all things.

Avoid bad company.

It is better to suffer wrong than to do wrong.

Falsehood; deception; prevarication.

Always safe to do right, — never safe to do wrong.

Guard against little sins and trifling errors.

Whatever is worth doing at all, is worth doing well.

On the above, and kindred topics, you may safely strive, by "word and example," to exert an influence which shall be for the true good of your pupils.

Your sincere friend,

C.

LETTER VIII.

ORAL TEACHING.

My dear Friend:—

You wish to know what prominence you shall attach to oral instruction, — to what extent you shall use it, and how, when, and where. The question, in all its bearings, is an important one. Let us consider the subject. Not many years ago it was the nearly universal practice in schools, to conduct all recitations in strict accordance with the language of the text-book, — the teacher asking the printed question, the pupil giving the printed answer. To some extent the same plan is adopted in many schools at the present time. The practice, whenever and wherever pursued, will not lead to true development of mind. The evil results of this course have become apparent, and educational lecturers and writers have called attention to the subject, and urged reform. They have declaimed and written against it, and wisely and strongly contended for a change. But, in education, as in other concerns, one extreme is very apt to follow another. In advocating the importance of oral teaching, many went too far, and gave undue prominence to the subject. Some teachers went so far as to contend that oral teaching was the only true method, and that text-books should be almost, if not altogether, discarded. I recollect a visit, many years ago, to a school kept by a man somewhat advanced in years, who was taken captive by the phrase "oral teaching." No pupil had a book before him, but the teacher was attempting to amuse and instruct them by telling stories, they very listlessly hearing. This he considered the very acme of oral instruction, and yet the stories he told had not the remotest bearing upon the school, or any of its appropriate exercises, nor were they in any sense adapted to awaken mind, or impart moral precepts. But you will readily see that this man was adopting a course quite as erroneous as the former,—tending, as it would, to relieve the pupil from true mental discipline, and to weaken his self-reliance.

The true course is a medium one,—a judicious blending of the two; and those teachers will be the most successful who properly unite the two modes. The objection to the old method was not so much to the use of the text-book, as to the improper and excessive use of it. The book should be used by the pupils, and its contents be learned. The important truths and principles of each lesson should, if possible, be comprehended. If they are clearly understood, they may be, and should be, clearly expressed. In order that a pupil's knowledge of a lesson may be ascertained, the teacher should freely use the oral method, and ask such questions as will thoroughly test the ability and comprehension of the pupil. In conducting a recitation, the teacher should not feel confined to the mere questions of the book. With a clear understanding of the subject, he should strive, by incidental remarks and illustrations, and by judicious questions, to awaken thought, and secure true mental discipline.

Even the simplest questions in geography, grammar, etc. may be expanded and varied, and made suggestive of other questions; and the oral method should be mainly applied to secure this expansion and variation. The first question in geography usually is, "What is geography?" and the printed answer is, "A description of the earth." But how few pupils, taught merely by rote, have any clear and well-defined knowledge of the subject. A pupil may give a word-definition of a *cape*, *an island*, *peninsula*, *isthmus*, etc., without really possessing any correct conception of the object or thing thus defined. It should be the duty and aim of the teacher to ask such questions, and use such illustrations, as will make an accurate and permanent impression on the mind.

If the lesson be in arithmetic, and some particular rule is under consideration, let the teacher propose such questions as will tend to elucidate the subject, and test the scholar's comprehension. For instance, if the lesson is in Interest, much of the time devoted to the recitation may be most profitably used by asking questions aside from those contained in the book, though involving the same principle. At every step the teacher may properly and profitably propose questions, uniformly remembering that his true object is to awaken thought, and promote right and wholesome mental development and discipline; or, in other words, to teach his pupils how to think, to investigate, to understand.

In attempting to favor oral teaching, some have fallen into an excess of talking. To tell a child a fact, is not half as valuable to him, in many instances, as some hint or indirect aid, by which he would be led to make the discovery himself, in part, if not entirely. In no case regard oral teaching as an entire substitute for the book, but merely as an accompaniment for the purpose of confirming, elucidating, and expanding the lessons of the book. With very small children, for a time, most of the instruction should be of the oral kind. But here, even, great caution is necessary, in order that oral teaching may not degenerate into mere *talk*. Objects should form the basis of many of the lessons for the youngest pupils in our schools; and it should be the constant aim of the teacher to ask such questions as will awaken thought in the mind of the child. Such lessons will be given without a book, and, of course, will be wholly oral. It is quite an error to suppose that a child must be told everything that he does not know. The true way is, for the teacher to ask questions and give suggestive hints; but, in most cases, to leave some point for further thought and investigation on the part of the pupil. The mechanic, who should hope to make an accomplished workman of an apprentice, by doing all the work for him, instead of requiring him to practise for himself, would be no more unreasonable than those teachers who attempt, by mere talking, to awaken thought and secure mental growth. I will illustrate my idea of an oral object lesson by giving an example. I will give other examples in a future letter. I will suppose that the teacher points to the side of the school-room, to the plaster wall, and that the following conversation takes place. I would, however, recommend that your usual practice be, to ask a question with the understanding that all who think they can answer will raise the right hand, and that some one be selected to give an answer, and if any have a different answer, let them be called upon to give it.

Teacher. "Now, children, give attention. I wish to ask you a few questions. Let us see who will answer the most. What do we call this?"

Pupils. "The wall, or side of the room."

Teacher. "Very well. Of what is it made?"

Pupils. "Of plaster."

Teacher. "Yes, we call it plaster. Of what is plaster made?"

Pupils. "Of lime."

Teacher. "Is lime the only article in plaster?"

One Pupil. "I saw the masons put in some hair."

Another. "And I saw them put in sand."

Teacher. "You are both right. Hair and sand

are both used in making plaster. Can you tell what it is called before it is placed upon the wall?"

One Pupil. "My father calls it *mortar*."

Teacher. "Yes, that 's right. In making mortar you say *lime*, *hair*, and *sand* are used. Can you tell me why hair is used?"

After some hesitation, one pupil says, "I guess it is used to hold the mortar together better."

Teacher. "Very good. Now can any one tell me why sand is used?"

All hesitate, and no one offers an answer. The teacher then says, "As no one knows why sand is used, we will wait until to-morrow, and see if you can find out. Perhaps your parents will tell you, or; if not, you must ask a mason. How many of you will try to find out why sand is used, and tell me to-morrow? (All hands raised.) I wish you would also try to tell me all you can about lime, of what, and how, it is made, where it is made, and for what used besides in making mortar. We will talk about lime at our next lesson."

It will be readily seen, that pupils would go home from a brief lesson of this kind abounding in inquisitive questions. Father and mother, brother and sister, and all whom they meet, will be interrogated for information; and the whole neighborhood will be made fully sensible that a school exists, and that an *active*, *efficient*, *live* teacher is at the head of it.

Your sincere friend,

C.

LETTER IX.

RECITATIONS.

My dear Friend: —

Much of your success and usefulness as a teacher will depend upon the manner in which you conduct recitations. In some schools but little benefit results from these exercises; indeed, in some cases they are prejudicial to the true advancement and improvement of the pupils.

For what are recitations designed? I answer, briefly, to afford the teacher an opportunity, not only for ascertaining what the pupil does know in relation to the passing lesson, but also (and this is more important) what he does *not* know, — that light may be imparted when and where really needed, and that more effort on the part of the learners may be required and encouraged, when and where it may seem desirable and essential. I will give you a few brief hints on several points.

Assignment of Lessons. — Much care and judgment should be used on this point. Lessons should be neither too long nor too short. It would not be well to assign a lesson that would severely tax the ability of the best pupil in the class, nor would it be well to give one that the dullest member could readily learn. A lesson adapted to the capacity of the medium talent of the class will be right, — one that will require close application on the part of the dullest members.

Regularity and System. — Have a regular time for each exercise, and let it receive attention at the right time. Let not one lesson encroach upon the time that belongs to another. After classifying your school, and learning what is to be done, strive judiciously to apportion your time and attention to the several classes as circumstances may require, — neglecting none, giving no undue prominence to any. See that your pupils move in an orderly and quiet way to and from the place of recitation.

Keep a Record of each Recitation. — This will have a good influence over the pupils, and incite them to diligence. It will also be a convenient form in which to exhibit to parents and visitors the character of the various recitations. The scale for marking may vary according to circumstances or range of studies. From 0 to 3 will answer in most schools. If a recitation is perfectly satisfactory, let it be indicated by 3; if a little defective, by 2; if unsatisfactory, by 1; and if entirely faulty, by 0. The scale of marking may in some cases be extended to 5, or even to 10. At another time I will give you a form of record. (See Appendix.)

Make Preparation for the Recitation. — Though the lesson may be one which has previously received attention, and occupy ground that may seem familiar to you, it will still be desirable for you to examine the same with reference to the anticipated recitation. Perhaps some new mode of explaining principles, or some anecdote for illustrating, may occur to your mind whereby you may impart fresh interest to the lesson. So far as possible, I would advise that you examine each lesson with a special reference to its proposed recitation.

Teach the Subject, and not mere Words. — It has been a very common fault of the teaching in our schools, that it has been too formal, — too much confined to the language of the text-books. Teachers have asked the questions from the books, and pupils have repeated the answers as contained in the book. This may be well to a certain extent, and yet such a course alone constitutes but a small part of a true recitation. Words without ideas are but little worth, — but little worth only as the clear exponents of ideas. A pupil may be able to repeat the words of a grammar from beginning to end, and yet have no clear and well-defined ideas of the structure or analysis of language. If he has learned mechanically, no thoughts have been awakened, no valuable impressions have been made. With a view to testing the understanding of your pupils, and awakening thoughts, ask many incidental questions, such as are not contained in the text-book, but such as are pertinent to the subject under consideration. It is not unfrequently the case that a pupil may perform certain operations with the text-book or a given model under his eye, and yet not clearly comprehend the principles involved. In all your teaching, consider that your true duty is to awaken thought, to encourage investigation, to lead your pupils to examine, to think for themselves.

Insist on Attention. — It is too often the case, that the benefits of a recitation are lost through the listlessness or inattention of members of the class. Let your pupils clearly understand that you will proceed with no exercise, unless you can have their strict attention. As one means of securing this, adopt no undeviating order for asking questions at a recitation. Ask the question, and then designate some one to answer the same. It should be deemed sufficient if the question is asked once distinctly, with the understanding that any and every member of the class is liable to be called upon for an answer. It is a good way to place the names of the class in a small box, and then, as you ask the question, take some name from the box, and have that decide from whom an answer is expected.

Insist on Exactness, Promptness, and Energy. — Pupils are prone to give partial or imperfect answers. These should not be regarded as satisfactory. One of the greatest advantages of a recitation consists in the accuracy, precision, and clearness with which questions are answered. Require answers that shall be perfectly intelligible to all, such as will give the clearest evidence that the pupil comprehends the subject, and is not merely repeating words that are to him meaningless. Also insist that answers be given promptly and energetically. Avoid, assiduously, a dull, monotonous, indistinct mode of reciting; and with equal care avoid the "drawing-out process," by means of which "piecemeal" answers are obtained, or drawn out, by asking certain leading questions. Let it be always remembered, that a pupil is not, in any true sense, prepared with his lesson unless he can promptly, and without aid from any one, give a clear and full answer to the question proposed.

Make all Explanations and Corrections plain and intelligible.—This is not always done by teachers. They seem not to realize the difference between their own minds and those of their pupils, and they are often too ready to believe that a principle or explanation must be as clear to the minds of their pupils as it is to their own, and yet the truth may be far otherwise. Two or three amusing illustrations occur to my mind. A certain teacher was preparing his pupils for examination, and, I am sorry to say, practising a little special drill preparatory to the occasion. One pupil was to define "Faith," and, with a view to prepare the boy for his part, the teacher illustrated by using a teacup and an apple.

He first placed the apple under the cup, in presence of the pupil, and then said, "You know the apple is under the cup, because you saw me place it there. Now, Faith would cause you to believe that it was there, if I told you so, though you might not see me place it there." With words like these the subject was left, and on examination day, when the lad was asked to define Faith, he very promptly said, "It is an apple under a teacup."

A little boy once came to the following passage in his reading lesson. "Abraham, Isaac, and Jacob were patriarchs." The little fellow read as follows: "Abraham, Isaac, and Jacob were *partridges*." "No," says the teacher, "not *partridges*, but *patriarchs*." Very soon the lad came to the same word again, when, after a little hesitation, he looks into his teacher's face and says, "Here 's another of those queer birds, and I forget what you called it." If the teacher had explained the meaning of patriarch, the pupil would not have made this error; but the very manner in which the correction had been made led the lad to suppose that *partridges* and *patriarchs* were both birds, though not the same bird.

A little girl was once called upon to define *ferment*, and gave as an answer, "to work," which was received as satisfactory. She was subsequently called upon to compose a sentence which should contain the word, and she wrote, "*I love to ferment in the garden*." From these instances you will not fail to draw practical hints and inferences.

Encourage Thoroughness. — If possible, cause your pupils to learn thoroughly whatever they undertake to learn. Often impress upon their minds the truth and importance of the maxim, "Whatever is worth doing at all, is worth doing well." Professor Davies, the distinguished mathematician, gives the following rules, which it would be well for every teacher to observe: —

1. Teach one thing at a time.
2. Teach that one thing well.
3. Teach its connections.
4. Feel, and teach, that it is better to know everything of something, than to know something of everything.

Encourage your pupils to ask questions in relation to the lesson, or some point in the lesson. Before they pass from the recitation-seat, say to them: "If there is any principle in the lesson which you do not comprehend, or if I have not been understood in my explanations, I wish you to say so freely. Our object is, not merely to attend to the recitation, but to understand the subject; and very likely they who are most anxious to know, to learn, will be most ready to ask questions." It may not always be advisable to give an immediate answer to every question that may be asked. You may think it best that the pupils investigate for themselves. In this case, give them a few suggestive hints, and, with words of encouragement, ask them to give more attention to the subject, and if they fail to discover all they wish, you will explain more fully at a

future time. Always bear in mind, that it is not that which you do directly for your pupils that most benefits them, but that which you incite them, by expressions of encouragement, to do for themselves. A simple hint, as a step to the desired information, will often be of more real benefit, than a direct communication of the knowledge sought.

Studiously avoid the "Drawing-out" Process. — This is so admirably described and illustrated by another,* that I shall quote at some length his language. The "drawing-out" process "consists in asking what the lawyers call *leading questions.* It is practised, usually, whenever the teacher desires to help along the pupil. 'John,' says the teacher, when conducting a recitation in Long Division, 'John, what is the number to be divided called?' John hesitates. 'Is it the dividend?' says the teacher. 'Yes, Sir, — the dividend.' 'Well, John, what is that which is left after dividing called? — the remainder — is it?' 'Yes, Sir.' A visitor now enters the room, and the teacher desires to show off John's talents. 'Well, John, of what denomination is the remainder?' John looks upon the floor. 'Is n't it always the same as the dividend, John?'

* From the "Theory and Practice of Teaching," by David P. Page, A. M.; a work of the highest merit, the twenty-fifth edition of which has already been issued by the publishers, A. S. Barnes and Burr, New York. It is a work which should be in the hands of every teacher, and will prove worth a hundred-fold its cost to any who will regard its hints.

'Yes, Sir.' 'Very well, John,' says the teacher, soothingly, 'what denomination is this dividend?' pointing to the work upon the board. 'Dollars, is it not?' 'Yes, Sir, — dollars.' 'Very well; now what is this remainder?' John hesitates. 'Why, *dollars*, too, is n't it?' says the teacher. 'O yes, Sir, *dollars!*' says John, energetically, while the teacher looks complacently at the visitor, to see if he has noticed how *correctly* John has answered!

"A class is called to be examined in History. They have committed the text-book to memory; that is, they have learned the *words*. They go on finely for a time. At length one hesitates. The teacher adroitly asks a question in the language of the text. Thus: '*Early in the morning, on the* 11*th of September*, what did *the whole British army do?*' The pupil, thus timely reassured, proceeds: '*Early in the morning, on the* 11*th of September*, the *whole British army*, drawn up in two divisions, commenced the expected assault.' Here again she pauses. The teacher proceeds to inquire: 'Well, — *Agreeably to the plan of Howe, the right wing* did what?'

Pupil. '*Agreeably to the plan of Howe*, the right wing —'

Teacher. '*The right wing, commanded by whom?*' *Pupil.* 'Oh! *Agreeably to the plan of Howe, the right wing, commanded by* Knyphausen, made a feint of crossing the Brandywine at Chad's Ford,' etc."

This is a very common way of helping a dull pupil out of a difficulty; and I have seen it done so adroitly, before a company of visitors, that it was wonderful to see how thoroughly the children had been instructed!

I may further illustrate this *drawing-out* process, by describing an occurrence, which, in company with a friend and fellow-laborer, I once witnessed. A teacher, whose school we visited, called upon the class in Colburn's First Lessons. They rose, and in single file marched to the usual place, with their books in hand, and stood erect. It was a very good-looking class.

"Where do you begin?" said the teacher, taking the book.

Pupils. "On the eightieth page, third question."

Teacher. "Read it, Charles."

Charles. (Reads.) "A man being asked how many sheep he had, said that he had them in two pastures; in one pasture he had eight; that three fourths of these were just one third of what he had in the other. How many were there in the other?"

Teacher. "Well, Charles, you must first get one fourth of eight, must you not?"

Charles. "Yes, Sir."

Teacher. "Well, one fourth of eight is two, is n't it?"

Charles. "Yes, Sir; one fourth of eight is two."

Teacher. "Well, then, three fourths will be three times two, won't it?"

Charles. "Yes, Sir."

Teacher. "Well, three times two are six, eh?"

Charles. "Yes, Sir."

Teacher. "Very well." (A pause.) "Now, the book says that this six is just one third of what he had in the other pasture, don't it?"

Charles. "Yes, Sir."

Teacher. "Then if six is one third, three thirds will be — three times six, won't it?"

Charles. "Yes, Sir."

Teacher. "And three times six are eighteen, are n't it?"

Charles. "Yes, Sir."

Teacher. "Then he had eighteen sheep in the other pasture, had he?"

Charles. "Yes, Sir."

In relation to the above-described process, Mr. Page very justly remarks: "The teacher should at once abandon this practice, and require the scholar *to do the talking* at recitation. I need hardly suggest, that such a course of *extraction* at recitation, aside from the waste of time by both parties, and the waste of strength by the teacher, has a direct tendency to make the scholar miserably superficial. For why should he study, if he knows from constant experience, that the teacher, by a leading question, will relieve him from all embarrassment? It has often been remarked, that 'the teacher makes the school.' Perhaps in no way can he more effectually make an inefficient school, than by this *drawing-out process.*"

Cultivate a Self-reliant Spirit. — While undue boldness should be discountenanced at all times, a true spirit of self-reliance, based on a well-grounded confidence, should be studiously cultivated. A diffident, self-distrusting spirit always causes its possessor to appear at great disadvantage, while a degree of manly confidence, based on a true consciousness of understanding a subject, will give power to him who exercises it. Some pupils are naturally reserved, afraid to give utterance to their thoughts and ideas. Such need much kindness and encouragement. A word or look of reproof will entirely crush out any feelings of confidence that may have existed. Deal gently with them, commending them for any approximation to what is desirable, rather than censuring them for defects and short-comings. Kind and cheering tones and words have a wonderful power for good, while captious tones and frowning looks are extremely dispiriting in their effects. Captain Basil Hall illustrates the same ideas in the case of two sea-captains. It was the habit of one, as he came on deck, to look about to discover points for his approval. As he glanced at the decks, he would, with smiling countenance, say: "How white and clean you have got the decks to-day! I think you must have been diligent all the morning, to have got them into such order." The other would, with sour looks and captious tones, seek for points to censure. If the decks were perfectly clean and white, instead of noticing the same, he would seek for some trifling defect, and, pointing to a bit of rope-yarn left under the truck of a gun, he would say: "I wish, Sir, you would teach these sweepers to clear away that bundle of shakings!" The influence of the former was like magic for promoting a kindly, co-operative spirit; that of the latter was promotive of a spirit of indifference, if not of opposition. Captain Hall very justly remarks: "It requires but very little experience of soldiers or sailors, children, servants, or any other kind of dependents, to show that this good-humor on our part towards those whom we wish to influence, is the best possible coadjutor to our schemes of management." Can you not profit from these hints?

Make Recitations Interesting.—This you may do in various ways, but in none more than in showing yourself to be interested. Indeed, if you feel deeply interested in the exercise, you will cause your pupils to feel the same. "As is the teacher, so will be the pupils," in this and many other particulars. Then be earnest, energetic, interested, if you would have your pupils be so. Seek to elucidate and enliven every lesson by appropriate illustration and pertinent anecdote. Expand the subject under consideration by stating facts and incidents additional to those contained in the book; and never feel satisfied with a recitation, unless you have full assurance that your pupils pass from the same with a clearer and more accurate comprehension of the subject, than they had when they came to it. Be sure that at each recitation some truth or principle, new to your pupils, is developed, or some additional light imparted in relation to a subject or principle previously considered in part.

Efforts in themselves uninviting, and laborious even, may be made pleasant and attractive, by connecting them with some agreeable object or association. The following anecdote will illustrate this point, and the same principle may often be used to advantage in school exercises.

A certain man directed his son, on a given afternoon, to pick up the stones, which abounded in a small lot of land, and place them in a pile under the wall. The lad considered this very dull work for a holiday afternoon; but, nevertheless, he went to work. His mates were happily playing in the street, not far distant. After working for a short time he left, and, joining the boys at their sports, took an early opportunity to suggest a new play; and that was "to throw stones at a mark." "O yes!" shouted the boys, "that 'll be nice sport; but where shall we go?" "Why," says the lad first named, "over in my father's lot will be a capital place. There are stones enough there, and my father will let us throw as many as we please." At this the whole company rushed to the lot. The mark was placed by the *interested* lad in the very spot where he had already so tediously placed many of the stones, and in a very short time the lot was cleared of stones, and all the lads felt that they had had fine sport; and no one enjoyed it with more relish, or participated more earnestly, than the very lad who had planned "the sport." From this learn a lesson.

Your sincere friend,

C.

LETTER X.

OBJECT LESSONS.

My dear Friend:—

In a previous letter I alluded to the value of lessons on objects, and promised to give you two or three specimens of such lessons. For young pupils these may be frequent, but not long; and with pupils of all ages they may be made profitable, if judiciously conducted. The true design of such lessons should be to cultivate habits of attention and observation, and at the same time lead pupils to give expression to their thoughts and views; in other words, to train them to see and describe what they see. They will even do more than this;—they will cause pupils to think, to compare, to investigate. If, however, you would have exercises of this description productive of the highest good, make it a point to secure accuracy and propriety in the answers given, remembering that it is a prominent object to train children to give correct and lucid expression to their ideas. After giving you two or three sample exercises, I will enumerate a list of objects, each of which may be the basis of a lesson. Let me advise, however, that you commence such lessons by a few simple questions that may be pretty readily answered. It greatly encourages children to feel that they can answer questions proposed by their teacher, and the mere fact that they have answered some correctly, will give them confidence to continue their efforts; while an opposite course, in which a few difficult questions are asked at the outset, will tend to embarrass and discourage them. It will also be well, near the close of every lesson, to ask one question, or more, to which you will not be likely to obtain correct answers. By leaving some question or questions unanswered till a future time, you may do much towards awakening a spirit of investigation and inquiry. Two ideas should be made clear to the pupils by these lessons; one, that they know some facts in relation to the objects you present for their attention; the other, that there is something more to be learned on every subject. In this way you may encourage a becoming confidence, and at the same time check a spirit of self-conceit.

The following lesson I take from the Canada Journal of Public Instruction, making a few changes. The object is a "Feather," which the teacher holds in view of the class, when the following conversation takes place.

Teacher. "What have I in my hand?"

Pupils. "A feather."

Teacher. "Whence did it come?"

Pupils. "From a bird."

Teacher. "How do you think a bird would feel without feathers?"

Pupils. "It would be very cold."

Teacher. "What do we wear to keep ourselves warm?"

Pupils. "Coats, jackets, stockings, etc."

Teacher. "What do we call these?"

Pupils. "Clothes."

Teacher. "What do birds have for clothes?"

Pupils. "Feathers."

Teacher. "Can you think of any animals that wear clothing different from that we wear, and also different from that worn by birds?"

Pupils. "The sheep wears wool; the dog and horse have hair."

Teacher. "Now look." (Throwing the feather into the air.) "What do you see?"

Pupils. "It flies, or floats in the air."

Teacher. "If I toss a penny into the air, will it do the same?"

Pupils. "No, it will fall to the floor."

Teacher. "Why does the feather float, and the penny fall?"

Pupils. "Because the feather is light, and the penny heavy."

Teacher. "Can any of you tell me why feathers are better for birds than clothing like ours, or wool like the sheep's?"

Pupils. "Because they are light, and birds can fly better with them."

Teacher. "Very well. If they had heavy covering, they could not rise into the air, or if they did, they would soon fall down. From this we may see how wise and good our Heavenly Father is. He even cares for the birds. He says in the Bible, that a little bird shall not fall to the ground without his notice. Now if God sees all the little birds, and takes care of them, do you think he will ever forget little children? In the same passage in the Gospel, which tells of God's care of the little birds, it says, he takes still greater care of his children. I wish you would all try to find the verse I mean, and learn it to say to-morrow. Boys sometimes kill birds and destroy their nests, — is that right?"

Pupils. "It is not."

Teacher. "No, it is very cruel, and I hope you will never do so. Now, children, examine these feathers, — are they all alike?"

Pupils. "One is white, one is black, and one is brown."

Teacher. "What, then, will you say of the color of feathers?"

Pupils. "They have different colors."

Teacher. "Now take one in your hand, and tell me how it feels?"

Pupils. "It is soft."

Teacher. "Are all parts soft?"

Pupils. "No, the middle part is hard."

Teacher. "Yes, the middle part, which we call the stem, is hard, while the down, or feathery part, is soft. Is there any other difference between the two parts?"

Pupils. "The stem is bright and smooth, but the rest is not."

Teacher. "What do we say of those things that shine?"

Pupils. "We sometimes call them brilliant."

Teacher. "And what of things that do not shine?"

Pupils. "We call them dull."

Teacher. "Do you notice any other difference between the two parts? Will all parts bend alike?"

Pupils. "No, the quill or stem part does not bend easily,—it is more stiff."

Teacher. "Name some other things that are stiff."

Pupils. "Wood; stone; slate."

Teacher. "For what are feathers used?"

Pupils. "For making beds."

Teacher. "Why are they good for making beds?"

Pupil. "Because they are soft."

Teacher. "There are many other curious things about feathers which I will tell you at another time. You may now repeat what you have learned about feathers."

Pupils. "Feathers are the clothing of birds. They are very light and soft. God takes care of the little birds, and still more care of us. Feathers are of different colors. The stem of the feather is hard and stiff and shining; but the down is soft and dull. They make good beds, because they are soft."

Teacher. "You may now repeat the names of

the different kinds of birds you have seen, and I will write them upon the blackboard; and at our next lesson I shall call upon you to spell them and to describe them, or tell what you know of them."

Pupils. (Repeat as the teacher writes.) "Robin; Canary; Sparrow; Hawk; Crow; Eagle; Blackbird; Thrush; Owl; Linnet; Lark; Chickadee; Bobolink; Wren; Woodpecker; Oriole; Parrot; Swallow; Martin," etc.

I will now give one of a different nature, — or, rather, three or four brief ones connected, and adapted to children who have not learned their letters.* "If they are given to children who have learned to read, the names should be spelled, — written on the board by the teacher, and on the slates by the pupils. What has been learned of the lines, should be applied in learning the alphabet; referring to a list of plain capitals, and pointing to the parts of different letters, ask the pupils to say whether the part designated is curved or straight. Then request them to point to the letters which have no straight lines, and those which have no curve lines."

In the lessons on Lines, which follow, the answers of the pupils are not always given. The main purpose is to give the teacher's part, merely as suggestive. Each will expand and vary according to circumstances, or according to his own peculiar views.

* By J. D. Philbrick, in "The Massachusetts Teacher."

OBJECT LESSONS.—LINES.

FOR PRIMARY SCHOOLS.

Lesson I.

Straight Line. Curve Line.

You see what I have drawn on the board.

Are these lines alike?

How do they differ from each other?

One is straight and the other is not.

We call the one which is not straight, a curve line.

You may tell me the names as I point to them.

Which is this? Repeat it.

And this? Repeat it.

James may come and point to the *straight* line. Now to the *curve* line.

You may now make them on your slates.

If I stretch this thread thus, what line does it make?

Now if I bring the ends nearer together, and let it bend down thus, what line does it make?

A line that is not bent in any part of it, is called a straight line. Repeat together.

A line that bends in every part, but has no sharp corners in it, is a curve line. Repeat together.

Lesson II.

Having reviewed the preceding lesson, the teacher proceeds.

10*

Perpendicular Line.

You see I have made a line straight up and down. When a line is made in this direction, we call it a perpendicular line.

You may say *perpendicular line.*

We will analyze the word *perpendicular.*

You may make four on your slates.

I will look at some of your slates.

Jane has made them very well.

Look at Jane's; you see they are straight up and down.

Now erase them, and try again.

Now see me make one on the board (an oblique one).

Is it right?

It is *not* straight up and down.

It is not *perpendicular*, you mean.

Well, I will make this one right.

You may try again.

Edward may come up and hold this pointer in a perpendicular direction.

Tell me what you see in the room that is perpendicular.

The sides of the door, and of the windows, and of the blackboard.

Lesson III.

Review the preceding lesson.

Horizontal Line.

Now I have made a straight line across the board. When a line is made in this direction, we call it a horizontal line.

You may say *horizontal line.*

Analyze the word *horizontal.*

The pointer is now horizontal.

Who will come and hold it in a horizontal direction?

You may make four horizontal lines on your slates.

(Proceed as in Lesson II.)

Lesson IV.

Review as before.

Is this straight line perpendicular?

Is it horizontal?

Oblique Line. This is a slanting or oblique line.

You may call it an oblique line. Say *oblique line.*

Analyze the word *oblique.*

You see it leans towards the right.

Now I will make one leaning towards the left.

Mary may come and point to the one that leans to the right; to the left.

(Illustrate with the pointer. Proceed as in Lesson II.)

Lesson V.

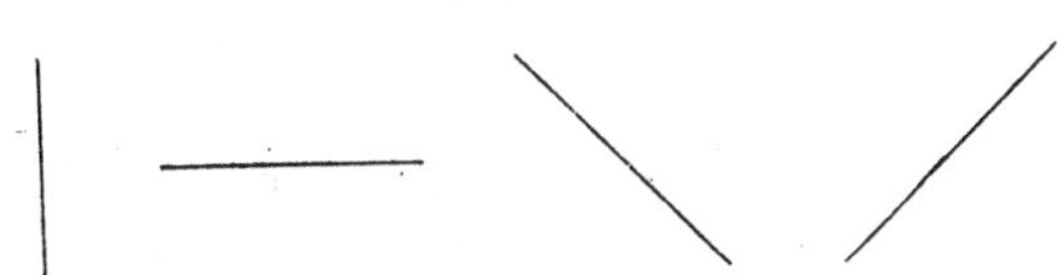

Here are a perpendicular line, a horizontal line, and two oblique lines.

Which is this (pointing to the horizontal line)?

A horizontal line.

This ?

A perpendicular line.

This ?

An oblique line, leaning or inclining towards the right.

This ?

An oblique line inclining towards the left.

You may all lean towards the right; — left. Stand up straight, in a perpendicular position.

Hold out your arms in a horizontal position.

Make these lines on your slates.

Tell the names as I point to them.

Lesson VI.

Parallel Lines.

I have made two straight lines. You see they are just as far apart in one place as in another; they run in the same direction.

If two straight lines are just as far apart in one place as in another, they are parallel.

Do you see any things in the room parallel ?

The two sides of my slate, the two sides of the door, of the window, of a pane of glass; the wires of the numeral frame.

Now I will make three parallel lines.

Make three just like them on your slate.

(Practise on these some time; then proceed in the same way with the horizontal and oblique parallel lines.)

The following I take from an English work entitled "Object Lessons," — a very useful book for the teacher.

GLASS.

Glass has been selected as a proper substance to be presented to the children, because the qualities which characterize it are quite obvious to the senses. The pupils should be arranged before a blackboard or slate, upon which the result of their observations should be written. The utility of having the lessons presented to the eyes of the children, with the power of thus recalling attention to what has occurred, will very soon be appreciated by the instructor.

The glass should be passed round the party, to be examined by each individual.*

Teacher. "What is this I hold in my hand?"

Children. "A piece of glass."

Teacher. "Can you spell the word *glass?*"

(The teacher then writes the word "glass" upon the slate, which is thus presented to the whole class as the subject of the lesson.) "You have all examined this glass; what do you observe? What can you say it is?" †

---

* By this means each individual in the class is called upon to exercise his own powers on the object presented; the subsequent questions of the teacher tend only to draw out the ideas of the children, which he corrects if wrong.

† This question is put, instead of asking, "What are its quali-

Children. "It is bright."

Teacher. (The teacher having written the word "qualities," writes under it, "It is bright."). "Take it in your hand and *feel* it." *

Children. "It is cold." (Written on the board under the former quality.)

Teacher. "Feel it again, and compare it with the piece of sponge that is tied to your slate, and then tell me what you perceive in the glass." †

Children. "It is smooth, — it is hard."

Teacher. "What other glass is there in the room?"

Children. "The windows."

Teacher. "Look out at the window, and tell me what you see?"

Children. "We see the garden."

Teacher. (Closes the shutters.) "Look out again, and tell me what you now observe?"

Children. "We cannot see anything."

Teacher. "Why cannot you see anything?"

Children. "We cannot see through the shutters."

---

ties?" because the children would not, at first, in all probability, understand the meaning of the term; its frequent application, however, to the answer of this question, will shortly familiarize them with it, and teach them its meaning.

* The art of the teacher is to put such questions as may lead successfully to the exercise of the different senses.

† The object of the teacher here is to lead the pupil to the observation of the quality *smooth,* and he does so by making him contrast it with the *opposite* quality in another substance; a mode of suggestion of which frequent use may be made.

Teacher. "What difference do you observe between the shutters and the glass?"

Children. "We cannot see through the shutters, but we can through the glass.'

Teacher. "Can you tell me any word that will express this quality which you observe in the glass?"

Children. "No."

Teacher. "I will tell you then; pay attention, that you may recollect it. It is *transparent.** What shall you now understand when I tell you that a substance is transparent?"

Children. "That you can see through it."

Teacher. "You are right.† Try and recollect something that is transparent."

Children. "Water."

Teacher. "If I were to let this glass fall, or you were to throw a ball at the window, what would be the consequence?"

Children. "The glass would be broken. It is brittle."

---

* The fact of the glass being transparent is so familiar to the children, they will probably not observe it till its great use in consequence of that quality brings it forcibly before their minds. They then feel the want of a term to express the idea thus formed, and the teacher gives them the name, as a sign for it, and in order to impress it upon their minds. To ascertain whether they have rightly comprehended the meaning of the word, they are called upon to give examples of its application.

† It is but too common a practice to call a child *good* because he gives a right answer; thus confounding intellectual truth and moral virtue.

Teacher. "If I used the shutter in the same manner, what would be the consequence?"

Children. "It would not break."

Teacher. "If I gave it a sharp blow with a very hard substance, what would happen?"

Children. "It would then break."

Teacher. "Would you, therefore, call the wood brittle?"

Children. "No."

Teacher. "What substances, then, do you call brittle?"

Children. "Those which are *easily* broken."

These are probably as many qualities as would occur to children at their first attempt: they should be arranged on the slate, and thus form an exercise in spelling. They should then be effaced: and if the pupils are able to write, they may endeavor to remember the lesson, and put it down on their slates.

OBJECT LESSON.—FOR OLDER PUPILS.

IRON.

Teacher. (Holding up a piece of iron.) "Can you tell me what this is?"

Pupils. "It is iron, Sir."

Teacher. "And what is iron,—mineral, animal, or vegetable?"

Pupils. "It belongs to the mineral kingdom."

Teacher. "Can you tell me some of its uses,— or name some articles * that are made of iron?"

Pupils. "Nails, screws, bolts, bars, locks, keys, stoves, ploughs, hammers, wheels, axletrees, shovels, tongs, pincers, hinges, latches, horse-shoes, chains, knives, forks, axes, planes, saws, chisels, doors, chairs, bedsteads, buildings, boats, steam-engines, locomotives, boilers, pumps, etc."

Teacher. "You see that you have named a great many articles which are made of iron, and many others might be named. You say that knives, and other edge-tools, or cutlery, are made of iron. Are they made wholly of common iron?"

Pupils. "No, Sir, they are composed partly of steel, which is iron refined and hardened."

Teacher. "Yes,—we will talk more about steel at another time. You say that *nails* are made of iron. Are all nails alike? If not, name some different kinds?"

Pupils. "Tack-nails, shingle-nails, clapboard-nails, board-nails, spike-nails, horse-shoe nails, wrought nails, cut nails." †

Teacher. "What are the principal forms in which iron is used?"

Pupils. "Cast-iron, wrought-iron, sheet-iron, and steel." (Here the teacher may ask questions in relation to each kind, and its uses.)

* It will be well for the teacher to write these on the blackboard, as they are given, and let the list be taken for a spelling lesson.

† Ask the purpose for which each is used; the difference between a cut-nail and a wrought-nail, etc.

Teacher. "Can you name some particulars in which iron and wood are alike?"

Pupils. "Both have solidity, strength, firmness, durability,—though wood has less than iron."

Teacher. "Name some points of difference."

Pupils. "Iron is mineral, wood is vegetable; iron is not inflammable, wood is; iron is ductile and malleable, wood is neither." (Call for a definition of the words used in the answers to the last two questions.)

Teacher. "In what respects are iron and glass alike?"

Pupils. "They are both solid, both have weight, neither of them will burn, both may be melted," etc.

Teacher. "Can you name some particulars in which they are unlike?"

Pupils. "Glass is smooth, iron is rough; glass is brittle, iron is not; glass is transparent, iron is not."

Teacher. "Which do you think more useful and important, iron or gold?"

Pupils. (Variously.) "Gold,—iron."

Teacher. "I see you have different views on this point, and I will leave the subject for your reflection until another day. I shall also wish you to inform me where iron is found, the form or condition in which it is found, how it is obtained, how it is prepared for use, etc. To obtain information on these points you can consult books, or ask your parents and friends. Let us see who will be able to tell us the most about iron at our next lesson."

I will add only one more exercise of this kind, and that I take from Page's "Theory and Practice of Teaching," a work previously alluded to, and one that every teacher should own and read. In this the object is

"AN EAR OF CORN.

"*Teacher.* 'Now, children,' holding up the corn, and addressing himself to the youngest, 'I am going to ask you only one question to-day about this ear of corn. If you can answer it, I shall be very glad; if the little boys and girls upon the front seat cannot give the answer, I will let those in the next seat try; and so on till all have tried, unless our time should expire before the right answer is given. I shall not be surprised if none of you give the answer I am thinking of. As soon as I ask the question, those who are under seven years old, that think they can give an answer, may raise their hand. *What is this ear of corn for?*'

"Several of the children raise their hands, and the teacher points to one after another in order, and they rise and give their answers.

"*Mary.* 'It is to feed the geese with.'

"*John.* 'Yes, and the hens too, and the pigs.

"*Sarah.* 'My father gives corn to the cows.'

"By this time the hands of the youngest scholars are all down, for, having been taken a little by surprise, their knowledge is exhausted. So the teacher says that those between seven and ten years of age may raise their hands. Several instantly appear.

The teacher again indicates, by pointing, those who may give the answer.

"*Charles*. 'My father gives corn to the horses when the oats are all gone.'

"*Daniel*. 'We give it to the oxen and cows, and we fat the hogs upon corn.'

"*Laura*. 'It is good to eat. They shell it from the cobs and send it to mill, and it is ground into meal. They make bread of the meal, and we eat it.'

"This last pupil has looked a little further into domestic economy than those who answered before her. But by this time, perhaps before, the five minutes have been nearly expended, and yet several hands are up, and the faces of several are beaming with eagerness to tell their thoughts. Let the teacher then say, 'We will have no more answers to-day. You may think of this matter till to-morrow, and then I will let you try again. I am sorry to tell you that none of you have mentioned the use I was thinking of, though I confess I expected it every minute. I shall not be surprised if no one of you give this answer to-morrow. I shall now put the ear of corn in my desk, and no one of you must speak to me about it till to-morrow. You may now take your studies.'

"The children now breathe more freely, while the older ones take their studies, and the next class is called. In order to success, it is absolutely necessary that the teacher should positively refuse to hold any conversation with the children on the subject till the next time for 'general exercise.'

"During the remainder of the forenoon the teacher will very likely observe some signs of thoughtfulness on the part of those little children who have been habitually dull before. And perhaps some child, eager to impart a new discovery, will seek an opportunity to make it known during the forenoon. 'Wait till to-morrow,' should be the teacher's only reply.

"Now let us follow these children as they are dismissed, while they bend their steps toward home. They cluster together in groups as they go down the hill, and they seem to be earnestly engaged in conversation.

"'I don't believe it has any other use,' says John. 'O yes, it has,' says Susan; 'our teacher would not say so if it had not. Besides, did you not see what a knowing look he had, when he drew up his brow, and said he guessed we could n't find it out?'

"'Well, I mean to ask my mother,' says little Mary; 'I guess she can tell.'

"By and by, as they pass a field of corn, Samuel sees a squirrel running across the street, with both his cheeks distended with '*plunder*.'

"At home, too, the ear of corn is made the subject of conversation. 'What is an ear of corn for, mother?' says little Mary, as soon as they have taken a seat at the dinner-table.

"*Mother*. 'An ear of corn, child? why, don't you know? It is to feed the fowls, and the pigs, and the cattle; and we make bread of it, too —'

"*Mary.* 'Yes, we told all that, but the teacher says that is not all.'

"*Mother.* 'The *teacher?*'

"*Mary.* 'Yes, ma'am; the teacher had an ear of corn at school, and he asked us what it was for; and after we had told him everything we could think of, he said there was another thing still. Now I want to find out, so that I can tell him.'

"The consequence of this would be that the family, father, mother, and older brothers and sisters, would resolve themselves into a committee of the whole on the ear of corn. The same, or something like this, would be true in other families in the district; and by the next morning, several children would have something further to communicate on the subject. The hour would this day be awaited with great interest, and the first signal would produce perfect silence.

"The teacher now takes the ear of corn from the desk, and displays it before the school; and quite a number of hands are instantly raised, as if eager to be the first to tell what other use they have discovered for it.

"The teacher now says, pleasantly, 'The use I am thinking of, you have all observed, I have no doubt; it is a very important use indeed; but as it is a little out of the common course, I shall not be surprised if you cannot give it. However, you may try.'

"'It is good to boil!' says little Susan, almost springing from the floor as she speaks.

"'And it is for squirrels to eat,' says little Samuel. 'I saw one carry away a whole mouthful yesterday from the cornfield.'

"Others still mention other uses, which they have observed. They mention other animals which feed upon it, or other modes of cooking it. The older pupils begin to be interested, and they add to the list of uses named. Perhaps, however, none will name the one the teacher has in his own mind; he should cordially welcome the answer, if perchance it is given; if none should give it, he may do as he thinks best about giving it himself on this occasion. Perhaps, if there is time, he may do so, — after the following manner.

"'I have told you that the answer I was seeking was a very simple one; it is something you have all observed, and you may be a little disappointed when I tell you. The use I have been thinking of for the ear of corn is this, — *It is to plant. It is for seed*, to propagate that species of plant called corn.' Here the children may look disappointed, as much as to say, 'We knew that before.'

"The teacher continues: 'And this is a very important use for the corn; for if for one year none should be planted, and all the ears that grew the year before should be consumed, we should have no more corn. This, then, was the great primary design of the corn; the other uses you have named were merely secondary.'"

I will now close with a list of objects suitable for lessons of this kind.

Glass.
India-rubber.
Leather.
Sponge.
Wool.
Wax.
Whalebone.
Bread.
Ivory.
Chalk.
A pin.
A pencil.
A pen.
A chair.
A stove.
A brick.
A key.
A knife.
A piece of sugar.
An acorn.
A cork.
A piece of glue.
A stone.
A bell.
A wheel.
Cinnamon.
Nutmeg.
Ginger.
Cloves.
Water.
Oil.

Vinegar.
Butter.
Cheese.
Coffee.
Tea.
Rice.
Paper.
Cotton.
Flax.
Hemp
Silk.
Table.
Gold.
Silver.
Mercury.
Lead.
Copper.
Iron.
Tin.
Lime.
Coal.
Granite.
Salt.
Slate.
Feather.
Coral.
Gutta-percha.
A book.
A piece of fur.
A hat.
A door.

The list of objects might be greatly extended, but it will not be necessary. Take one at a time, and have its qualities, uses, color, shape, origin, etc. carefully considered. Each question asked will be suggestive of another, so that after you have fairly commenced you will find no difficulty, and I am sure you will be satisfied that such lessons will both please and benefit your pupils. As very useful aids in lessons of this kind, I will name two small works: "The Treasury of Knowledge," by Chambers, and an excellent work entitled "Common Things," by Worthington Hooker, M. D. The two books will cost but little, and will be worth much.

Your sincere friend,

C.

LETTER XI.

READING.

MY DEAR FRIEND:—

OF all the branches you will be called to teach, none will be more important than that of reading. It lies at the very foundation of all learning, and all must know something of this as a key to other branches. All who enter the school-room,—from the little ones, just beginning to lisp the letters of the alphabet, up to those who are about to close their school days,—all will require training in this department. How small the number of those who can be properly called accomplished readers, and how large the number who read quite indifferently or very poorly! One who can read a piece with ease and right effect will always be listened to with interest and delight, while one who reads in a hesitating, lifeless, meaningless style, will have no power over his hearers, and may even become a subject of ridicule.

As a general thing, it must be admitted that reading has not been well taught in our schools. It has received formal attention and frequent *in*attention.

This remark may be more properly true of schools as they were a score of years ago, than of those of the present day; and yet it is, to a certain extent, true of our schools as a whole, even now. I well recollect when it was customary for teachers to hear every member of their schools read four times a day, — twice in the forenoon, and twice in the afternoon. This was the established law, and seemingly as unalterably fixed as that of the Medes and Persians. In imagination I can see the school-dame of my boyhood days, as she called her several pupils and classes. First came the little alphabetarians, one by one, to whom, in regular order, the whole twenty-six letters were administered at a dose, — just four times daily; — the teacher pointing at the letter and pronouncing it, and the pupil repeating it after her, — the only variation consisting in an occasional snap upon the ear for inattention. For days, and weeks, and months, — perhaps for years, — was this operation continued before the letters were fairly understood. Then came the little boys and girls in b-a, ba, b-e, be, b-i, bi, b-o, bo, b-u, bu, etc., up through *baker* and *cider*, until the oldest had received their turn. If the performance was attended to just four times daily, the requirements of parents and committees were met, and all was considered right. But so far as real benefit was concerned, it would have been just as well if the pupils had been called upon to whistle just four times a day, — twice in the forenoon, and twice in the afternoon. Really it would have been better; for if they had, each time, whistled wrong, it would have done no harm. But to be required to go through the form of reading, as it was done, without any true regard to emphasis, inflection, punctuation, or sense, was only making a bad matter worse at every repetition that was made, as bad habits were only confirmed thereby. The prominent requirement seemed to be to read rapidly, —and this was essential, in order that the regular "round" might be accomplished. The whole exercise was a formal, unmeaning affair; and the result a monotonous, blundering, unmeaning style of reading. We were, it is true, commanded to "mind our stops," but it was only in an arbitrary way, which admitted of no modification on account of the sense. At a comma we were to stop long enough to count *one;* at a semicolon long enough to count *two*, etc. The following anecdote illustrates in an amusing manner the absurdity of the old rule for "minding the stops."

"A country schoolmaster, who found it rather difficult to make his pupils observe the difference in reading between a comma and a full-point, adopted a plan of his own, which, he flattered himself, would make them proficients in the art of punctuation; thus, in reading, when they came to a comma, they were to say *tick*, and read on to a semicolon, and say *tick*, *tick*, to a colon, and say *tick*, *tick*, *tick*, and when a full-point, *tick*, *tick*, *tick*, *tick*. Now, it so happened that the worthy Dominie received notice that the parish minister was to pay a visit of examination to his school; and, as he was desirous that his pupils should show to the best advantage, he gave them an extra drill the day before the examination. 'Now,' said he, addressing his pupils, 'when you read before the minister to-morrow, you may leave out the *ticks*, though you must think them as you go along, for the sake of elocution.' So far, so good. Next day came, and with it the minister, ushered into the school-room by the Dominie, who, with smiles and bows, hoped that the training of the scholars would meet his approval. Now it so happened, that the first boy called up by the minister had been absent the preceding day, and, in the hurry, the master had forgotten to give him his instructions how to act. The minister asked the boy to read a chapter in the Old Testament, which he pointed out. The boy complied, and in his best accent began to read: 'And the Lord spake unto Moses, saying *tick*, Speak unto the children of Israel, saying *tick*, *tick*, and thus shalt thou say unto them, *tick*, *tick*, *tick*, *tick*.' This unfortunate sally, in his own style, acted like a shower-bath on the poor Dominie, whilst the minister and his friends almost died of laughter."

It is not my intention to give you any specific hints, or directions, in relation to the elocutionary part of reading, but rather to offer such hints as may be of service to you in the every-day work of the school-room. I must leave the strictly oratorical part, and take up reading as an intellectual exercise, and, if possible, offer such thoughts and suggestions as may be truly practical. With so many under your training, you cannot be expected to go into all the minutiæ of elocutionary drilling. Your aim must be to teach well what you undertake to teach. If you cannot hope to make all your pupils accomplished elocutionists, you may hope and strive to make them good and intelligent readers. Perhaps you will wish to know what I consider good reading. I call that good reading where a person reads distinctly and clearly, and with such intonation and emphasis as to be pleasant to the hearer, and in such manner as to be easily heard and readily understood. That person may be called a good reader who can, from the columns of a common newspaper, read the several items and articles in a clear and intelligible style, without seeming effort on his part, and without requiring painfully or unpleasantly close attention on the part of the hearer.

You have some among your pupils who are yet strangers to the letters of the alphabet. The old method of teaching it was a tedious one both for teachers and children. Of course you have a blackboard in your school-room, as this is one of the really essential articles for every school. Call your little ones in front of the blackboard. If possible let each be furnished with a slate. Now draw upon the blackboard the picture of some animal or object, — a dog, for instance. With a pointing-stick in hand, call attention, and have an exercise somewhat as follows : —

Teacher. "What animal is this ?"

Children. "A dog."

Teacher. "Are all dogs alike?"

Children. "No, ma'am; some are small and some are large."

Teacher. "Are they alike in all but size?"

Children. "No, ma'am; they don't have the same color."

Teacher. "How many legs has a dog?"

Children. "Four."

Teacher. "What can a dog do?"

Children. "He can run fast, and he can catch squirrels."

You will readily see that these questions may be continued indefinitely. They will tend to awaken thought and interest in the little ones. After you have extended the questioning sufficiently, ask them if they would like to know another way to express the animal besides by a picture. They will all be anxious to know. Now print DOG under the picture on the board, and require them to do the same on their slates. Then tell them the name of each letter, and have it repeated several times. After having fixed their attention for a minute, make D only on the board, and ask its name, and so with each of the other letters, and in a short time they will be able to give their names readily. It will be well also, at the right time, to give them the powers of the letters, or their appropriate sounds. You will readily see, that some object of interest to children may be connected with these early lessons, and that, by judicious questioning, they may be trained to think and express their thoughts at the same time they are learning their letters.

The following excellent specimen lesson for teaching the alphabet just meets my attention. It is from the pen of a distinguished educator,* and will commend itself as sensible and practical.

TEACHING THE ALPHABET. — A SPECIMEN LESSON.

Apparatus. — A blackboard; a chart of easy words of one syllable; an alphabet chart; a set of alphabet cards, with a grooved stick, called spelling-stick, in which the cards may be inserted in spelling words; and a slate and pencil for each child.

Preliminary Training. — Children should not be put to reading immediately upon entering school for the first time. Judicious preliminary exercises will render subsequent progress, not only in this, but in other branches, more rapid and satisfactory. The object of these exercises should be to train the ear to distinguish sounds, and the organs of speech to utter them; to form habits of attention and of prompt obedience to all directions; and to excite the curiosity, or desire to learn something. Such being the objects, the judgment of the teacher must guide in the selection and adaptation of the exercises.

Lesson. — The proper preparatory training having been given, the teacher will select a single letter to begin with; it matters little which. Suppose it

* John D. Philbrick.

to be *ă*. The card containing it is placed in the spelling-stick, in view of all the class.

Teacher. "You see this letter. Now look at me. You all know me when you see me. Now I wish you to look at this letter, so that you will know it whenever you see it. It stands for a *sound.* Listen, and hear me give the sound."

Having enunciated the sound distinctly several times, taking care to secure the attention of all, the teacher might ask if any one has ever heard the sound before. Some may remember it, as given among the elementary sounds of the language. If so, they are pleased to find that the lesson is connected with something learned before. If it is not recalled, give the vowel-sounds promiscuously, requesting all to put up hands when they hear it.

Teacher. "Now all give the sound after me; again; again. That is what this letter says. When you read it, you give the sound. You may take your slates, and see if you can make one like it."

Only a few, perhaps, will try at first. But the teacher passes rapidly around, giving a glance at slates, bestowing commendation on the best efforts.

Teacher. "Erase it. See me make it on the blackboard. I begin here, and go round in this way. You may try it again on your slates."

The slates are inspected as before; the timid are encouraged, and the letter written for them on their slates. Then the drill on the sound is repeated, and afterwards individuals called up to give it.

If this is found to be enough for one lesson, when the course is resumed, the exercises on *ă* should be reviewed. The teacher will then proceed with another letter in a similar manner, taking one that, with the preceding, will make a duo-literal word. Suppose it is *t*. The letters are placed together.

Teacher. "You see I have put together the two letters you have learned, and they make a word; would n't you like to read the word? Hear me say the sounds, and see if you can tell what the word is. I will give them slowly,—*ă*, *t*. Can you tell the word?"

After several repetitions, perhaps some one will combine them and say, "*at*."

Teacher. "Yes, *at;* that is right. Now you have read a word. You often use the word. I am *at* the desk; you are *at* school. Say, 'We are *at* school.' I will write both letters on the board. I begin thus, and make the first; and then you see how I make the other, and cross it thus. You may take your slates, and make them."

Now the reading lesson is changed for writing or printing. This having been pursued long enough, the alphabet chart is suspended before the class, and the pupils requested to see if they can find the word. The first who raises his hand is allowed to come out and point to it.

If any time is allowed to elapse before presenting another letter, these steps should be reviewed. The next letter to be learned should be one which, with *at*, will form another word. Let it be *r*. The same course as before is pursued. First, the attention is called to the *form*. Next, the sound is learned. Then, it is written, exercising the conception and imitation, and fixing the form in the memory. The three letters are then placed in order, to form the word *rat*.

Teacher. "You see the three letters you have learned. They make another word. Hear me give the sounds, and then see if you can tell the word; *r-ă-t*. You may give the sounds after me."

If this process is well managed, some one will catch the word. Now, as many individuals as possible should be called upon to repeat the sounds, while pointing to the letters, and then pronounce the word. It is then written as before. This might be followed by some simple story read or related about the rat. Then the pupils might be asked to tell anything they know of the rat. The same process as before with the charts. Keep in mind the maxims, — one short step at a time, constant reviews, vigorous exercise of the mind during the lesson.

In the same way make the words, *bat*, *cat*, *fat*, *hat*, *mat*, *sat*, *vat*.

The letter *n* might come next. This, placed after *a*, will give the word *an*. Then *m*, which placed before makes *man*. And so make *tan*, *ran*, *fan*, *pan*, *can*. For the next vowel, take *i*, with *n* making *in*. Then as before form *pin*, *bin*, *din*, *fin*, *sin*, *win*.

Thus proceeding, go through the first reading chart, — always using every word learned in oral sentences, and training the class to make them for themselves.

The same general plan may be continued as the pupils progress. Suppose you have a class reading in short and simple sentences; as, *The dog ran after the fox.* Ask them questions like the following: Why did the dog run after the fox? Which has the most legs, a dog or a fox? Which do you think can run the fastest? What do we call all animals that have four legs? Which do you think can run fastest, a man or a dog? For what is a dog useful? How many kinds of dogs do you know of? You say one kind is called a Newfoundland dog, — why? Of what use are foxes? Of what use are dogs? What is the difference between a wild animal and a domestic animal? Which is the dog? Which the fox? etc.

It often happens that children acquire drawling habits and unnatural tones in reading. See to it that your pupils do not err in these particulars. Bad habits of pronunciation, intonation, or enunciation, formed at the outset, will, if indulged, soon become confirmed and disagreeable. A wrong intonation or inflection may sometimes be rectified by requiring the pupil to close his book, and to repeat the phrase or sentence after you, being careful yourself to give a natural and correct expression and tone. After he has done this three or four times, let him open his book and read the same again. If the first trial does not prove effectual, make another attempt, and continue until the error is fully eradicated.

I would urge that you strive to make every exercise interesting and instructive. This you may do by asking numerous questions. See to it that every word and expression is comprehended clearly. It will be well frequently to require all the members of the class to read, in turn, the same sentence, paragraph, or stanza, making the performance of each a subject of pleasant criticism. Your own active and ready mind will see to what extent this course may be pursued, and its advantages will be obvious to you. Always make your criticisms in that pleasant spirit which will not discourage, but rather lure them to renewed and more careful effort.

The hints I have given are mainly for beginners. I will now pass to offer some suggestions in reference to the more advanced classes. And here I may advise, that you take special care to cultivate a correct taste. Unless you can lead your pupils to appreciate the difference between good reading and that which is faulty, they will not be apt to make improvement. Make them understand that the mere calling of words does no more to constitute correct reading, than the mere daubing a canvas with paint constitutes a finished and lifelike picture. What the variations and shades are to the true beauty of the picture, such are inflections, emphasis, accent, etc. to good reading; and it would be just as sensible to hope to represent a beautiful landscape by a single color, uniformly applied, as to produce good reading with a monotonous, unchanging tone of voice. It will be well for you, occasionally, to read a stanza or sentence in different styles, — each, perhaps, exemplifying some common error, — and call upon your pupils to designate such faults as they may notice. If you can only succeed in arousing a critical spirit, and leading them to discriminate, the remainder of the work will be comparatively trifling.

If a pupil reads too rapidly, too low, too indistinctly, too monotonously, or in any way faulty, call upon others in the class to read the same passage, and read it yourself, — and again call upon the first one to make another attempt. It is not enough to say to a pupil, "You read too fast, or too low, or gave the wrong emphasis." If there was some prominent defect, not only cause it to be seen, but corrected. Object not that it requires time. It will require more time, if you let these habits become confirmed. It is nót *how much* nor *how often* your pupils read, but *how* they read, that is most important. It is better that they read once a week carefully and properly, than to read ten times a day in a heedless and improper manner. Every repetition of a bad habit or act only renders it the more difficult of correction. Just remember this in all your teaching.

I have before suggested the importance of making every reading exercise a subject for questioning and criticising. Some teachers will make a single paragraph suggestive of numerous useful questions, and of much valuable information. It will be well, so far as possible, to have your pupils give a sketch of the author of the piece they are about to read, and an account of the circumstances under which it was written. This will tend to bring the subject home to their hearts, and, as it were, make the piece their own. This is essential. Take, for example, the following beautiful and expressive extract from "The Wreck of the Arctic," written by Rev. H. Ward Beecher, and see how many pertinent questions may be raised in reference to it.

"It was autumn. Hundreds had wended their way from pilgrimages; from Rome and its treasures of dead art, and its glory of living nature; from the sides of the Switzer's mountains, from the capitals of various nations; all of them saying in their hearts, 'We will wait for the September gales to have done with their equinoctial fury, and then we will embark; we will slide across the appeased ocean, and in the gorgeous month of October we will greet our longed-for native land, and our heart-loved homes.'

"And so the throng streamed along from Berlin, from Paris, from the Orient, converging upon London, still hastening toward the welcome ship, and narrowing every day the circle of engagements and preparations. They crowded aboard. Never had the Arctic borne such a host of passengers, nor passengers so nearly related to so many of us.

"The hour was come. The signal ball fell at

Greenwich. It was noon also at Liverpool. The anchors were weighed; the great hull swayed to the current; the national colors streamed abroad, as if themselves instinct with life and national sympathy. The bell strikes; the wheels revolve; the signal-gun beats its echoes in upon every structure along the shore, and the Arctic glides joyfully forth from the Mersey, and turns her prow to the winding channel, and begins her homeward run. The pilot stood at the wheel, and men saw him. Death sat upon the prow, and no eye beheld him."

How much of interest and profit may be obtained from the few lines above quoted, by asking the following questions, and others that may be suggested by them: —

What do you know of the author of this piece? What was the Arctic? Where was she? Whither was she bound? What is the meaning of "wended"? of "pilgrimage"? Where is Rome? What is meant by "the treasures of dead art"? Where does the Switzer live? What are his mountains called? What is meant by "September gales"? by "equinoctial"? What is meant by "we will slide over the ocean"? Meaning of "appeased"? What is meant by the "appeased ocean"? Meaning of "gorgeous"? Why is October called a gorgeous month? Can you give some other sentence containing the word "gorgeous"? Where is Berlin? Paris? London? The Orient? Meaning of "converging"? Why spoken of as "welcome ship"? "The hour was come," — what hour? Where is Greenwich?

What is meant by the expression, "the signal-ball fell at Greenwich"? Where is Liverpool? What would be the course of a vessel from New York to Liverpool? What is meant by the expression, "the anchors were weighed"? What is meant by "national colors"? What and where is the Mersey? Why the expression "the Arctic glides joyfully"? What is the meaning of "prow"? Who is the pilot, or what are his duties? What is meant by "Death sat upon the prow"? etc.

The same plan is recommended in the following extract from a well-prepared article in The Massachusetts Teacher.

"Imagine a class of sixteen or eighteen girls, ready to begin their recitation, their reading-books open at a description of the river Nile. One of them reads as follows: —

"'For many an hour have I stood upon the city-crowning citadel of Cairo, and gazed unweariedly upon the scene of matchless beauty and wonder that lay stretched beneath my view, — cities and ruins of cities, palm-forests and green savannas, gardens, and palaces, and groves of olive. On one side, the boundless desert with its pyramids; on the other, the land of Goshen, with its luxuriant plains, stretching far away to the horizon. Yet this is an exotic country. That river winding through its paradise, has brought it from far regions, unknown to man. That strange and richly varied panorama has had a long voyage of it! Those quiet plains have tumbled down the cataracts: those demure gardens have flirted with the Isle of Flowers, five hundred miles away; and those very pyramids have floated down the waves of the Nile. In short, to speak chemically, that river is a solution of Ethiopia's richest regions, and that vast country is merely a precipitate.'

"After analyzing the sentences and defining the more important words, various questions are asked. For example: Give some account of Cairo. What is a pyramid? Describe the Egyptian pyramids. What do you know of the land of Goshen? What is an exotic, and what is meant by an exotic land? In what form did those plains come down the cataracts? Give us some account of the Cataracts of the Nile. How were those vast pyramids floated down the river? 'In short, to speak chemically, that river is a solution of Ethiopia's richest regions, and that vast country is merely a precipitate.' Explain this sentence. What is it to speak *chemically?* What is a solution and a precipitate? Why is it correct to use such terms here?

"Another paragraph describes the annual inundation of the Nile: —

"'The stream is economized within its channel until it reaches Egypt, when it spreads abroad over the vast valley. Then it is that the country presents the most striking of its Protean aspects; it becomes an archipelago, studded with green islands, and bounded only by the Libyan Hills and the purple range of the Mokattan Mountains. Every island is covered with a village or an antique temple, and shadowy with palm-trees, or acacia groves. Every city becomes a Venice, and the bazaars display their richest and gayest cloths and tapestries to the illuminations that are reflected from the streaming streets.'

"Many interesting questions are here suggested. What are *Protean* aspects, and why so called? Where are the Libyan Hills and the Mokattan Mountains? Describe an Arab village,—an ancient Egyptian temple,—a palm-tree,—an acacia. Give some account of Venice. How does every city become a Venice? What is a bazaar?

"We followed the study of 'The Nile' with that of the poetical 'Address to the Mummy in Belzoni's Exhibition.' The manner of treating the first stanza will show the way in which the whole was studied.

> 'And thou hast walked about — how strange a story! —
> In Thebes' streets, three thousand years ago;
> When the Memnonium was in all its glory,
> And time had not begun to overthrow
> Those temples, palaces, and piles stupendous,
> Of which the very ruins are tremendous.'

"The class are asked if they know anything of the author of these lines, and of the traveller Belzoni; and having stated such facts as they have been able to procure respecting them, one is called upon to explain the first words of the poem.

"'And thou hast walked about.' The writer speaks as if the mummy were actually before him, while writing. Do you think that this was the case? Lucy may answer.

"'I suppose that he wrote the poem after returning from a visit to the exhibition, but remembered so perfectly how it looked, that he seemed still to be where he could see it.'

"Has any one a different opinion? Maria, you may give yours.

"'I think that he might have composed a part, at least, of the poem while at the exhibition, and then have written it after returning home.'

"'How strange a story!' Harriet may tell why it was strange.

"'Bodies usually decay in a short time, but this body had lasted thousands of years, owing to its having been embalmed. It seemed very strange to look at it, and remember that so many years had passed away since it was alive, and yet it looked as it did when it used to walk through the streets of Thebes.'

"Alice, you may give some account of Thebes.

"'Thebes was anciently the capital of Egypt. It is not known when it was founded; but the time of its greatest prosperity was, probably, when David and Solomon reigned in Judæa. Its ruins are wonderful. They extend seven or eight miles on both sides of the Nile, from each bank to the enclosing mountains. The most remarkable are the temple of Karnac, the palace of Luxor, and the Memnonium. The mountains are pierced with tombs, many of which are richly adorned with paintings and sculptures."

"The Memnonium is mentioned in the next line. Helen may tell us what she knows about it.

"'The Memnonium was the temple-palace of Rameses the Great. Its ruins show that it must have been a most beautiful specimen of architecture. There is in its grand hall a double row of pillars, crowned with capitals resembling the bell-shaped lotus-flowers. These are very large and of a solid stone, but the light and graceful shape of the flower is perfectly imitated. In the outer court, the fragments of an immense statue lie around its pedestal. Once it must have weighed nearly nine hundred tons; and the head was so large that, although several mill-stones have been cut out of it, its size does not appear to have been lessened.'

"Emma may explain the next three lines.

"'Time is here compared to a giant of such immense strength that he could throw down the magnificent palaces and temples that had been built with so much labor. But when the mummy was a living man, they were in all their splendor: Time had not even begun to destroy them.'

"It is proper for me to say, as I conclude, that I have no desire that such a study of reading-lessons should take the place of practice in elocution. I am aware that some time must be given to this alone; but the frequent or occasional study of reading-lessons in this manner will, I think, be attended with two advantages. Our pupils will read them far better, for they will have a more genial sympathy with the writer, and a more intelligent perception of his meaning. At the same time, they will form a habit which will be of indescribable benefit to them in after life, — the habit of comparing different views and statements, of trying an author by the great, eternal standard of Truth, and of earnestly questioning the Past, the Present, and the Future."

Sometimes these questions may be asked before the reading, and sometimes after. This may depend upon circumstances. The answering of the questions will prove very serviceable, by unfolding the sense of the piece, and thus enabling one to read it more understandingly. It will be well if you will often give illustrations of reading. This you may do for the purpose of exemplifying prominent errors and faults, and also for giving specimens of correct style. The importance of emphasis may be clearly manifested by a few illustrations, by which the entire force, if not meaning, may be affected by changing the emphasis. Let us take one or two examples. The oft-used line, "Do you ride to town to-day?" is a very good one. Write it upon the blackboard in the following different ways: —

Do *you* ride to town to-day?
Do you *ride* to town to-day?
Do you ride to *town* to-day?
Do you ride to town *to-day?*

This will give an idea of the variations that may be made merely by change of the emphasis. The following amusing, and perhaps I may say extreme cases, will show what a ridiculous import wrong emphasis sometimes gives to an otherwise expressive sentence.

"Do you imagine me to be a scoundrel, Sir?" demanded one man indignantly of another. "No," was the reply, "I do not *imagine* you to be one."

A careless reader once gave this passage from the Bible, with the following emphasis and pauses: "And the old man said unto his sons, Saddle *me*, the ass; and they saddled *him*."

A clergyman once told his congregation that they "had not followed a *cunningly* devised fable." The natural inference from his remark would be that he did not deny the fable, but only that it was not a *cunning* fable.

"Another clergyman, noted for reading hymns with an abrupt emphasis, once uttered the word *bears* in the following lines so that it seemed to his congregation a noun instead of a verb:

"He takes young children in his arms,
And in his bosom *bears* —"

I might say much more on the subject of reading, but it may not be necessary. If you carefully regard the hints already given, you will do much better than the majority of teachers who have preceded you. Hoping that you will not only regard these, but that you will, also, aim to devise new plans for securing the improvement of your pupils in the highly useful and pleasing art of reading, I am, as ever,

Your friend,

C.

LETTER XII.

SPELLING.

My dear Friend:—

Though the number of spelling-books has greatly increased during the last few years, it is still true that poor spellers do greatly abound. I have recently seen a few cases of false orthography, which I will give, both to amuse you and to convince you, if need be, that the subject of spelling calls for attention. The specimens I give are only a few of many. A bookseller recently received, from a person occupying a teacher's desk, the following order:—

"Plese scend me
4 secund Readors
4 primari Readors
and 2 sheats of stiffacets,"—
(meaning Certificates.)

Another received an order for "wun sam buk" (meaning one Psalm-Book).

A gentleman once wrote to a friend in India, requesting him to send him two specimens of the genus monkey. By the combination of indistinct writing and poor spelling the request seemed to be for 100 (*too*) monkeys, and the order was duly answered according to this understanding, much to the amazement of the gentleman, whose highest ambition was to become the owner of *two* of the chattering quadrupeds.

A merchant in London wrote to his agent in Scotland, requesting him to purchase a ton of copper, but being a poor speller, as well as writer, he omitted one of the *p*'s, and made a word which seemed more like *capers* than any other word. So the agent understood it, and, after much effort, he succeeded in procuring a full ton of capers, and wrote to the merchant, saying that "he had found it very difficult to obtain the required amount, but that he had finally filled the order, and the capers were subject to his order." The merchant was not a little surprised and mortified that so queer a *caper* should result from his illegible writing and poor spelling.

Again I urge you to give prominence to spelling, and I hope I may never receive a letter from any pupil of yours commencing, as a letter to another did, "My dear *Cur*." And should I ever have occasion to invite any of them to make me a visit, I should be very sorry to receive, as I once did, an answer thus: "It will afford me great pleasure to *except* your kind invitation," etc.

I might fill a volume with similar specimens, were it necessary. These defects are not chargeable to you. I have only instanced them as a proof of past neglect in teaching. I trust *your* pupils will be so trained and instructed that they will never be guilty of adding to the examples I have given. After speaking of two or three of the causes of poor spelling, I will give you a few hints and methods for conducting the spelling exercise. It is often regarded as dull and uninteresting, but, by adopting variety, it may be made pleasant and profitable.

One cause of the frequency of poor spelling may be found in the neglect with which the spelling lesson is treated in school. It is often crowded into a few minutes, and passed over in a very hurried and imperfect manner, and if any exercise must be omitted, the spelling lesson is the neglected one. Another cause may be found in a feeling, not very uncommon, that spelling is undeserving the attention of any but very young pupils. Many feel as the young man did, who, on commencing a course at an academy, demurred at the idea of joining the spelling class, notwithstanding he was a very poor speller. On being informed that all the pupils were required to join in the exercise, he very condescendingly consented to do so, provided the words should be taken from Webster's Unabridged Dictionary,—feeling that it would be quite derogatory if they should be selected from any spelling or reading book. These and some other erroneous notions must be eradicated. From the beginning, let your pupils see that the spelling lesson will always receive its due share of attention, and at its due time, and also cause them to feel that the only thing really derogatory is the inability to spell correctly. But I will proceed to describe a few methods for conducting the exercise,—both in the oral and written exercises,—for the latter of which I give a decided preference. I would, however, recommend a union of the two. But, first, I will allude to two very common errors.

One is that of giving out the words with an improper pronunciation, or an undue emphasis on a particular syllable or vowel; as, in-tī-mate, in-hab-ī-tant, im-me-dī-āte-ly, sep-ā-rate, sim-ī-lar-ī-ty, op-ē-ra-tion, etc. The only correct way is to pronounce a word precisely as it would be spoken by a good speaker; giving no undue emphasis to any letter or syllable; and, if distinctly pronounced once, it should suffice.

The other error to which I allude is that of allowing pupils to try more than once on a word in oral spelling. This is wrong, and I trust you will guard against it. One trial is sufficient, and all beyond is mere guessing. If pupils feel that they may make two or three attempts to spell a word, they will never become accurate spellers.

Some are strong advocates for the use of the spelling-book, while others entirely discard its use. My own impression is that it may be used to a certain extent; but if you would make a spelling lesson truly interesting and profitable, you must draw exercises from every proper source. It is an excellent plan to devote some time daily—a few minutes will suffice—to spelling the names of familiar objects.

Ask your pupils to give you the names of all the objects they saw on the way to school, and as they repeat, write the words legibly upon the blackboard, and say to them that the list thus written will constitute the next spelling lesson. Let us suppose the following to be a list of the words given by your pupils, as names of objects they have seen on the way to school: —

horse	collar	barrel
wagon	wheel	teamster
harness	carriage	mail-coach
bridle	whip	trunk
saddle	axletree	box.

Now, that you may call particular attention to these words, spend five minutes in making some of them subjects for object lessons, somewhat as follows: * —

Teacher. "What is the meaning of harness?"

Pupil. "It is something put on horses for them to draw by."

Teacher. "Of what is it made?"

Pupil. "Of leather." (Here you may expand the subject by asking what leather is, how made, and why better for making harnesses than rope or other materials, etc.)

Teacher. "Of how many principal parts does a harness consist?"

* In asking questions in this way, I would not often allow concert answers. Require all who feel prepared to answer to raise the hand, and then designate some one to give his answer, after which others who have a different definition may be called upon.

Pupil. "Four,—*collar*, *hames*, saddle, and bridle."

Teacher. "What is sometimes used instead of a collar?"

Pupil. "*Breastplate.*"

You will readily see that such an exercise may be extended almost indefinitely, and be made interesting and profitable. If desirable to add to the number of words, given in the columns above, the italicized words will be very good ones. The word *wheel* may be taken, and used somewhat as follows:—

Teacher. "What is a wheel?"

Pupil. "A round frame which turns round."

Teacher. "On what does it turn?"

Pupils. "On its axis; we say a wagon-wheel turns on an axletree."

Teacher. "Yes,—but not *exle*tree, as some say. Can you name the parts of a wheel?"

Pupil. "*Hub* or *nave*, *felloe* or *felly*, *spokes*, *tire*."

Here you may call for a description of each, and explain the process of setting tire, etc. You may, also, question them on the different kinds of wheels which they have seen or heard of, etc.

The word *mail-coach* may be taken and explained. So too *box*, *wagon*, *barrel*, *axletree*, may, each, be made a topic for a lesson. For variety's sake, as well as for profit, suppose you call upon your pupils to name sentences containing the word *box*. The following may be the examples given:—

The driver sat upon the *box* of the coach.

The garden walk had a border of *box.*

John kept his money in a *box.*

The boy received a *box* on the ear.

Sailors can *box* the compass.

This will be sufficient to explain my meaning. Your active mind will readily expand the exercise, and make it highly interesting and instructive. Such questions in connection with the spelling lesson will do much to give it life and meaning; and with such exercises, well devised and continued, pupils will become good spellers, though they may never study the spelling-book for an hour. The words thus selected can be left upon the blackboard until within a few minutes of the time for spelling them.

At another time you may collect a list of words from the school-room, as follows: —

book	inkstand	philosophy	penmanship
library	desk	astronomy	composition
arithmetic	platform	physiology	declamation
geography	blackboard	botany	orthography
grammar	crayon	aisle	discipline
dictionary	shelf	ventilator	paper
slate	chair	furnace	scholar
pencil	algebra	recitation	teacher.

The names of objects which pupils may see at their respective homes, may constitute a list sufficiently long for two or three lessons, and include such articles as may be found in nearly every house.

These names will be the very words all should know how to spell, and yet such as are very frequently misspelled. The articles kept for sale, in different kinds of stores, would also form a very appropriate and long list. The names of the various trees to be found in the gardens, fields, and forests, and the names of flowers, would, also, be fruitful sources from which to draw many useful spelling and object lessons.

Make a drawing of some familiar object upon the blackboard, as the basis of a spelling lesson. For example, the picture of a book. Call upon your pupils to name the different parts of the book, and you will get something like the following: —

outside	preface	contents
inside	title-page	letters
binding	running-title	words
leaves	folio	sentences
edges	quarto (4to)	paragraphs
margin	octavo (8vo)	printing
page	duodecimo (12mo)	stereotyping.

Let us suppose you call upon your pupils to give the names of the different trees they have seen, and the following are given and written upon the blackboard: *oak*, *walnut*, *elm*, *chestnut*, *hemlock*, *birch*, *cedar*, *pine*, *spruce*, *maple*, *beech*, *locust*, *ash*, *sycamore*, *poplar*, *willow*, *cypress*, *fir*, *larch*, *apple*, *pear*, *plum*, *peach*, *cherry*, *mulberry*, *apricot*. After these are distinctly written, ask questions like the following: —

Which of the trees named are fruit-bearing? Which produce nuts? For what purposes is the *oak* valuable? How many kinds of oak, and what called? For what is the *walnut* valuable? Which of the trees named are most prized as ornamental trees?

After calling for the uses and properties of the different trees, let the names be studied for a future spelling lesson. The same course may be pursued in regard to flowers, shrubs, vegetables, etc.

At another time, you may make a plain drawing of a house.

Teacher. "Can you tell me the names of some of the parts of a house?"

Pupil. "*Roof, eaves, ridgepole, cornice, doors, windows, chimney, rafters, sill, sash, parlor, kitchen, pantry, cupboard, closet, sitting-room, chamber, garret, cellar, stairs, hall* or *entry, piazza.*"

Teacher. "Can you name some of the materials used in building houses?"

Pupil. "*Timber, joist, boards, laths, nails, lime, brick, clapboards, shingles, glass, paint, screws, hinges, stone, zinc,* etc."

The particular use of each of these objects or materials may be explained at the same time that its name is spelled. A prominent advantage in these methods is, that it connects the subject of spelling with actual objects, and gives it a meaning and a force. Pupils trained in this way will soon form the habit of spelling the name of every object they meet with.

Another Method.

I will now name one or two other methods which may be well for occasional use and for the sake of variety. In all exercises in oral spelling, I would recommend that you pronounce the words distinctly, once only, require the class to pronounce the same in concert, and then call upon some one to spell. This will help to secure the attention, and make it sure that the word is understood.

In giving out long words it may be well, at times, to let the pupils spell by each giving a letter in its order, or pronouncing a syllable when finished. For example, let us take the word *orthography*. You pronounce the word and the whole class repeats it. In rapid succession the pupils spell thus, the figure indicating the number of pupil:

1 2 3 4 5 6 7 8 9 10 11 12 13
O-r—or—t-h-o-g—thog—orthog—r-a—ra—orthogra-
14 15 16 17
p-h-y—phy—orthography (by whole class.)

Another method which has its advantages is the following. Let the teacher dictate some thirty or forty words to a class, requiring the members to write them upon their slates. These words are to be carefully examined and studied by the pupils, who are also to be required to incorporate each word into a sentence, which shall illustrate its meaning and show that it is understood by them. After these sentences have been read, and erased from the slates, let the words be again dictated, to be written and examined with special reference to the orthography. An exercise of this kind will answer very well to fill up time that would otherwise be unimproved. The words may be given on one afternoon, and the written exercises and the spelling receive attention on the next afternoon.

It will be well if the teacher will have a small blank-book in which to write such words as are frequently misspelt, or such as are not of very common occurrence, and make use of these words for the method above named.

*"In order to secure the perfect attention of a class, the following methods will be found valuable; and, at the same time, they will aid in awakening an interest, and causing improvement.

"1. Read a short sentence distinctly, and require every word to be spelt by the class, — the first scholar pronouncing and spelling the first word, the next scholar the second, and so on, until all the words in the sentence have been spelt. After a little practice in this method, scholars will be able to go through with quite long sentences, with a good degree of accuracy and promptness. Many valuable truths and proverbs may in this way be impressed upon the mind, while attention is more directly given to orthography. The following may be samples: —

A good scholar will be industrious and obedient.

If sinners entice thee, consent thou not.

Take care of the minutes, and the hours will take care of themselves.

A soft answer turneth away wrath.

---

* From "The Teacher and Parent," published by A. S. Barnes & Burr, New York.

"2. It will be well, often, to make all the members of a class feel responsible for the accurate spelling of each and every word. If the first member of a class misspells the word given to him, let the teacher proceed and give out the next word, without intimating whether the first was correctly or incorrectly spelt. If the second scholar thinks the first word was not correctly spelt, he will spell it instead of the one given to him; and so on, through the class, each being expected to correct any error that may have been committed. If the first spells a word wrong, and no one corrects it, let all be charged with a failure. This method will amply compensate for its frequent adoption.

"I will now proceed to speak of some points in relation to the mode of conducting an exercise with the slate. Most experienced teachers have, latterly, often adopted the plan of writing words; but, for the benefit of others, I will specify one or two modes.

"Let the teacher select words from some studied exercise, either in the reading-book or spelling-book, pronounce them distinctly, allowing time, after each word, for all to write it *legibly*. After all the words have been given out, each slate may be examined separately, and all errors noted; or, the members of a class may exchange slates, and each examine his companion's slate, — while the teacher spells the words correctly, — and mark the number wrong upon each slate. Or, instead of either of these, the instructor may call upon some one to spell a word as he has written it, and then request those who have written differently to signify it by raising the hand. Neither of these methods will consume much time, and either of them will be preferable to the oral method.

"It will sometimes be the case, that scholars will prove themselves quite expert in spelling long or difficult words, and yet make sad mistakes in spelling those that are shorter, and apparently much easier. To remedy this, it will be well, occasionally, to read slowly an entire stanza or paragraph, and require the members of a class to write the same upon their slates. This course has its advantages.

"Again, it is frequently the case that scholars are exceedingly deficient in ability to spell the names of countries, states, counties, towns, mountains, rivers, individuals, etc. Any teacher, who has not exercised his pupils on such words, will be astonished at the number and nature of the errors that will be committed by a class on the first trial. Let teachers who have overlooked words of this description, in conducting the spelling exercise, commence by requesting their pupils to write all the *Christian* names of their schoolmates, the names of the counties in their native State, towns in the county, and States in the Union. Though the result, at first, may be neither very satisfactory nor gratifying, the plan, if frequently adopted, will cause much improvement.

"It may be profitable, sometimes, to request the members of a class to select, from a certain number of pages in a book, some ten or twelve words, which may seem to them of most difficult orthographical construction, which shall, subsequently, be given to the class as a spelling exercise. The prominent advantage in this plan results from the fact that each scholar will, in searching for a few words, notice the orthography of a much larger number, — selecting such only as appear to him peculiarly difficult. In this way pupils will, unconsciously as it were, study with interest a lesson in itself unattractive to them. Favorable results will attend such a course.

"If a school-room is well furnished with blackboards, the words or sentences for the spelling exercise may be written on them. In this case, it may be well to have the exercise occur during the last half-hour of the day. Let the scholars be required to write the words, legibly, as soon as pronounced by the teacher. After all have written, let the teacher examine the work, and draw a line over such words as are incorrectly written, and request that all errors be corrected immediately after school is dismissed. It is very important that pupils should be required to write all such exercises in a neat and distinct manner.

"At times it may be well to require scholars to divide the words into their appropriate syllables, and to designate the accented syllable of each word; as, an-ni-ver′-sa-ry, me-men′-to, la′-bor, la-bo′-ri-ous.

"Another method of conducting the exercise of spelling is the following, — and we may add, that, for more advanced schools, it possesses some advantages over either of the others named. Let the teacher write, legibly, upon the blackboard, some twenty or more difficult words, and allow them to remain long enough to be carefully studied by the school. A few minutes before the close of the school, let all the words be removed from the board. Now let each scholar put aside his books, and provide himself with a narrow slip of paper. At the top of this, or upon one side, let him write his name, and then the words, as dictated by the instructor. After all have written the list of words that had previously been placed upon the blackboard, let the slips be collected, and taken by the teacher, who may himself, aided perhaps by some of his best spellers, examine the slips, and mark those wrong upon each. At some hour of the next day, let the teacher read the result to the whole school, stating the number of errors committed by the several pupils; after which, the papers may be returned for correction. We will suppose, for illustration, that, on some day, the teacher gives out the names of the months, days of the week, and seasons of the year; and that the following is a sample of one of the papers, as returned by the teacher, with errors marked:

AMOS MASON.

Eleven Errors.

January.	Feberwary.*	March.
April.	May.	June.
July.	August.	Septembur.*
Octobur.*	Novembur.*	Decembur.*
Sundy.*	Monddy.*	Tuesday.

Wensday.*	Thursday.	Friday.
Saterday.*	Spring.	Sumer.*
Autum.*	Winter.	

"In conducting this exercise, let the teacher insist upon perfect distinctness in the writing of the words, and let it be understood that every letter not perfectly plain will be considered as wrong, and marked accordingly. It will be readily seen, that a little skill, on the part of the teacher, in the selection of words, will make this a highly useful and interesting exercise; and the time for the announcement of the number of errors will be looked for with interest.

"An attractive method, which may answer for oral or written spelling, is the following. The instructor pronounces a word, which is to be spelt by the first in the class, who will immediately name another, commencing with the final letter of the first word, which is to be spelt by the next scholar; and he, in turn, will name another word, and so on, through the class. If the words are to be written upon the slate, the same course may be taken, as to naming of words. Let us take, for illustration, the following words: —

Commotion.	Rhetoric.
Nourishment.	Circumstances.
Theoretical.	Sympathy.
Language.	Yellow.
Endeavor.	Wandering.

An exercise of this kind will have its peculiar advantages, the more prominent of which will be, the awakening of thought and interest. After a little practice, the members of a class will be able to name words with a great degree of promptness; and an exercise of this kind will be made highly interesting and profitable.

"Another method, and the last I shall name, is the following, which may prove very useful in the higher classes of most schools. Let the teacher pronounce to a class several words of difficult orthography, or short sentences containing such words, the pupils writing the same upon their slates as fast as dictated. After the desired number of words and sentences have been written, the instructor may address his class as follows: 'Scholars, the words and sentences which I have just pronounced may require from you some study. Examine them carefully, ascertain the correct spelling and meaning of each; and when you have studied them sufficiently, erase them from your slates. To-morrow I shall give you the same exercise, and shall then expect you to write them accurately.'

"Let us suppose that the following words and sentences should be given for an exercise of this kind:

Aeronaut.	Colporteur.
Armistice.	Hemorrhage.
Anchovy.	Beau ideal.
Acoustics.	Guillotine.
Bronchitis.	Hemistich.

Thomas has an excellent daguerreotype likeness of his mother.

The dahlia is a beautiful flower.

He was a successful merchant and a skilful financier.

The glaciers of Switzerland.

There is a beautiful *jet d'eau* on the common.

There was a beautiful giraffe in the menagerie.

His loss caused great poignancy of grief.

It was a successful *ruse de guerre.*

The police exercised strict surveillance.

"This mode is well adapted for presenting words and phrases whose orthography is peculiarly difficult, and which occur less frequently than most words."

By a judicious use of the methods I have named, and of others which may suggest themselves to your mind, I cannot but think you will succeed in your attempts to make your pupils good spellers. That such may be the case is the earnest wish of

Your sincere friend,

C.

LETTER XIII.

PENMANSHIP.

My dear Friend:—

Your pupils will all be anxious to write, and those foolish parents who have been duped into the belief that a finished style of writing may be given in "twelve lessons of one hour each," will be rather unreasonable in their demands; but you have too much sense to feel any sympathy with such notions, and, of course, will neither attempt nor pretend to be one of the impostors.

A good handwriting is often spoken of as quite an accomplishment. It is more. Its utility is its chief value, and for this, mainly, should it be taught. Whatever is worth knowing at all, is worth knowing well; and whatever is worthy to be taught, is worthy to be thoroughly taught. All reasonable people believe this, and yet how few practise it! How many there are who write so illegibly as to make it almost impossible to decipher their meaning! How often do we find it necessary to spend more minutes in reading a letter, than the writer used in penning it! This should not so be, and certainly there is no reasonable excuse for it. With proper care and right instruction, every pupil on leaving school may be, and should be, able to write a fair and legible hand, — I mean every one who attends school regularly. Some, of course, will write a more finished and elegant style than others, and learn much more readily; but if a boy leaves school at the age of fourteen years, without the ability to write a plain, readable hand, *he* must have been grossly heedless, or his *teacher* a very incompetent one.

But you wish for hints and directions. I can point out no royal road, — designate no way in which you can hope to make good writers without continued care on your part, and persevering effort and practice on the part of your pupils. This should be understood at the outset by you and by them. I think it may also be understood, that a due regard to the directions and suggestions which I am about to give will secure satisfactory results in the branch under consideration.

A definite, desirable, and attainable end should be kept before the mind. It is too often the case that pupils commence writing with no well-defined views, and with no object beyond that of spending the required time in making "pen-and-ink marks" upon paper; and many teachers, I am sorry to add, feel that their whole duty is performed if they require their pupils to devote a half-hour daily to the making of these marks. No right taste is cultivated, no directions given, no instruction imparted, and, of course, no improvement is made. Week after week the pupils sit in the same improper position, holding the pen wrong, making and remaking very imperfect letters, — both teacher and pupils attaching more consideration to the quantity written than to the quality.

I will now, in a familiar way, proceed to give a few hints and directions on specific points.

I. *The Position.* — Pupils are very apt to sit in an awkward and bent position. They should be required to sit nearly erect, and with the right or left side towards the table. If you find that your pupils have acquired a bad position, it may require considerable effort for you to cause a change; but it should be effected, whatever amount of labor and time it may cost. It is not uncommon to find pupils in schools who bend over so much as to bring their eyes very near the paper. Though this is really an unhealthy and uncomfortable position, it will be no easy matter to cause a change, especially if the improper position has been long allowed.

II. *Holding the Pen.* — You cannot be too particular in your efforts on this point. Very bad habits are often formed, and become so established that the most patient and decided effort will be necessary in order to eradicate the old habit and introduce a new and correct one. But you must do it, if you would hope to be a successful teacher in this department. Bad habits in pen-holding are frequently the result of the improper construction of seats and desks. It is sometimes the case that the seat is so far from the desk, or the desk so high, as to render it impossible to sit erect, or hold the pen in a proper position. Effort should be made to have these right. If you find that any of your pupils have formed bad habits in holding the pen, give attention to the subject, and not lose sight of it until all is right. Sit at your table in view of your school, with your body and pen in proper position. Require them to observe how you sit and hold your pen, and then require them to imitate your example. It may seem awkward to them at first. If so, repeat the operation frequently, requiring them to imitate you in movements similar to those made in actual writing. The following cuts will show the correct position of the hand and pen.

III. *A correct Taste and quick Perception.*—These are very important points. It is very essential that we know precisely what is to be done before we attempt to do it. A farmer once sent an ignorant man to work in his field, who spent most of the day in plying the hoe, but doing little good and much harm, simply because he knew not the difference between the weeds to be cut up and the corn to be cultured.

So, often, it is with pupils in writing, — they have no clear idea of what they should do, and the longer they use the pen, the more paper they waste, and the more bad habits they confirm. After devoting the requisite time and attention to the two particulars previously named, — position and holding the pen, — spend a little time in an effort to cultivate a correct taste and judgment. I will tell you how this may be done, and would suggest that a few minutes be given daily to this point, — the main thing being to lead the pupils to see that the same letter may be made in several different ways, and at the same time cause them to feel that one way is the best, and that they should always aim to secure the best way. Let us go to the blackboard, in imagination, with the following : —

m m m m m m
1 2 3 4 5 6

Teacher. "Scholars, can you tell me what letters these are ?"

Scholars. "Yes, Sir ; they are *m*'s."

Teacher. "What, all *m*'s ? Are they all alike ?"

Scholars. "No, Sir ; some are made better than others, but they are all *m*'s."

Teacher. "Which do you think is made best ?"

Scholars. "The fourth one."

Teacher. "Those who think the fourth is the best, may raise their hands." (All hands up.) "Very well ; I think so too. Now let us see what fault there is with the others. George, what do you think of No. 1 ?"

George. "The different parts are not of the same height, and the turns are not good."

Teacher. "Very well; but is that all? Thomas, can you name any other faults?"

Thomas. "I should think they all ought to have the same slope and be better spaced."

Teacher. "Very good. I am glad you understand so well about these letters. Now if you were going to make one, which should you try to imitate?"

Scholars. "The fourth."

This might be extended, but the idea will be readily seen. Each of the other *m*'s may be treated in the same manner, — the particular defects in each being pointed out.

A similar course may be pursued with more advanced classes. A line like the following may be presented for criticism: —

A good name is better than riches

A course of questioning on this line would lead pupils to see the prominent faults, and induce them to study to avoid them. Such a plan will afford an opportunity for explaining the difference between the looped and unlooped letters; the effects of unequal spacing; want of uniformity in height; and of evenness in the down marks, etc. In examining the writing-books of one day, you will find a sufficient number of errors to afford you material for a lesson the next. Two particulars should be kept constantly and prominently before the mind of the pupils.

1st. That they should strive to imitate a good model.

2d. That the writing of each day should indicate an improvement upon that of the preceding day. Towards securing the first of these, the blackboard exercises above alluded to will do much. To promote the second, I would recommend the two following plans.

1. At the beginning of the term let each pupil write a few lines upon a page of a blank-book, provided for the purpose, and say to him that at the close of the term he will be required to write a few more lines on the same page, and that, if he is faithful and attentive, the lines last written will appear much better than those written at the commencement of the term. This will give you in one book — and a common writing-book will answer — a specimen of the handwriting of each pupil at the beginning and also at the close of the term. It will have a stimulating effect upon your pupils.

2. Let the pupils go through the book, writing one half of a page at a lesson, — and one half of a page well written will be better than ten pages carelessly written. After writing one half of each page in the book, let them re-commence and write the remaining half of each page. There will be two advantages in this, — one that it will relieve pupils of the monotony of writing the same copy, and the other, that

the time elapsing between writing the first and last half of each page will be sufficient to afford a criterion of improvement.

IV. *If possible, classify your Pupils in Writing, as well as in other Exercises.*—The pupils in most schools may be arranged in from two to four classes in writing. This classification may be governed by qualification, as in other branches. One of the prominent advantages of such an arrangement will be the opportunity of giving instruction to a number, at the same time, on the same copy. For this purpose the blackboard may be used with excellent effect. We will suppose that your first class is just commencing the book, and that the first copy is to be written. Go to the blackboard and write the copy, and call their attention to the particulars to which they should give special effort, and point out some of the errors which pupils most frequently make. To a class of ten or twenty members, more or less, you can make a brief exercise of this kind very profitable. After listening to your instruction and hints, they will commence writing with some definite object in view. In a late report to the School Committee of Boston, Superintendent Philbrick thus testifies in favor of the use of the blackboard for illustration in this branch: "Where the best results were produced, the blackboard was in constant use, and a whole section of pupils wrote the same copy at the same time." Perhaps you will say that your pupils are so irregular in their attendance, that you cannot classify them in writing. But you can just as well as in other branches. Every class suffers from the irregular attendance of members. Have the copies come in regular order, and if a pupil is absent when a particular page is written, either require him, on his return to school, to write the page after school, or leave it blank; and if at the end of the term there are several blank pages, just explain to the committee and parents the reason, and say to them that there are just as many *blank* pages in all other studies, only they are not so distinctly visible as in this particular. This may cause some to see the evils of irregular attendance in a new light.

It will frequently happen that a whole class will err in the same particular, or in making the same letter. When such is the case, go to the blackboard and imitate the wrong letter or letters, and show wherein the defect is. Then make a letter as nearly correct as possible, and require them to spend two or three minutes in forming the same letter on slips of paper.

The following sensible and judicious remarks and directions I take from the cover of one of the best systems of penmanship now before the public.* I commend them as worthy of observance.

"From an experience of many years, we are satisfied that there is no short and easy method of ac-

* Payson, Dunton, and Scribner's, published by Messrs. Crosby, Nichols, & Co., Boston.

quiring a rapid and graceful style of penmanship; and that those who profess to teach the art of writing in twelve, twenty-four, or double that number of lessons, may be justly regarded as empirics.

"Learning to write well must always be a work of much time and effort, since it involves a careful training of the eye and hand, and a gradual development of the judgment and taste. Great natural obstacles are sometimes to be overcome; but by careful and well-directed efforts, with a good system, *any one* may learn to write well, and most persons may learn to write elegantly.

"Good writing is characterized by *legibility, rapidity, and beauty.* In order that these ends may be attained, the following rules must be carefully studied and implicitly observed, — all of which the authors submit to the careful attention of the public.

"1. Of Position. — Sit with either the right or left side turned a little towards the desk, in an easy, natural position, but do not lean against the desk.

"2. Hold the pen with a gentle pressure, between the *thumb and the first and second fingers*, keeping the muscles of the hand and arm so relieved that the motions may be free and easy.

"3. Of Position of Hand and Arm. — The hand and arm should rest very lightly upon the desk, in order to secure freedom of motion and rapidity of execution.

"4. Remarks. — Before commencing to write after a copy, the pupil should carefully notice the form and proportion of each letter, and he should also *examine each word* as soon as it is written, to see wherein it differs from, or agrees with, the copy, and then try to improve it the next time. This course, diligently pursued, will certainly secure a good degree of improvement; while, by an opposite course, the time of the pupil and the labor of the teacher will be entirely wasted.

"5. Of Order and Neatness. — Write nothing but the copy on the book, unless directed to do so by the teacher; but try to keep the book clean and free from *blots*, and never cut out a leaf. Keep the pen clean, and ink thin. A habit of neatness and order is of very great value to a book-keeper or business man.

"6. The Pen. — Never touch the point of the pen with the fingers, nor wipe it on the hair, but on a *pen-wiper*, made of some kind of cloth. It should be wiped often, and always when you lay it aside. Do not hold the pen between the teeth while turning the leaves, etc., but place it over the right ear, where it will be less liable to make blots than elsewhere.

"7. Of Position of Left Hand. — The left hand may rest on the paper above the line on which you are writing, but never below it, as the oily matter of the perspiration, on the paper or the pen, will prevent the ink from flowing freely."

LETTER XIV.

GRAMMAR.

MY DEAR FRIEND: —

MUCH time has been devoted, in most schools, to the subject of Grammar; yet the real attainments of pupils, for all practical purposes, have been very limited and unsatisfactory. In this branch, more than in any other, have pupils been allowed to repeat words, definitions, and rules, which were to them but empty sounds, — meaningless expressions. In many cases, scholars have committed to memory the entire contents of a text-book, without gaining any true knowledge of language or grammatical science. What I have said of geography is quite as true of grammar, — that words are too often learned and repeated on the recitation-seat, without imparting any definite ideas. "What is a vowel?" asked a teacher of a girl. "A vowel is an articulate sound," was the ready answer, in the language of the book. "And what is an *articulate* sound?" "A melodeon," answered the girl. To her mind, a vowel was but another name for a musical instrument, or melodeon.

Some of the most discouraging cases you will meet with will be those in which pupils have "been through the Grammar," and learned little but words. Professor Russell gives a case in point. "A boy, who had studied grammar a long time, got tired of it, and did not wish to go over the definitions again under the guidance of another teacher. To test him, the teacher said: 'Do you think you understand all that you have studied?' 'Yes, Sir; I know it all.' 'Well, here is the definition of an indefinite article; what is that?' '*A* or *an* is styled the indefinite article, and is used in a vague sense; in other respects indeterminate.' (So he learned from his Grammar.) 'Do you understand that fully?' 'O yes, Sir.' 'Will you tell me what "styled" means?' 'Why, it means something sort of grand, stylish.' 'What does "article" mean?' 'It means — why, it means anything that we see.' 'What does "vague" mean?' 'I don't know, Sir.' 'Well, what does "indeterminate" mean?' 'Being very determined about it, Sir.'"

And yet this lad, like hundreds of others, had a sort of impression that he knew all about grammar, and felt it almost derogatory to his standing as a scholar to have his attention called to it as a suitable branch for him to study. If you meet with such a case, as you undoubtedly will, your first effort must be directed to convincing the pupil that he does not comprehend the subject. This will be no easy task, and yet it must be accomplished. You must strive to convince him both of his lack and need of knowledge, before you can expect to have him study with a will.

You wish to know what I consider the proper age for commencing the study of grammar. This will depend on circumstances. Many lessons may be given to very young pupils. The parts of speech, kinds of sentences, and many other points, may be treated of in a familiar style of oral lessons by the teacher, and much information may be imparted to pupils of the ages of eight or nine years, before they take the text-book. The "when" to commence, therefore, will depend much upon the "how" of commencing. The very youngest pupils should have the benefit of correct examples of speech. But it would be better that the study of grammar never be commenced, than to have it improperly treated.

My object, in this letter, will be to caution you against the tendency, on the part of scholars, to learn words only, and also to give you a few hints on teaching grammar. Mr. Tower, in his preface to a valuable work entitled "Grammar of Composition," uses the following sensible and truthful language: — "English Grammar has been defined as 'the art of speaking and writing the English language correctly'; and this definition has been accepted and retained by grammarians, notwithstanding it has become a matter of public notoriety that pupils may excel in grammar and 'parsing,' as taught in our schools, and yet be unable to form grammatical sentences, either orally or in writing. Where, then, is the fault? in the definition, or in the method of teaching? In the latter, we fully believe. The very fact that it is an *art* shows the absurdity of supposing that it can be acquired without *practice*. Who ever became a skilful musician simply by studying the principles and rules of music?"

If teachers would regard the truth contained in the brief extract just made, it would be sufficient. And yet, for years and tens of years, a sort of word-repeating and formal round of technical parsing have constituted the sum and substance of grammar in many of our schools, though within the last ten years the study has been more wisely taught by most good teachers. Many of my suggestions, at this time, will be directed to giving the subject a more practical bearing.

Be careful to speak correctly yourself, and require your pupils to do the same. — This is all-important. If, in all your conversation, your commands and requests, you speak with propriety, you will, as it were, be a living grammar to your pupils. Your example will be felt for good. On the other hand, if you are careless in the use of language, and are guilty of frequent grammatical inaccuracies, you can hardly hope to have your pupils speak correctly. One great difficulty in the way of teaching grammar is, that the pupils out of the school-room often hear expressions and language at variance with any correct standard. If all persons were in the habit of "speaking the

English language correctly," the teacher's efforts to impart instruction in the school-room would be far more successful. But every pupil has twofold instruction, — that in the school-room and that outside the school; and often the two are directly antagonistic in their influence and results. This point is not duly considered, and the faithful teacher is often charged with errors or defects in his pupils, which are in no true or just sense chargeable to him.

Let us suppose a portrait-painter undertakes to perfect the likeness of some person. During a part of the hours of each day he devotes his time and skill, most assiduously, to make the painting life-like and accurate. Faithfully and well he performs his part, making no errors, but constantly developing true shades and right points. Every touch is made at the right time, and in the right place and manner. Now suppose this unfinished painting should be daily brought in contact with those who are no artists, and that each should give a touch with his own unskilled hand. It would be easy to predict the result. And yet the teacher's work is thus exposed and tampered with; and in no point does it suffer so much as in that under consideration. Be sure that the errors of the street find no countenance in the practice of the school-room. "Speak correctly" yourself, if you would hope to have your labors in teaching grammar successful, and insist on correct speaking on the part of your pupils. By the exercise of care and judgment, you will soon succeed in creating a sort of popular school-sentiment in favor of the right; and when you have secured this, your success will be sure.

Make your teaching thorough and clear.—One of the most common errors has been that of attempting to advance too rapidly. The pupil's mind is often so perplexed with the variety before him, that he receives no definite and accurate view of any one topic. I have known a class of beginners who have been required to give the definitions of all the parts of speech at a single lesson. Of course they could not receive any clear impression of either. The result would naturally be vague and confusing. Suppose one individual should attempt to enlighten a friend in relation to the trees in a dense forest, not one of which was known to the second party. The two enter the forest, and the first, as they pass rapidly along, says to his friend: "This is an oak; this, a pine; this, a hickory; this, a hemlock; this, a chestnut," &c.;—without any attempt to point out the distinctive peculiarities of each, and not even allowing time for the learner to take a fair look at each tree as its name is given. How many such forest walks would it require to give to the man the needed information? Yet a course equally unreasonable has often been taken with beginners in grammar. See that you commit no such error. From the beginning, teach one thing at a time, and teach that thoroughly. Make one step familiar before another is attempted.

In teaching the several parts of speech, deal with one singly, at first, and dwell upon it until the class understands it. The old definition of a noun was as follows: "A noun is the name of anything that exists, or of which we have any notion; as, London, man, virtue." I have heard this repeated scores of times, when I was satisfied that those who gave the definition had not the slightest correct "notion" of the part of speech defined. To them a noun was "London-man-virtue," — but what "London-man-virtue" was, they knew not. Most of the Grammars of the present day define a noun as "the name of an object," — and yet even this may be repeated, and not be understood. I have, in many instances, known pupils to confound the object with its name. The word *book* is a noun, but not the book itself. See that your pupils discriminate, and, after using proper effort to make the point plain, call upon them for a list of nouns. Ask them to give you the names of all the objects in the school-room, and write them as they are spoken. The list may be something as follows: Desk, chair, book, stove, inkstand, pencil, slate, pen, window, floor, wall, nail, hat, etc. They may also be called upon to give the names of objects that they have seen on their way to school. Continue exercises of this kind, requiring your pupils to write them upon their slates, until they are fully comprehended. The same course may be pursued to explain what is meant by "common and proper," as applied to nouns. Require the pupils to make lists of each until they shall be able to do so with promptness and correctness. Number, person, gender, and case may be taken in the same manner. If a term has been properly explained, require your pupils to give a practical illustration by some written exercises. After the noun and its several modifications have been considered, in the manner alluded to, your class will be prepared to write sentences exemplifying the following: —

A sentence containing one proper and two common nouns.

A sentence with a proper noun in the nominative case, and two common nouns in the objective case and singular number.

A sentence with two common nouns, one in the nominative and the other in the possessive case.

A sentence with a proper noun in the nominative case, masculine gender, and a common noun in the plural number, objective case, and feminine gender.

These exercises will please the pupils, and they should be continued until the several points and modifications are made perfectly plain.

The same general plan may be taken with the several parts of speech, and their various modifications. Have every definition followed by some written exercises illustrative of the same. The different kinds of sentences may be explained in the same manner.

On the subject of grammar, important as it is, it is hardly necessary that I should enlarge. The hints I have already given will be of some service if duly regarded. On many points teachers differ in opinion. A score of years ago most of the grammatical exercises consisted in the parsing of words. These were conducted in a manner so set and formal, that but little good resulted from them. The analysis of sentences received no attention. But there has been a change, and now, with many, the old mode of parsing is entirely discarded, and analysis substituted therefor. The true course, I think, is to give attention to both methods. Combine the two in practice, and the results will be satisfactory.

Much of grammar, in its practical use, will enter into the exercise of composition, — of which I shall speak more particularly in my next letter, — and I would urge you to give much attention to that branch of the subject. Indeed, in all your attempts to teach the subject, do not forget that it is only by frequent practice that one can reasonably hope to become skilled and ready in "speaking and writing the English language correctly."

Before closing, I will speak of two other exercises in this connection. The first is the correction of false syntax. It will be well, occasionally, to place upon the blackboard a few ungrammatical sentences and require your pupils to correct them, and also to tell what is wrong, and why wrong, in the example given. I will add a few sentences for the purpose named. You will find that pupils will feel pleased in attempting their correction, and the effort will cultivate a critical and observing spirit.

Charles did it unbeknown to me.

It is him. It is her.

Let every scholar attend to their studies.

May John and me go to walk?

Please to let John and I go to walk.

You should have went with me.

He said how he would go.

I have not seen him this ten days.

I expect you reached home safely.

John and George was to home.

I saw that James had been abused with half an eye.

A newspaper has the following: —

"*Wanted.* — A young man to take charge of a pair of horses of a religious turn of mind."

A carpenter once rendered the following bill to a farmer, for whom he had worked: "To hanging two barn-doors and myself seven hours, one dollar and a half."

A newspaper says: "A child was run over by a wagon three years old and cross-eyed, with pantalets on which never spoke afterward."

A man writes: "We have two school-rooms sufficiently large to accommodate three hundred scholars one above another."

Another writes: "We have a new school-house large enough to accommodate four hundred pupils three stories high."

Make a memorandum of errors, like the above, as you hear or see them, and occasionally make one the subject of a brief criticism by the school, guarding against any improper spirit on the part of your pupils. Aim to have all criticisms made in a friendly, and not in a censorious or supercilious spirit.

The only remaining point, to which I will call your attention in this letter, is punctuation. This has been sadly neglected in our schools; and yet its importance, as affecting the import of what is written, is such as to demand for it special attention. Of course I cannot consider the subject in detail. I will merely urge its claims to your attention, and give a few examples illustrating the entire change, in meaning, caused by a change of punctuation. These examples will assist you in showing the effect of punctuation, and in awaking an interest in the right direction.*

"Lord Palmerston then entered; on his head, a white hat; upon his feet, large, but well-polished boots; upon his brow, a dark cloud; in his hand, his faithful walking-stick; in his eye, a meaning glare; saying nothing, he sat down."

With a slight change in punctuation, it will read thus: "Lord Palmerston then entered on his head; a white hat upon his feet; large, but well-polished boots upon his brow; a dark cloud in his hand; his faithful walking-stick in his eye; a meaning glare saying nothing. He sat down."

* A Treatise on Punctuation, by John Wilson, is the best work on the subject within my knowledge. Indeed, it seems to be a complete treatise on the subject, and it should be used in all our schools. I am indebted to it for two or three of the illustrations.

In the priory of Ramessa there dwelt a prior who was very liberal, and who caused these verses to be written over his door:

> "Be open evermore, O thou my door,
> To none be shut, to honest or to poor."

But after his death, there succeeded him another, whose name was Raymond, as greedy and covetous as the other was bountiful and liberal, who kept the same lines there still, changing nothing therein but one point, which made them run after this manner:

> "Be open evermore, O thou my door,
> To none; be shut to honest or to poor."

Afterward, being driven thence for his extreme niggardliness, it grew into a proverb, that for *one point* Raymond lost his priory.

Observe the difference in the following: "The persons inside the coach were Mr. Miller; a clergyman; his son; a lawyer; Mr. Angelo; a foreigner; his lady; and a little child."

As here punctuated, with a semicolon after each noun, the number of individuals is eight. Arranging the names in pairs, thus: "The persons inside the coach were Mr. Miller, a clergyman; his son, a lawyer; Mr. Angelo, a foreigner; his lady; and a little child," — we reduce the number to five, and entirely change the meaning of the sentence.

Varying the punctuation a third time, we find that "the persons inside the coach were Mr. Miller; a clergyman, his son; a lawyer, Mr. Angelo; a foreigner, his lady; and a little child."

The following lines will furnish another instance. By placing the semicolon, now at the end of each line, after the first noun in the line, quite a change will be made in the sense.

"I saw a pigeon making bread;
I saw a girl composed of thread;
I saw a towel one mile square;
I saw a meadow in the air;
I saw a rocket walk a mile;
I saw a pony make a file;
I saw a blacksmith in a box;
I saw an orange kill an ox;
I saw a butcher made of steel
I saw a penknife dance a reel;
I saw a sailor twelve feet high;
I saw a ladder in a pie;
I saw an apple fly away;
I saw a sparrow making hay;
I saw a farmer like a dog;
I saw a puppy mixing grog;
I saw three men who saw these too;
And will confirm what I tell you."

A clergyman was lately depicting before a deeply interested audience the alarming increase of intemperance, when he astonished his hearers by saying: "A young woman in my neigborhood died very suddenly last Sabbath, while I was preaching the gospel in a state of beastly intoxication!"

From the work of Mr. Wilson I take the following illustrations of the value of correct punctuation.

"A blacksmith, passing by a hair-dresser's shop, observed in the window an unpointed placard, which he read as follows: —

'What do you think? —
I'll shave you for nothing,
And give you some drink.'

"The son of Vulcan, with a huge black beard on his chin and a little spark in his throat, considered the opportunity too good to be lost. He accordingly entered; and, after the shaving had been duly performed, asked with the utmost *sang froid* for the liquor. But the shaver of beards demanded payment; when the smith, in a stentorian voice, referred him to the placard, which the barber very good-humoredly produced, and read thus: —

'What! do you think
I'll shave you for nothing,
And give you some drink?'"

"The following request is said to have been made at church: 'A man going to sea, his wife desires the prayers of this congregation for his safety.' But, by an unhappy transposition of the comma, and the misspelling of one word, the note was thus read: "A man, going to see his wife, desires the prayers of this congregation for his safety."

"Witness the entire change caused by punctuation in the following: —

'Every lady in this land
Hath twenty nails upon each hand;
Five and twenty on hands and feet.
And this is true without deceit.'

'Every lady in this land
Hath twenty nails: upon each hand
Five; and twenty on hands and feet
And this is true without deceit.'"

"The well-known speech of Norval, for instance, in the tragedy of 'Douglas,' may, by an erroneous use of the pauses, be delivered in such a manner as to affect or destroy the meaning; as,—

'My name is Norval on the Grampian hills.
My father feeds his flock a frugal swain;
Whose constant cares were to increase his store.
. . . .
We fought and conquered ere a sword was drawn.
An arrow from my bow, had pierced their chief
Who wore that day the arms which now I wear.'

"A change in punctuation restores the meaning thus:—

'My name is Norval. On the Grampian hills
My father feeds his flock; a frugal swain,
Whose constant cares were to increase his store.
. . . .
We fought and conquered. Ere a sword was drawn,
An arrow from my bow had pierced their chief,
Who wore, that day, the arms which now I wear.'"

Trusting that you will be able to make a good use of these illustrations, and be aided by them in causing your pupils to see the importance of the subject, I remain

Your sincere friend,

C.

LETTER XV.

COMPOSITION.

My dear Friend:—

You ask if you shall make the writing of composition a regular exercise in your school. I answer, most emphatically, Yes. It is one of the most important subjects, and well deserves your care and thought. It has often been sadly neglected,—more frequently improperly treated. You also ask at what age pupils should commence the exercise, and for some hints in regard to it.

In answer to this I would say, if it is regarded by you as it is by some teachers, it would be better never to commence; but, properly viewed and conducted, it can hardly be commenced too early. As soon as a child can write words, he may begin the writing of composition, provided his first lessons are of the right kind. I well recollect some of my first themes for composition, given when I was a mere boy. They were such as these: *Temperance*, *Friendship*, *Virtue*, *Happiness*, *Charity*, &c.,—all themes entirely unsuitable for beginners. Pupils cannot write upon a subject beyond their comprehension, or in which they feel no special interest; and whenever such themes are given, pupils will be very apt to examine books to ascertain what others have thought or written. In this way, many early become plagiarists, and try to pass as their own what they have wholly, or partly, borrowed from others. I recollect an instance of this kind, in which the ready wit of the offender saved him from punishment and exposure. He took a nicely written article to his teacher, who, after reading it, opened a volume written by Mrs. Barbauld, containing the same views, expressed in precisely the same words. After reading this to the pupil, the teacher remarked: "What have you to say to this?" "Why," said the lad, "all I have to say is, that Mrs. Barbauld and I think exactly alike."

The better way is to give suitable subjects, and thus afford no temptation for pupils to borrow thoughts or words from the writings of others. You have, I doubt not, often heard compositions read in schools, whose whole style and expression afforded the most convincing proof that they were not original. I recently heard one, many words of which were so shockingly mispronounced, that it was perfectly obvious that the piece was a borrowed one, and that the meaning of many of the words was not comprehended. The word "receptacle" was repeatedly called "respectacle." But I have said enough on this point, and will now offer a few suggestive hints.

You know very well with what a feeling of dread

pupils engage in the exercise under consideration. The very word *composition* seems to cause a shudder; and the longer the subject is deferred, the greater will be the reluctance with which it will be commenced. With a little care and prudence, you may fairly initiate your pupils into the mysteries of the exercise before they realize that they have taken the first step, and before you make any allusion to it as a step, even, in the much-dreaded exercise. Take a class of little ones, and ask them to write the word *horse* upon their slates. For three or four minutes ask them questions about a horse, somewhat as follows: How many of you ever saw a horse? Of what color are horses? How many legs has a horse? What do we call animals which have four legs? For what is the horse used? Of what does his food consist? What do we sometimes call his feet? What is meant by a draft-horse? carriage-horse? race-horse? etc. Such questions as these will elicit thought, and prepare them for the next step, which is to write upon their slates something about the horse. As a result, you may get something like the following: —

"My father has a black horse.

"The feet of a horse are very hard, and are called hoofs.

"Some horses are very swift, and called race-horses. Some are large and strong, and called draft-horses, because they are used in drawing heavy loads.

"The horse is very useful, and it is cruel to whip him.

"Horses, and other animals that have four legs, are called quadrupeds."

These sentences may not all be as correctly written as they are printed. There may be errors in spelling, use of capitals, etc. Still each of them expresses an idea, and is a first step in composition writing. At first it will be well rather to commend them for what they have done properly, than to censure them for any errors they may have made. A little encouragement will do much good, while a slight reproof at the beginning may prove quite dispiriting. At the first attempt, each will write but a single sentence. This may be as much as it will be well to require, and if they do this fairly, commend them, and as a next step ask them to see how many sentences each of them can write about a horse. After a few exercises you may receive something like the following:—

"The horse is a very useful animal. My father has a good horse. His color is white. He eats hay and oats, and sometimes he feeds on grass. He is very gentle, and I can drive him. He is not afraid of the cars, but a gun frightens him some. He wears iron shoes, which are nailed to his feet. His foot is called a *hoof*. We ought to use a horse very kindly."

If, instead of this, you should give to a beginner *virtue* as a subject, he would not write, because he would have nothing to write,—no ideas on the subject. The fault is not in the pupil, that he does not write, but in the subject, or rather in yourself, if you assign him such a subject. So much depends upon the selection of subjects, and the manner of treating the few first efforts, that you should make a special point to give them suitable themes, and furnish encouragement by commending the first productions.

Quite young pupils may commence writing sentences, as soon as they can write legibly. It will amuse them, and serve to keep them usefully employed. For such pupils the subject should, of course, be very simple; such as *horse*, *cow*, *dog*, *kitten*, *house*, *garden*, etc.

To more advanced pupils a different class of subjects may be given, but they should be subjects in which they feel an interest, and about which they should be expected to have some thoughts and ideas. An account of some *journey*, a *vacation*, a *holiday*, a *walk*, a *visit*, etc. might be very appropriate subjects. *Letter-writing* may very profitably be introduced as an exercise in composition. To be able to write a good letter is, in itself, quite an accomplishment, and constitutes, in the true sense, an exercise in composition. I would advise you to make the writing of a letter a special lesson occasionally. If it had heretofore received more attention in all our schools, we should not see so many miserably written letters. By using the blackboard you may give directions as to date, address, closing, superscription, etc.

The following may serve as specimens of subjects for letter-writing.

1. Write to a cousin, and give an account of your school and studies.

2. Write to your parents, and give them an account of your studies, deportment, etc. for the last week or month.

3. Write to an absent brother, sister, or friend, and give an account of whatever you may deem interesting.

4. Write to a former schoolmate, and tell him about your school, your amusements, and companions.

5. Write to your teacher, and tell how you have spent your vacation.

6. Write to some absent friend or relative, and tell about your home, your friends, your school, etc.

It will make a very pleasant and useful exercise for pupils, to require them to change poetry into prose in such manner as to retain the same meaning. I will give an example.

> "Across the rolling ocean
> Our Pilgrim Fathers came,
> And here, in rapt devotion,
> Adored their Maker's name.
> Amid New England's mountains
> Their temple sites they chose,
> And by its streams and fountains
> The choral song arose."

Changed to prose, the above might read thus: "Our Pilgrim Fathers crossed the rough ocean that they might, on these shores, engage in earnest and devout worship of their Creator. They erected churches among the hills and mountains of New England, and on the banks of the streams and rivers they sung anthems of praise to Him who had sustained and guarded them."

The ideas expressed might be expanded, and given in many different modes of expression.

Another method for giving pupils a start in the exercise of composition is to read to them some interesting story, or relate to them an account of some journey, and require them, on a subsequent day, to express the leading incidents in their own language and style. From the outset encourage simplicity of style and manner of expression, and discourage every attempt at high-sounding words and phrases.

Give to a class a few words, requesting them to write as many sentences as there are words, and to incorporate one word into each sentence. For example, let us suppose you give the following words, by dictation, or by writing them upon the blackboard: *good*, *lesson*, *scholar*, *obedient*, *teacher*, *diligently*. No two scholars will be likely to write precisely the same sentences. The variety itself will be useful in illustrating the different ways in which the same word may be employed. Perhaps one pupil may write as follows: —

"*Good* boys will obey their parents in all things.

"The idle boy will not learn his *lesson*.

"An industrious *scholar* will improve.

"The *obedient* pupil will love to do right.

"The faithful *teacher* will be happy.

"We should all study *diligently*."

The word *good* may be used as follows by different pupils: —

"We should all try to be good."

"John gave me a very good apple."

"The good scholar will obey his teacher."

"I had a good time last vacation."

"School will do us no good if we are idle."

As another exercise, requiring more effort and thought, require a class to write a sentence which shall contain all the words. One may write thus: "A good scholar will be obedient to his teacher, and will study his lesson diligently."

So far as time will permit, read the several sentences aloud, or require the pupils to do so, and make such criticisms as you may think proper, always being careful not to subject any pupil to the ridicule of the class. If a boy has done as well as he could, commend him, though his performance may fall far short of what you might wish. This hint should pertain to all exercises of the schoolroom.

I have alluded to the correction of errors. It must be expected that beginners will make many mistakes in their early productions. If they could write without making errors, it would not be necessary for them to write as a school exercise. The very object for which they write in school is that they may learn how to correct their errors, — learn how to express their thoughts properly. It will be your duty to assist and encourage them. Very much will depend upon the manner in which you perform your part. At the outset, it may not be well to be over-critical; for, if beginners should have all their mistakes arrayed before them at once, they might feel discouraged. In a kindly way point out some of the more prominent ones first, — often uttering words of cheer, so far as you can do so consistently. Many of the first exercises may be written upon slates; but after sufficient practice, let paper be used, and always require a margin of an inch on the left for the designation of errors. It will be most profitable to require pupils to correct their own errors, — you merely indicating the lines in which they exist, and also their nature. A few simple characters may be used as expressive of the nature of the mistake. Perhaps the first four or five figures will answer the purpose. Let it be understood that (1) placed opposite a line denotes an error in spelling; (2) an error in use of capital, or neglect of same; (3) the omission of a word, or the repetition of a word; (4) false syntax; (5) a wrong word. If two or more errors are in the same line, use the figures that indicate all that exist. To illustrate my meaning more clearly, let us suppose the following to be a composition, with the errors designated according to the above method.

"Vacation.

1 *"It is very pleasent to have vacation*
come, for we get tired of studying all the
2, 5 *Time. If we have studied studiously*
during school time we will enjoy our vaca-

3 *tion more than if we had idle. I love*
1, 2 *to go to the country in vacasion as i always*
5, 1 *have a good time at picking berrys and in*
1 *riding with my cusins. When vacation*
4 *is over we should return at school and*
5 *studying."*

This will be sufficient to explain what I mean. You will readily see that the above will be at once simple and effective. It will prove very beneficial for pupils to search for, and correct, these errors. I would recommend that at first they correct the errors upon the paper which contains them, and that they then be required to rewrite the whole in the right form; and I would also advise that you make the chirography itself a subject for criticism. As an incitement to effort in this department, it is well to have a "paper," into which the best written articles shall be copied, and that, occasionally, extracts be read from this paper to parents and others who may come to listen. In some schools an hour is devoted to this semi-monthly.

As aids to the subject of composition, a few useful treatises have been prepared, and are now before the public. For beginners Brookfield's work, published by S. A. Rollo, New York, will be found an excellent work. For more advanced pupils, Parker's "Aids to Composition," published by R.

S. Davis, Boston, and a work by Quackenboss, published by the Messrs. Appleton, New York, will prove very valuable. But I would have you feel that in yourself are the chief aid and moving power. If you are judicious in the selection of subjects and in the general management of the exercise, you will do your pupils great good without any of these aids; but if you have not the right feeling, or if you err in your instruction, all other aids cannot compensate therefor.

I will close this letter by giving you a list of topics for exercises in composition.

SUBJECTS FOR COMPOSITION.

1. A description of my home.
2. A description of my school-house and its location.
3. An account of the village or town in which I live.
4. A description of a garden, with its trees, plants, and flowers.
5. A description of a ship.
6. A description of the ocean and its uses.
7. The Dog.
8. The Cat.
9. The Horse.
10. The Cow.
11. The Pig.
12. The Sheep.
13. The Ox.

Note.—These and other domestic animals may form themes for Composition. A description of each may be given, in which the habits, mode of living, uses, etc. may be considered.

14. The Lion.
15. The Elephant.
16. The Leopard.
17. The Panther.
18. The Giraffe.

Note. — The countries in which they live, their appearance, habits, disposition, mode of living, etc. may be named.

19. The names and description of the wild animals I have seen.
20. The Whale.
21. The Seal.
22. The Walrus.

Note. — Where found, how captured, and for what valuable.

23. The fishes I have seen, and their uses.
24. The names of the common domestic fowls, and an account of their food, habits, uses, etc.
25. A list of the different birds I have seen, and something about them.
26. Reflections at the beginning of a year.
27. Reflections at the close of a year.
28. Thoughts at the commencement of a school term.
29. Thoughts at the close of a school term.
30. Thoughts on the death of a friend.
31. Duties to parents.
32. Duties to teachers.
33. Duties to brothers and sisters.
34. Duties to schoolmates and associates.
35. Duties to the poor and unfortunate.
36. Some of the ways for promoting happiness.
37. An evening at home.
38. A day at school.
39. The importance of forming good habits.
40. Learning is better than wealth.

41. How to improve time.

42. Spring.
43. Summer.
44. Autumn.
45. Winter.

Note. — Some of the peculiar and appropriate pleasures and duties of each season may be mentioned, and preferences expressed.

46. An account of the fruits I have seen.

47. A description of the different trees I have seen, their names, appearance, uses, etc.

48. Some of the most common vegetables, — manner of cultivating, uses and modes of use.

49. An account of the different grains and grasses I have seen, etc.

50. A description of the flowers I have seen.

51. The materials used in building houses, and how used.

52. Articles of furniture in a house, and their uses.

53. Uses of knowledge.

54. The Puritans.

55. Fourth of July.

56. What should I aim to be and do?

57. Industry.

58. Perseverance.

59. Idleness, and its evils.

60. Disobedience.

61. Right use of time.

62. Delays are dangerous; — why?

63. Pleasures of school.

64. The good scholar.

65. The bad scholar.

66. Good deportment.

67. Cruelty to animals.
68. Pleasures of home.
69. Order; or, "A place for everything, and everything in its place."
70. Cheerfulness.
71. Politeness.
72. Punctuality.
73. The evils of war.
74. The farmer.
75. The blacksmith.
76. The shoemaker.
77. The tanner.
78. The currier.
79. The printer.
80. The carpenter.
81. The sculptor.
82. The mason.
83. The cabinet-maker.
84. The merchant.
85. The sailor.

Note.—Let a description of each be given,—their duties named, the tools or implements used described, etc.

86. Pleasures of travelling.
87. An account of a journey to ——.
88. Honesty.
89. Truth.
90. Falsehood.
91. Thoughts on visiting a cemetery.
92. Reflections on witnessing a funeral procession.
93. Thoughts on seeing a ship "set sail" on a long voyage.
94. Thoughts on leaving school.

95. The past, — the present, — the future.
96. Attention.
97. Adversity.
98. Affectation.
99. Benevolence.
100. True courage.
101. Cruelty.
102. Carelessness.
103. Curiosity.
104. Diligence.
105. Education.
106. Early impressions.
107. Friendship.
108. Flattery.
109. Gambling.
110. Intemperance.
111. Force of habit.
112. Honesty.
113. Happiness.
114. Kindness.
115. Music.
116. Sincerity.
117. System.
118. Every man the architect of his own fortune.
119. Never too old to learn.
120. Selfishness.
121. Avoid extremes.
122. Example better than precept.
123. Our country.
124. Ambition.
125. Contentment.

126. The art of printing.
127. Commerce.
128. Fashion.
129. Silent influence.
130. A soft answer turneth away wrath.
131. The true object of life.
132. "Be not overcome of evil, but overcome evil with good."
133. Gratitude.
134. Our duties to God.
135. "Labor conquers all things."

Your sincere friend,

C.

LETTER XVI.

GEOGRAPHY.

My dear Friend: —

The dictionary tells us that geography is a description of the earth; and in all our schools the pupils commence the study of this branch by committing the definition to memory. This is all well as far as it goes; but too often the words are repeated without having any definite idea connected with them. Hence it is true that children study geography for weeks and months without gaining any correct and practical views. In all your teaching, it should be your aim to impart or awaken ideas. Cause your pupils to feel that words are useless, except as symbols of ideas, and that they are but unmeaning sounds, unless they convey ideas. The definition of a peninsula, for example, may be repeated by a pupil for the hundredth time, and yet give no accurate impression of the thing defined. If possible, awaken thoughts in the minds of your pupils, and then lead them to use right words as expressive of those thoughts. It would greatly amaze you to know how much some pupils are able to recite from the Geography, while, for all available, practical purposes, they are as ignorant as untutored children. A gentleman once took an apple, for the purpose of illustrating to his niece, sixteen years of age, who had studied geography for several years, the shape and motion of the earth. She looked at him a few minutes, and said, with much earnestness: "Why, uncle, you don't really mean to say that the earth turns round, do you?" "Certainly," he replied; "did you not learn that several years ago?" "Why yes," said she, "I *learned* it, but I never *knew* it before." So it is with many pupils in our schools; they *learn* without *knowing*.

A late writer in an English paper gives the following, which admirably illustrates our point. "One little incident we must mention, as illustrating education by rote. Walking to church, one Sunday, in Skye, we were followed by a slip of a lad some ten or eleven years of age, who, on putting some questions to him, volunteered to name all the capitals in Europe, which he did with marvellous dexterity. From Europe he crossed to South America, and rattled out the names of the capitals with the accuracy of a calculating machine. From South America he started off to Asia, and finally brought up at Jeddo, in Japan. We were rather sceptical as to the value of such acquirements, and, indeed, as to the reality of any information having been conveyed to the lad's mind by the formidable muster-roll of words that had been stuffed into his mouth. We there-

fore asked him, 'Can you tell us the name of the island on which you live?' But, notwithstanding his lore, he had not learned that he lived in the Isle of Skye. To make quite sure of the fact, we requested the captain of the steamer to repeat the question in Gaelic, but there was no "Skye" forthcoming. He knew the name of the parish, and of all the capitals in the world, but not of the island he lived in. There being a schoolmaster present, accidentally, we thought the occasion too good to be lost to show the worthlessness of word-stuffing, and ventured another question: 'Now, my lad, you have told us the names of nearly all the capitals in the world; is a capital a man or a beast?' 'It 's a beast,' said the boy, quite decisively. So much for words without understanding. In the next school inspection, that boy will probably pass for a prodigy, and will figure in statistical reports as an example of what good education can do."

From these derive a lesson, and be sure that your pupils *know* what they *learn*. True *learning* implies the possession of *knowledge*. True teaching implies the giving of information; and when this is attempted by means of illustrations, they should be made simple and expressive. An English teacher was once drilling his pupils preparatory to an anticipated visit from the committee. "Very likely," said the master, "you will be asked of what shape the earth is; and if you forget, look towards me, and I will show you my snuff-box to remind you of its shape." It so happened that the teacher had two snuff-boxes, — a round one, which he used on Sundays, and a square one, that he used on other days. As was expected, the committee-man asked one of the lads, "What is the earth's shape?" After a moment's embarrassment, he turned his eye towards the teacher, and, seeing the snuff-box, said: "It is round on Sundays, but square the rest of the week."

It will be my object in this letter to give you some hints on teaching geography. In many schools, it is the custom for pupils to commit to memory the answers in the book, and if these are repeated accurately, it is sufficient. If, in answer to the question, "What is an isthmus?" the pupil says, "A neck of land uniting a peninsula to the mainland," it is perfectly satisfactory, notwithstanding the pupil may have no well-defined idea either of "peninsula" or "mainland." Let me advise you not to be satisfied with mere word answers, but, by asking questions, ascertain that definite and correct ideas accompany the utterance of those words.

Aim to bring every term and definition within the comprehension of your pupils. So far as possible, do this by using familiar illustrations, — the simpler, the better. For a child to say that the earth is round, conveys no true impression. A dollar is round; the trunk of a tree is round; a cup is round; but neither of them round like the earth. If you have a globe, you can readily explain the earth's rotundity; but if you have none, use an apple, an orange, or a ball. All our maps represent the earth as on a flat surface. Explain this, and cause your pupils to see that these maps simply represent the surface of the globe, spread out for our convenience; and that, if a globe of the right size should be prepared, these several maps could be made to cover it in proper form. See to it that all the geographical terms are perfectly understood. Question your pupils concerning island, peninsula, continent, isthmus, cape, promontory, mountain, valley, ocean, sea, lake, river, gulf, bay, &c., until you are satisfied they know precisely what is meant when either of these terms is used. In this connection, I would commend to your attention a series of geographical cards, published by Messrs. J. H. Colton & Co., New York. These cards convey through the eye a clear impression of the object defined. No. 1 represents a beautiful island, with trees and dwellings upon it, and boats and vessels around it. From a moment's glance at this picture a mere child will understand what an island is. All the other terms above alluded to are clearly illustrated in the same way. If you have not these cards at hand, take a little time, and, by use of maps or blackboard, make each term as plain as possible.

In commencing geography, it will be well to begin near home. The idea of boundary, location, relative position, and distance, may be given by some simple illustration. The school-house, or its yard, — if you are so fortunate as to have one, —

may be taken for a lesson. Its north, east, south, and west boundaries may be given. Tell your pupils that their fathers' gardens or farms are bounded by those farms or gardens or streets which adjoin them, and that to give the boundaries of a town, state, or country, is to give the towns, states, countries, or waters which lie next to them. For the sake of system, require all boundaries to be given commencing with the north, and then proceeding to east, south, and west.

In giving some idea of location and relative position of places, require them to draw a representation of the street from their homes to the schoolroom; or, in the first place, give them an example by representing upon the blackboard some prominent street, with the dwellings and other objects of general interest. This exercise of drawing may be commenced quite early, and continued through the whole period of studying geography. The benefits will be many and great.

The following extract* contains many valuable suggestions.

"In order to impart clear ideas in teaching geography, it is indispensable, first, that the figure and motions of the earth be clearly understood. To accomplish this, the teacher must have at hand maps and globes, to which reference should be constantly had. A knowledge of the definitions, also, is indis-

* From a late report of J. W. Bulkley, Superintendent of Schools in the city of Brooklyn.

pensable. But verbal definitions are of little worth, unless the thing defined, and its relations, use, &c. are understood. Much time is usually spent on Descriptive Geography. This department of the subject should receive attention, but it is by no means the most important, because, in its nature, it is the most liable to change. What is true of a particular locality or district to-day, may have materially changed in the course of a single year. Attention should be directed rather to *principles*. These change not; and without a knowledge of them, no one can lay claim to anything of geographical science.

"The earth being one of the planets of the solar system, the pupil should be made acquainted, after he has gained some knowledge of maps and the globe, with so much of Mathematical Geography and Astronomy as may be necessary to give him an idea of the relations of the earth to the system, and the general phenomena pertaining to this body. He may be easily taught how to find north and south by showing him the polar star and the sun at noon, the shadow then falling towards the north. The other points of the compass would be clearly understood; and then he would know the true meaning of these in nature as well as on the map, which is an important point gained.

"The form of the earth, and the reasons and evidences of its rotundity, could here be explained in such a way as to interest and awaken thought in the pupil, and carry conviction to his understanding.

The motion of the earth on its axis, and rotation in its orbit, will claim attention also. Here let such models as represent a sphere and hemisphere, and such lines as represent a circle, diameter, and right, curved, and parallel lines, be exhibited, explained, and their use and application shown. An idea of the axis of the earth may be given by running a wire through an apple, and turning the same upon it; the diameter of the apple representing the axis, and the ends of the axis the poles; and these not extending beyond the surface, as often represented on maps, but terminating thêre. Care should here be taken to have the pupil understand that the axis is *not* a real, but an imaginary line. Next let the equator be described; and let it be seen that, notwithstanding it *appears* like a straight line on the map, it is nevertheless a true circle. This can easily be shown by tracing this line on a globe, or winding a thread around an apple or ball.

"This line (the equator) would furnish the teacher with thoughts which would not only interest and instruct his pupils, but be of importance in understanding the general subject. Here, the days and nights are *always* equal, the sun rising and setting at six o'clock, with a very short twilight; consequently, darkness comes on almost immediately after sunset. Here, the temperature is nearly the same at all seasons, being generally as high as eighty or eighty-two degrees. This would be understood by reference to our hot days in summer. Here, animals and plants differ much from our own. The teacher would name some of the most important, and describe them. Here, the sun is vertical at noon on the 20th of March and the 23d of September, when bodies cast no shadow. Here, the polar star is in the horizon, and the Great Bear near the same line or below it. Here, the story of the old '*Salts*' to the young sailors, on approaching the ***burning line***, concerning old 'Father Neptune,' and the terrible ordeal to which he subjects all who cross it the first time, may be told.

"Again, the subjects of latitude and longitude, the tropics, polar circles, and the zones, each in order, should be carefully explained and well understood. The pupil should distinctly understand that latitude must be measured on the meridian, and that the meridian line is that which runs north and south of a given place; that all places on the same parallel must have the same latitude; that these on the globe are marked on the brass meridian, and in maps on their sides; and that a degree is about sixty-nine miles. The tropics may be the next subject presented. Their distance from the equator shown, and why; the space included between them, its name, why so called; its productions, animal and vegetable; its climate; and that, when the sun is vertical at the tropic of Cancer, the northern hemisphere has the long day of summer, and the southern the long day of winter, at the same time; and that, when the sun is vertical at Capricorn, the opposite takes place, as to length of day and season, in the northern hemisphere. Here the question may be answered in relation to the polar circles, why drawn the same distance from the poles as the tropics from the equator? The temperate and frigid zones, in their climate, seasons, length of the days and nights, and other important facts, may be described, and the same contrasted with the torrid. An interesting fact for the pupil to understand, namely, how it is that the earth's surface has two divisions of constantly equal day and night, at the poles six months each, and at the equator of twelve hours each, while the other parts of the earth's surface have unequal day and night, should here be explained.

"Instruction in longitude should be given, in connection with time, as all places under the same meridian have the same time, and opposite meridians a difference of twelve hours. Let it be explained, that longitude must be reckoned in degrees, minutes, and seconds, along the parallel of the given place, and marked on the equator, on the globe, or on maps at the top or bottom. An interesting problem may now be explained,—the difference of time at different places. The earth makes a revolution in twenty-four hours. A circle contains three hundred and sixty degrees. Now, if we divide three hundred and sixty by twenty-four, we obtain fifteen. An hour is equal, then, to fifteen degrees of longitude. Or, if we divide an hour (sixty minutes) by fifteen, we get four minutes, which is equal to one degree, a result corresponding with the first. The time of the place farthest east will be in advance of the one in the opposite direction. Thus the pupil has the elements by which to ascertain the time of any given place, and the difference between it and his own and other places."

In teaching geography, a set of outline maps will be found of great value. With a set of such maps, the subject may be taken up by topics, and made very interesting and profitable. I know not how I can better express my views as to the beginning of instruction in geography, and also in relation to the use of outline maps, than in the language of Professor Camp, in his hints to teachers as contained in his Geography, prepared to accompany Mitchell's excellent set of Outline Maps. Any teacher who will follow the plan thus pointed out can hardly fail of success.

"In introducing the study of geography to a class of young pupils, their attention should first be directed to the school-yard, or a portion of the road, or fields; prominent objects should be pointed out, and their relative position and distance noted. The whole should then be represented on the blackboard, by the teacher. Thus would be conveyed to the child the idea of a map. This map should be copied on a slate, by each member of the class, and recited from as a lesson. Additions of surrounding fields, roads, etc. should be made at successive lessons, till a map of the district, village, town, or city be completed.

"Various natural features should be described when located, such as brooks, ponds, hills, and islands; the points of the compass indicated; the boundaries, peculiarities, and general features of the whole taught orally, and by actual view of the same, if possible.

"By similar and successive steps, the geography of the county or parish should be taught, while an outline of the same is made upon the board and copied by the class.

"The excellent State maps now published, will give the teacher an opportunity to teach well the geography of the pupil's own State.

"When this is done, the class or school will be prepared to study with advantage from the text-book.

"The geographical definitions should be thoroughly committed to memory, and illustrated from the maps, and by a globe.

"In the use of the outline maps, it is desirable that the class be so arranged that they will face the north, with the map before them. The teacher should point out the country or part of the world to be studied, calling the attention of the class to any peculiarities of configuration or position.

"The pupils should then become so familiar with each map, the natural features represented, the political divisions, and the locality of places, as to recognize them by their forms or positions, without their names accompanying.

"This can be secured by oral instruction, by a careful study of the map with the key in the Geography, and by drawing the map on the slate or paper, putting down the parallels and meridians, and accurately filling up the outline with the natural and political divisions.

"The principle of association, according to some particular order of arrangement, will aid the memory in retaining the name of each place or division. The following order has long been used by some of the best teachers of New England, and has been adopted in the arrangement of the maps and key. Commencing with each map at the upper left-hand corner, or northwest part, and proceeding around the map to the right, let the pupil in recitation pronounce distinctly the names classified as follows.

1. Countries.
2. Oceans, seas, gulfs, and bays.
3. Straits, channels, and sounds.
4. Islands.
5. Capes, peninsulas, and isthmuses.
6. Mountains and deserts.
7. Lakes and rivers.

"Or the teacher may pronounce the name, and let the pupil point out the thing named, on the map.

"Each map is to be reviewed by promiscuous questions. A few of these have been given. But the teacher should multiply and vary them, as circumstances require.

"For classes of advanced scholars, topical instruction will be productive of very beneficial results. The country to be studied having been selected, the teacher should assign a topic to each pupil, who, with a given and definite subject before him, should consult reference-books, public and private libraries, and all sources of available information.

"The following list of topics can be used, or so much of it as is adapted to the attainments of the class, or their means of obtaining the facts required.

"LIST OF TOPICS FOR ADVANCED CLASS.

1. Situation, extent, and boundaries.
2. Coast (indentations and projections).
3. Rivers and lakes.
4. Surface (mountains, plains, plateaus, etc.).
5. Soil and climate.
6. Productions (animal, vegetable, and mineral).
7. Manufactures.
8. Commerce (exports and imports).
9. Cities and towns (capital, seaports, and manufacturing towns).
10. Travelling facilities.
11. Inhabitants (population, manners, and customs).
12. Government.
13. Education and religion.
14. History (colonial possessions).
15. Miscellaneous (natural curiosities, places and objects of interest, distinguished persons, etc.)."

For reviews in geography, the following arrangement of topics will be found a good one.

1. Situation, boundary, latitude, and longitude.

2. General divisions.
3. Islands, peninsulas, capes, and isthmuses.
4. Mountains, plateaus, and deserts.
5. Capitals, cities, and important towns.
6. Oceans, seas, and archipelagos.
7. Gulfs, bays, and harbors.
8. Straits, channels, and sounds.
9. Rivers and lakes.
10. Government, — in whom vested, and how administered.
11. Religion and education.
12. Agricultural productions.
13. Mechanical productions.
14. Miscellaneous, — as, modes of travel, objects of interest, etc.

Let us suppose that North America is to receive attention according to the above order, and that the class has studied with reference to the same. One pupil is called upon for an answer to the first. If you have outline maps, require him to go to the same, and, with a pointer, to trace the outlines, — give the boundaries, latitude, and longitude. The pupil called upon to answer No. 4 should be required to point out the several places as he names them. The list of topics treated in this way will embrace all the important points in relation to the country under consideration.

Here let me caution you against the very common error of indistinct or incorrect pronunciation of geographical terms and names. How often do we hear *Artic* for *Arctic*, *Missippy* for *Mississippi*,

Carlina for *Carolina*, *Fellydelfy* for *Philadelphia*, *Ashee* for *Asia*, *Mederanean* for *Mediterranean*, etc. It will be well occasionally to devote an hour to the pronouncing and spelling of geographical names, and especially such as are often mispronounced.

In addition to the hints named, you will find it an excellent plan, occasionally, to require your pupils to describe the course of a ship from one country to another. For example, —

From New York to Manilla.
" Boston to Melbourne.
" Philadelphia to Constantinople.
" New York to San Francisco.
" Boston to the Sandwich Islands.

Let them go to the outline maps, and, with a pointer, designate the route of a ship, and give such information as they can in relation to these places, naming their imports and exports, the probable length of the voyage, etc. It may be well to call upon some pupil, daily, for an exercise of this kind. It will occupy but a few minutes, and may be made both interesting and profitable. After one pupil has given all the information he possesses, give others an opportunity to add other particulars.

Another exercise may be, to require a class to write, in letter form, some geographical account of a State or country. For instance, a letter relating to Massachusetts, in which its situation, boundaries, chief rivers, mountains, productions, exports, imports, educational condition, etc. may be stated.

This may be made a useful exercise in composition, as well as in geography.

Much interest may be excited in a class by the following plan, which I have often seen adopted with pleasing results. Let the first in order name some city, state, country, mountain, river, etc.; let the next in order tell where it is, and give all the information he can concerning it; and then give to the next some place commencing with the last letter of his own topic, and so on. Sometimes it will be well to limit the names or topics to cities, sometimes to countries or rivers, etc. An exercise of this kind, once or twice weekly, will excite much interest in a class, and lead to investigation.

If one is unable to give any information, or gives it incorrectly, let him pass to his seat, and the next in order make the trial. To illustrate this let us suppose a class of six members, whom we will designate by the figures 1, 2, 3, 4, 5, 6.

1. *London?*

2. London, the most important and largest city in the world, is situated on the river Thames, in England, and is the capital of the British empire. It contains a population of nearly 3,000,000, and is in all respects a city of immense influence. (To the next.) *New York?*

3. New York is the name of one of the United States, and also of the largest city in the Union. The city of New York is situated on Manhattan Island, and it is the most important and influential city of the New World. The island, on which it is

situated, is thirteen and a half miles long, and about two miles wide in its widest part. The population is about 650,000. It was first settled by the Dutch, in 1612. (To the next.) *Knoxville?*

4. Knoxville is a flourishing city in Tennessee. It is on the Holston River, and was formerly the capital of the State. It has a university and an asylum for the deaf and dumb. (To the next.) *Edinburgh?*

5. Edinburgh is the capital and metropolis of Scotland. As the centre of learning, it is the most distinguished town in the British empire. It is in many respects an important city. It is particularly noted for its excellent and elegant buildings. The name Edinburgh ("Edwin's castle or fort") is supposed to be derived from Edwin a Saxon prince. It was anciently written Edwinsburgh, etc. (To the next.) *Hartford?*

6. Hartford is one of the capitals of Connecticut. It is on the west bank of the Connecticut River, and is a city of much enterprise. Trinity College is located at Hartford. The American Asylum for the Deaf and Dumb is in this city. There is also an asylum for the insane, — which is one of the most noted and best conducted in the United States, etc.

These are merely given as examples. You will readily see to what extent an exercise of this kind may be carried, — and especially if the class is large. It will be well, after a few trials, to require all the prominent particulars in relation to each topic or place to be given; but at first, if a few are correctly given, it may answer. After one has stated what he may have to say, an opportunity may be given for others to add any particulars not already given. An additional interest and advantage may be secured by making the spelling of the names given a part of the exercise.

Another interesting, useful, and practical lesson may be obtained from the items in a common "Marine Journal." Let us take, for illustration, the following, which I find in a New York newspaper.

MARINE JOURNAL.

PORT OF NEW YORK, AUGUST 5.

Cleared.

Steamships — Roanoke, Skinner, Norfolk, Ludlam & Pleasants; Kangaroo, Jeffrey, Liverpool, J. G. Dale; Illinois, Boggs, Aspinwall, M. O. Roberts.

Ships — Ocean Pearl, Chandler, New Orleans, N. H. Brigham; Matoro, Dillingham, Valparaiso, A. Ladd; H. Von Gagen, Reimer, Hamburg, W. F. Schmidt; Horatio, Hathaway, Cowes and a market, Jas. E. Ward & Co.

Barks — William, Heath, Gibara, C. & E. J. Peters; Cavallo, Washington, Lavacca, J. H. Brower & Co.; Nazarine, Smith, Benaventura, M. M. Bachey.

Brigs — Lydia Francis, Hall, Philadelphia, Yates & Porterfield; Crimea, Hickborn, Philadelphia, Walsh, Carver, & Chase; Wilhelmina (Brem.), Howyer, Laguayra, Burchard & Burk; Edinburgh, Bartlett, Philadelphia, T. H. Sandford; Flying Eagle, Conant, Alicante, R. P. Buck & Co.; Vulcan (Br.), Card, Windsor, D. R. DeWolff; A. B. Cook, Leighton, Philadelphia, G. W. Simpson.

Arrived.

R. M. steamship Persia (Br.), Judkins, Liverpool, July 25, mdse. and pass. to E. Cunard. July 25, passed ship Countess (of England), bound in; Aug. 1, lat. 47 20, lon. 50 16, passed a cutter steering W., showing Spanish colors; 2d, lat. 44 40, lon. 57 32, exchanged signals with Br. ship Onward, bound E.; 3d, at 8 a. m., lat. 42 26, lon. 62 56, passed steamship Vanderbilt, hence for Southampton; same day, at 9½ a. m., lat. 42 18, lon. 61 21, passed steamship Atlantic, hence for Liverpool; the Persia arr. off Sandy Hook on the 4th, at 8 p. m.; Aug. 1, wind easterly, light breeze and cloudy, at 8 p. m., Cape Race Light abeam; 4th, at 6½ a. m., lat. 40 23, lon. 71 25, calm, with dense fog, took a pilot from the Edwin Forrest, No. 14.

Steamship New York (Br. screw), Craig, Glasgow, July 22, mdse. and pass. to J. McSymon. Has experienced strong westerly gales for the first 5 days; on the 25th, had a heavy gale from W. N. W.; 26th, signalled Brem. ship Janson, Smidt, bound W.; 29th, at 5½ a. m., signalled steamship Arabia, for Liverpool; 30th, at 9 p. m., a large steamer passed, bound W.; Aug. 4, at 11½ a. m., signalled steamship Atlantic, hence; same day, saw a Brem. bark, showing private flag, blue swallow and white cross.

Ship Don Quixote (of Boston), Elwell, Foo-Chow-Foo April 23, teas to order. Sailed in company with Br. ship Glencoe, for London; left Angier May 21, in company with bark Reindeer, Townsend, from Singapore for New York; April 26, lat. 18, lon. 115, passed Br. ship Bio Bio, from Shanghae; May 21, 20 miles from Angier, signalled ship Mandarin; 26th, exchanged signals with a ship supposed the Fearless; 29th, spoke Fr. ship Thetis, from Pondicherry for Bourbon; June 15, lat. 34 28, lon. 29, spoke ship Jennie W. Paine, from Batavia for London; 18th, lat. 34, lon. 23, spoke bark Vernon, for Table Bay; 27, lat. 29, lon. 12, signalled Br. ship Anglo American; 28th, lat. 27, lon. 9, signalled Br. ship Alice Jane; same day, signalled ship Fleetwood Dale, from Calcutta, 71 days out; 21st, lat. 35, lon. 13, spoke the C. W. Wappers, from Batavia, 72 days out; 22d, lat. 33 30, lon. 15, spoke brig Helena, for Hamburg; July 24, lat. 13, lon. 50, spoke bark Emblem, from Rio for Philadelphia, 25 days out; passed St. Helena July 3.

You will readily see that you may make the above extracts from a "Marine Journal" — such as you may always find in newspapers printed at important seaports — the basis of several interesting lessons. These lessons, too, will have a practical bearing. Let us propose the following questions to your class: —

What is meant by "Marine Journal"? "Port of New York," — where is it, and what can you say of it? What is meant by "Cleared"? What is the name of the steamship first cleared? her captain's name? whither bound? by whom cleared? Where is Norfolk? Where is Liverpool? How would you go from New York to Liverpool? Where is Aspinwall? Is it an old or new town? To what does it owe its origin? Where is New Orleans, and what can you say of it? Where is Valparaiso? Where is Hamburg? (Let pupils go to the outline maps and point out these places, and designate the course of a vessel from Boston or New York, etc.) Where is Cowes? What is meant by "Cowes and a market"?

You will at once perceive to what extent these questions may be proposed.

Under the head "Arrived," the lessons may be still more interesting and varied. The places of meeting may be pointed out; the meaning of phrase "showing Spanish colors." This will open a new and instructive field. "Cape Race Light abeam," what is meant? what by "took a pilot"? etc.

But in your efforts to teach the geography of other and distant sections, do not overlook less remote sections. Occasionally take *imaginary* journeys with your pupils. Let us suppose you have a school in New York city. Say to your class, when sufficiently advanced: "To-morrow's lesson will be an imaginary journey to the city of Boston. There are three or four different routes. You may confine your attention to either of those which consists partly of water. I shall wish you to describe the course, tell where you leave the steamer for the cars, the prominent places through which you pass, and about how long it will require to make the journey. At another time, we will make the return over a route wholly by railroad." The idea you will readily see, and also the extent to which this course may be carried.

If the interesting volumes of Dr. Kane have been read, his perilous travels, daring adventures, and many hardships, may be made to invest many a geography lesson with an interest before unthought of. Let the various points spoken of be pointed out upon the map, and let the members of your class be called on to state all the incidents that may occur to them as worthy of note. This course will tend to awaken a spirit of attention and investigation in relation to their reading.

I would again advise that you make the drawing of maps a prominent exercise; and, if rightly conducted, it will prove a very pleasant and profitable one. If the lesson is about a certain country, let its outlines be drawn upon the blackboard, together with the prominent features, mountains, rivers, etc. Frequent and careful practice will give results highly useful and satisfactory.

As a valuable aid to you in the department of map-drawing, I would call your attention to a small work just published, entitled "Elements of Map-drawing, with Plans for Sketching Maps by Triangulation, and Improved Methods of Projection." The author is Cornelius S. Cartée, a successful instructor in Charlestown, Mass. The work is a valuable one, and original in its plan.

Your sincere friend,

C.

LETTER XVII.

ARITHMETIC.

My dear Friend:—

I now come to consider the subject of Arithmetic. This has been made a very prominent branch, in most of our schools. In this age of money-getting and calculation, there is a strong tendency to give it an undue prominence. I have sometimes thought it did receive more than its just share of time and attention. It is urged that the science of numbers is deserving of special consideration, on account of the mental discipline it will give. This may be urged in favor of other branches, though, it may be, not to the same extent. The amount and quality of mental drill and development depend more upon the teacher's manner of teaching, and the pupil's habits of learning, than upon the mere subject taught.

Let me say, at the outset, that it will be hardly possible for you to overestimate the value of mental arithmetic. This should be commenced at an early period in the child's education, and be continued through a series of years. Indeed, it would be well if the pupils in all our schools and academies should be required to devote a short time, daily or weekly, to operations in mental arithmetic. A little daily practice, in the right way, will secure results of the most satisfactory nature. I have heard children of the age of nine or ten years perform mental operations with a degree of rapidity and accuracy far greater than most adults could perform similar exercises with the use of slate and pencil. If, then, you wish to have your pupils make true progress in numbers, give them frequent and thorough drilling in mental arithmetic. If you devote an hour, daily, to the study of arithmetic, give at least one half of it to mental operations. I have no hesitation in saying that a lad, who has been thoroughly and properly trained in all the exercises in Colburn's First Lessons, or in those of the mental Arithmetics of Davies, Thompson, Greenleaf, Stoddard, or any other well-prepared book of the kind, without having received an hour's training in written arithmetic, — that such a lad will be better fitted for any common business, so far as arithmetic is concerned, than he would be if he had devoted months merely to written arithmetic, without giving any attention to mental exercises.

In teaching mental arithmetic, the Numeral Frame will be found almost invaluable. No primary or intermediate school should be without one of these simple articles of apparatus. It is alike useful in teaching the little ones to count, and in illustrating operations in addition, subtraction, division, and also in explaining fractions. It will prove worth tenfold its cost in the hands of any active and judicious teacher. A set of blocks and solids for the illustration of square and cubic measure will be found very useful, both in mental and written arithmetic.

In the performance of mental exercises, it will be well to require the pupils to recite without the book. Read the question distinctly, and let the pupils give the answer and explain the process, — giving the reason for every step. This course will tend to secure attention, and prove a more desirable mental discipline. From the beginning, cause your pupils to feel that they must recite the lesson without your aid. You may, of course, solve one or two problems, as a specimen of the mode in which you wish to have them solved. It is often the case that much of the benefit of such examples is lost by the careless and immethodical manner of performing them. Then let me urge you to train your pupils to be accurate and self-reliant. Train them to think and act for themselves. Says Bishop Potter: "If I were to reduce to a single maxim the concentrated wisdom of the world on the subject of practical education, I should enunciate a proposition, which, I think, is not incorporated as it should be into the practices of schools and families. That principle is, that, in educating the young, you serve them most effectually, not by what you do to them or for them, but by what you *teach them to do for themselves*. This is the true secret of educational development."

Exercises like the following — in which the whole school may take part — will be found of great value, and a few minutes of daily practice will, in a short time, lead to a wonderful degree of rapidity and accuracy in mental operations. In these exercises, the pupils are expected to follow the dictation of the teacher, so that they will be able to give the answer the instant he pauses. The terms *plus*, *minus*, and *square* should be well understood.

Square $5 + 6 \times 3 \div 2 - 5 \div 8 + 6 \times 5 = ?$*
$7 + 5 \times 2 \div 6 \times 4 \times 2 - 12 \times 5 - 25 = ?$
Square $8 \times 2 \div 4 \times 10 - 40 + 20 - 80 = ?$
$\frac{3}{4}$ of $20 \times 2 + 20 \times 5 - 50 \times 2 - 300 = ?$
$\frac{1}{7}$ of $49 \times 4 + 2 \div 5 \times 6 \div 9 - 4 = ?$
$15 + 10 + 5 + 12 \times 2 + 16 \div 2 - 20 \times 3 = ?$

The above may be varied and extended almost indefinitely. I merely give the hint. In treating of written arithmetic it will not be necessary for me to go fully into the details of teaching the various rules and principles. Most of the modern textbooks on this subject usually contain good formulas and a sufficient number of rules. I have sometimes thought that the rules and explanations, the formulas and directions, were too numerous, — leaving too little for the pupils to accomplish, and thus failing to secure that mental growth which is so essential to true progress.

* In dictating this, the teacher would say, Square 5, add (or plus) 6, multiply by 3, divide by 2, subtract (or minus) 5, divide by 8, add 6, multiply by 5, — how many ?

It will be my aim to caution you against two or three of the common errors of teachers, in relation to arithmetic, and, in passing, to give a few hints touching miscellaneous exercises that may be found useful, for the purpose of general drill and review.

Avoid undue Haste. — Many teachers seem to think that, if they can only say they have "taken a class through the text-book," they will have accomplished all that is required, — and under this impression they "take" their pupils along at a surprisingly rapid gait. Scholars, too, seem to imagine that the degree of their proficiency will be augmented by every new page "gone over" in the text-book, and they "hurry on," impatient of delay. And, in addition to this, parents and committees often "harp on the same string," so that, with all, the amount "passed over" is made the only criterion of the teacher's ability or of the pupil's progress.

I once visited a school in which the feeling just spoken of greatly prevailed. It was a showy school, and, to a superficial observer, might present a good appearance. The teacher was one of your wordy men. He blew his own trumpet loud enough, and long enough, and, I am sorry to say, he deceived many whose ears had never been properly tuned to such blasts. Many supposed he kept an excellent school, and his pupils considered themselves of the *ne plus ultra* order. In speaking of his first class, he said: "This is the finest class you ever saw. I have taken this class over more ground than any other class was ever taken in the same time. I took them through Davies's Arithmetic in three months, and they can do anything within the covers of that book." This was said in that positive manner which would be sure proof to some that the statement made was true. Without in the least questioning the truth of what had been said, I remarked: "That is a very intelligent class, and they must have been well trained to accomplish so much." "O yes, I have done well by them, and they have done well for themselves." "Are you willing to have me ask them a few questions?" said I. Somewhat "taken aback" by the question, he hesitated a moment, and then said: "Why, yes, I have no objection, but I don't know how they will get along with questions from a stranger." "My questions shall not be difficult," said I; "I do not wish to puzzle or trouble them." I then proceeded to ask a few questions on the ground rules, and the answers were mostly wrong or very defective. I gave them a few examples in addition, subtraction, etc. These were performed very slowly, and not more than one in ten gave the correct answers; and not a single one could give a clear reason for what he did. I passed to fractions, and there found a total lack of knowledge. The same was true of interest, discount, mensuration, &c. They actually knew less than any intelligent boy of the same age would know after a week's proper instruction; and yet they really felt that they were quite expert in arithmetical operations. The teacher undertook to console himself, and satisfy me, by attributing their *seeming* ignorance to diffidence before a stranger; but a more self-conceited class I never saw. The pupils seemed to feel almost insulted that I should question them in the simple rules, and yet the result showed that they had not been properly or thoroughly drilled on those rules. Surely, thought I, you have been "*taken* through" the book; and a hard task will it be to take self-conceit away, and cause you to see your true position as arithmetical "know-nothings."

Now, my friend, let me say to you, "Make haste slowly." Be thorough. Teach one thing at a time, and be careful that you teach it properly, and that your teaching is understood. Be not ambitious to "take your pupils through the book," but rather aim so to teach and train them that they will be able, if necessary, to complete the book without the aid of a teacher, after they have been fairly started upon the right track.

Be sure that the simple or ground Rules are thoroughly comprehended. — Most teachers pass over these too rapidly. We frequently meet with persons who can, somewhat readily, perform many of the more difficult problems of arithmetic, and yet are very moderate and unreliable in adding columns of figures. I would recommend that you devote a few minutes nearly every day to some general exercises, for the entire school, in the elementary rules. The results of a little daily practice will be highly satisfactory. If the maxim, "Practice makes perfect," is ever true, it is strictly so in relation to operations in arithmetic. I would advise you to have daily exercises in notation, numeration, addition, multiplication, subtraction, division, fractions, &c. In such exercises, let all who are sufficiently advanced take part, and insist on promptness and energy in the performance of the work.

I will give you an example or two, as a specimen for the general exercise alluded to, and the same plan may be adopted in reference to the other rules. Calling for the attention of your pupils, you address them somewhat as follows: "Scholars, I wish you to give your entire attention to an exercise I am about to give. It is a simple exercise, — one in which all who have ciphered can take part. It is only a sum in simple addition. But in performing the example, I wish you to aim to excel in three or four particulars: —

1. Make your figures plain.
2. Put them down in straight columns.
3. Add accurately.
4. Add rapidly.

As I dictate the figures, you will write them; and when I say, '*Add,*' you will all commence. The pupil who first obtains an answer will speak distinctly and say, 'No. 1'; the second, 'No. 2'; and so on. I will note the time in which each performs the example, and will read to you the result. But remember that there will be no merit in obtaining an incorrect result; for that you can do without any attempt at adding the several columns. Rapidity and accuracy together will be very desirable. You may now write." *(Dictate either of the following:)*

24875	78564
95628	96875
76439	63987
87542	49563
94387	87459
62954	95386
45768	74321
89541	97487
97865	78965

As soon as you have repeated the last line, say, distinctly, "*Add,*" and be ready, with your watch in hand, to note·down the time required, by each, in obtaining an answer. After all have performed the work, call for answers, and then name the time occupied by each. If you have a liberal supply of blackboard, let a class occasionally take chalk, and perform similar operations upon the board. This will afford you a better opportunity for pointing out defects in figures and columns.

Exercises like the above will yield good results. If you will devote six or eight minutes, daily, for ten days, at the expiration of the time you will find that most of your pupils will obtain correct answers in about one half the amount of time at first required. When you commence, the time used in obtaining the answer to a sum having as many figures as there are in the examples given, will vary from one to three minutes; but at the end of the time named, you will find that many will be able to perform similar examples in thirty seconds, and less. And, moreover, you will find that the skill and accuracy gained here will be of service in all the more difficult operations of the Arithmetic. Of course, the number of figures and columns may be varied from time to time. It will be well, often, to give a single column, of some twenty or more figures, for the double purpose of giving discipline in addition, and training the eye in making straight columns of figures. The same general method may be adopted with examples in division, subtraction, multiplication, fractions, etc.

Do not be satisfied with the mere verbatim repetition of the rules of the Arithmetic, and the mechanical performance of the questions under the several rules. Vary the questions, and ask many not contained in the book. Do not abandon one rule or principle, and pass to another, until the former is perfectly clear. Move "step by step," never forgetting that practice tends to make perfect.

Do not render too much Help in the Performance of Problems. — It will be necessary for you to exercise much judgment and discretion on this point. Some aid you must render; but be very careful and not give too much or too soon. One prominent object, in all school exercises, should be to train pupils to overcome difficulties, — to surmount obstacles. In no branch will this hold more true than in that under consideration. It will scarcely ever be well for you to solve a difficult problem for a pupil. Give him one or two hints in the right direction, and then encourage him to persevere. If you can once succeed in arousing a true spirit of perseverance, you will find but little difficulty. "My teacher says I can do very hard problems if I will try long enough," said James Diligent, "and if I *can*, I know I *will;* for I can try as hard and as long as any one." With such a feeling, but very few insurmountable obstacles will be found. Give to your pupils as mottoes, *Labor omnia vincit*, and *Nil desperandum*.

Encourage your Pupils. — Utter words of cheer and expressions of kindly interest, and lead your pupils to feel that you are their sincere friend, and that you require them to learn hard lessons because you know it will do them good to learn such lessons. The following incident illustrates the power of encouraging words.

The teacher of a large school had a little girl under her care who was exceedingly backward in her lessons. She was at the bottom of the class, and seemed to care but little about what had passed in it.

During the school hours, singing was sometimes employed as a relaxation, and, noticing that this girl had a very clear, sweet voice, her teacher said to her: "Jane, you have a good voice, and you may lead in the singing."

She brightened up, and from that time her mind seemed more active. Her lessons were attended to, and she made steady progress. One day, as the teacher was going home, she overtook Jane and one of her schoolmates.

"Well, Jane," said she, "you are getting on very well at school. How is it that you do so much better now than you did at the beginning of the half-year?"

"I do not know why it is," replied Jane.

"I know what she told me the other day," said her companion.

"And what was that?" asked the teacher.

"Why, she said she was encouraged."

Yes, there was the secret, — she was encouraged. She felt she was not dull in everything; she had learned self-respect, and thus she was encouraged to self-improvement.

Take the hint, dear friend, and try to reach the intellect through the heart. Endeavor to draw out the dormant faculties of your scholars by discriminating culture and well-timed commendation. Give them the credit whenever you can, and allure them with hopeful words. Many a dull-minded child has been made irretrievably stupid by constant fault-finding or ungenerous sarcasm. And, on the other hand, how often has a genial smile or an approving remark awakened into new life some slow-learning pupil.

Make your Explanations plain and intelligible.— It is not unfrequently the case, that teachers fail to make their explanations sufficiently simple. At all times strive to awaken or impart ideas, and not merely to give words. Said a child to her teacher, "Will you please tell me why I carry one for every ten?" "Certainly," said the teacher, pleasantly, "it is because numbers increase from right to left in a decimal ratio." The child went to her seat, and, with a sad expression, sat repeating the words just quoted. She did not comprehend the answer of her teacher, and felt disappointed. The words "decimal" and "ratio" she did not understand. She sat thinking for a while, and then, utterly discouraged, she put aside her book, saying, "I do not like arithmetic; I cannot understand it."

See to it, my friend, that your pupils do not suffer in this way. When you give illustrations or explanations, have them such that they will convey to the pupil's mind the ideas or information intended by you and desired by them. As far as may be, use illustrations for the eye. Long measure, square measure, cubic measure, etc. may be illustrated by drawings and blocks. Let me suppose you ask a pupil the difference between ten square miles and ten miles square. A word answer may be given without conveying any clear idea; but if you go to the board and draw a figure, you may make all plain and clear. Let the following be used, considering each square the representative of a square mile: —

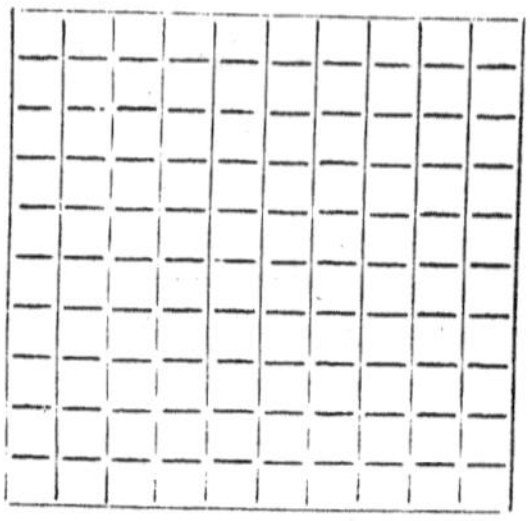

One mile long.

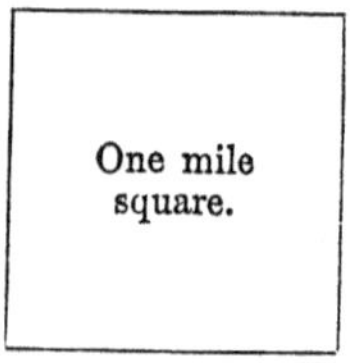

One mile square.

Many other definitions and principles you may readily explain by some simple drawing or illustration.

Aim to give a practical turn to every Exercise.— This you will best do by asking such incidental questions as shall have a bearing upon common business operations. So far as possible, require your pupils, not only to state the "how" of performing an example, but also to show that they fully comprehend the same, by solving problems given at the time, but not taken from the text-book. Let me suppose you have a class in mensuration. You ask a pupil how he will obtain the superficial feet in the floor of the school-room. His answer will be, "multiply the length by the width," and he may give these words without being able to perform the operation. That you may know whether he comprehends the definition, or not, give him a rule or measuring-tape, and ask him to get the contents of the room. If he can do that properly and accurately, you may feel sure that the words of the rule are understood. So let it be at every step; let the rule be elucidated and confirmed by the performance of some pertinent question. As another example on this point, let us take the subject of interest. The members of the class are able to repeat the rules and explanations with promptness. If you wish to ascertain if the words they have repeated convey the intended information, step to the blackboard, and write a note, as follows: —

New Britain, Ct., June 5th, 1858.

$ 457$\frac{62}{100}$.

On demand I promise to pay Frederic Churchill, or order, four hundred and fifty-seven dollars and sixty-two cents, with interest, value received.

Charles F. North.

Now call upon your class to tell how much it will require to pay the above note at the present time, on some previous day, or on some future day, that you may designate.

If the subject of indorsements is under consideration, prepare some notes in due form, note the payments upon the back in the usual and proper manner, and, passing them to members of the class, require them to ascertain the amount due on each at the present time. If results are correct, you may feel satisfied that the subject is clearly comprehended.

In fine, let it be a part of your daily practice to propose to your pupils practical questions, prepared by yourself for the purpose of illustrating and confirming the passing recitation. A lad may be able to give the rule for ascertaining the contents of a load or pile of wood, and not be able, by actual measurement and figures, to "carry the rule into practice"; and yet this is the more important part. In all your teaching, aim judiciously to combine theory and practice. Encourage your pupils to bring into the school-room such practical business operations as may come within their observation out of the school-room. In this way you will obtain a valuable variety, embracing such operations as the farmer, the merchant, the mechanic, etc. will have occasion to perform. By pursuing this course, your pupils will be so trained that they will not be confused and entirely thrown from the arithmetical track, if called upon to perform some simple business question outside of the school. How many there are among those who have professedly been through the Arithmetic, — even the "hardest Arithmetic you can name," — who would be completely nonplussed, if some farmer should ask them to cast the interest on a certain note, or ascertain the contents and worth of a load of wood at a specified amount per cord, or if some carpenter should ask them to estimate the cost of a pile of boards at a given sum per thousand feet!

Be sure that Fractions are well understood.— Most teachers and pupils fail in not giving sufficient attention to fractions. If the various operations in fractions are clearly explained by the teacher, and followed by frequent practice by the pupils, the results will be favorable. Let it be your aim to give thorough instruction and frequent drill in exercises involving the various principles of fractions. Facility and accuracy here will be of great service in all other arithmetical exercises. I once knew an entire school in which most of the pupils had been nearly through (that is, had been *taken* nearly through) written arithmetic, and yet not one could answer the following simple question proposed by a visitor: "If an apple and a half cost a cent and a half, what will one apple cost?" Who cannot see that in such a school the subject of fractions had not received merited attention?

But I have already sufficiently enlarged upon the subject under consideration. I hope the hints I have given may not prove entirely useless. In closing, I will say, if you would be a successful teacher of arithmetic, study to have fresh examples and new modes of illustration as often as possible, always endeavoring to teach the subject, and not the mere words of the book.

Your sincere friend,

C.

LETTER XVIII.

BOOK-KEEPING. — PHYSIOLOGY. — DRAWING. — HISTORY. — SINGING.

MY DEAR FRIEND: —

I HAVE already considered the several branches usually taught in our Common Schools. Pupils should be thoroughly instructed in these, and not be allowed to substitute other branches in their stead, nor to allow other studies to engross any part of the time and attention which should be devoted to the elementary branches already alluded to. If pupils are properly trained in these, they will have a firm and desirable foundation, on which a superstructure may be reared as circumstances may favor and require. But if these elementary branches are neglected, or but imperfectly taught, any superstructure will be in a toppling and unpleasant condition. Let me again urge you to be thorough in all your teaching, — but in no cases more so than in relation to those subjects which form the very basis of the educational structure. How many men may be found in each of the learned professions, who have suffered, and will suffer, their lives long, from a want of thoroughness in their early education! Be it, then, your motto, and that of your pupils,— "*Whatever is worth doing at all, is worth doing well.*"

As proof that I have not over-estimated the importance of the elementary branches, let me call your attention to the following remarks, made by Edward Everett, at the dedication of a school-house.

"I hold that to read the English language well, that is, with intelligence, feeling, spirit, and effect, —to write, with despatch, a neat, handsome, *legible* hand, (for it is, after all, a great object in writing to have others able to read what we write,) and to be master of the four rules of arithmetic, so as to dispose, at once, with accuracy, every question of figures which comes up in practical life,—I say I call this a good education. And if you add the ability to write pure, grammatical English, with the help of very few hard words, I regard it as an excellent education. These are the tools. You can do much with them, but you are helpless without them. They are the foundation; and, unless you begin with these, all your flashy attainments, a little natural philosophy, a little physiology, and a little geology, and all the other *ologies* and *osophies*, are ostentatious rubbish.

"Is it not a fact, that, in many of our common schools, spelling, reading, writing, geography, and grammar, combining with it the art of composition, are neglected in order to study the 'ologies and osophies'? How many college students have learnt

English grammar and English orthography? We know many who have not, and never will, because it is too late now to do what could only be well done in childhood, either in the family or primary school. A graduate of one of our colleges recently boasted that 'he never studied English grammar.' A person standing by remarked, 'No one would suppose you ever had, judging you by the manner you use the Queen's English.'"

I will now pass to consider, briefly, two or three other topics or branches, which should receive attention if circumstances will warrant. They are highly important, and if our schools were what they should be, as to organization and support, I should not hesitate to place the branches about to be considered among the really indispensable ones. But many of our schools are so large and so imperfect in classification, that but few teachers can find time or place for any studies additional to those named in previous letters. If, however, you cannot find time for a thorough and systematic course of instruction in them, you may give a few lessons and hints on each which will be of service; for, if the foundation is substantially laid, your pupils will be prepared, with but little help from their teacher, to make progress in other and higher branches as a fitting superstructure.

BOOK-KEEPING. — All should have some knowledge of accounts, and in many of our schools instruction in book-keeping should receive attention.

The exercises required in filling out a set of books will prove highly profitable and useful, — calling into practice, as it will, to some extent, knowledge already acquired in arithmetic, penmanship, and orthography. If, therefore, you can possibly find time — if it be only one hour per week — to devote to familiar instruction in the art of book-keeping, be sure to use it. In many schools nominal attention was given to this subject a score of years ago, but in such a manner as neither to interest nor instruct the pupils. I can well remember the amount and kind of attention it received when I attended school. The Arithmetics then used — more than those now in use — contained a few pages of accounts entered in Day-Book and Ledger form. These we were required to copy into blank-books, and in doing so we were made to feel that we were studying book-keeping. As well might one learn to compose by merely copying the compositions of others. A person might copy a thousand very excellent essays, and still not be able to compose ten lines with propriety of expression. So one might merely copy scores of pages from a printed account-book without gaining a clear and practical understanding of accounts.

There are now before the public several very good treatises on the subject of book-keeping, — either of which will be sufficient in the hands of a sensible teacher. But if you would give the subject a truly practical bearing, you must go beyond the book, and, by the use of the blackboard, expand, explain, illustrate, and apply the principles of the printed text-book.

Call upon your pupils, frequently, to go to the blackboard, and write in due form a note, a receipt, a common bill of goods, an order, etc. Name to them certain business transactions, real or imaginary, between two persons, and require them to express the same upon the blackboard as they should be recorded or expressed in an account-book. I see no reason why all, who attend school until the age of fourteen or fifteen years, may not receive a fair amount of instruction in accounts, certainly to such an extent that they will be able, with facility and correctness, to write any common business form, or to make proper record of any common business transaction. Let it be your aim to qualify your pupils to do thus much.

Physiology. — While I do not believe that an extended course of instruction in this branch should be attempted in our common schools, I do believe that some amount of information should be imparted in all our schools, — varying according to circumstances. If we cannot all gain a complete knowledge of "the house in which we live," we should certainly learn so much of its mechanism, its nature, its capabilities, and the dangers which threaten it, as will keep us from doing aught that will tend to mar or weaken our "tenement," and, if possible, so much as will enable us to impart unto it those influences which will tend to its true adornment, and lead to the real development of its powers and resources.

If one to whom a costly and well-finished dwelling has been presented should abuse the same, and pervert its use, by allowing, if not by enticing, " four-footed beasts and all manner of creeping things " to range through the various apartments, we should say that he was undeserving of the residence, and that it had fallen into bad hands. What, then, shall be said of those who so grossly pervert and abuse the temple in which they live, — that structure which an omnipotent hand has reared and intrusted to a single occupant? And yet how many there are who daily " live, move, and have their being " in that most wonderful structure, the human body, constantly, through design or ignorance, doing those things which at once tend to diminish its capacities and mar its beauty and symmetry! How many, through gross ignorance of the true laws of physical being and development, indulge in habits which are utterly at variance with the conditions of real existence and growth! Nay, more; in how many of our school-houses have the internal arrangements and fixtures been promotive of physical deformity! In how many has defective ventilation proved destructive of vitality and health, — often gradually, but surely! Now it is within your power, as a teacher, to diffuse much valuable information regarding some of the essentials for physical health and well-being. If you cannot find time for giving detailed and thorough instruction in the principles of physiology, you may and should find time for giving many valuable hints and suggestions bearing upon the subject. If you cannot teach anatomy, you may speak of some of the laws of health. The subjects of ventilation, diet, clothing, exercise, etc. may be considered, and much valuable information may be given in relation to each of them. Let the importance of the whole subject lead you to do what you can. It is to be hoped that the time will arrive, when our youth will remain in the school-room long enough to receive a more thorough course of instruction, than it would be practicable to undertake to give in many of our schools, under existing circumstances. But something you may do in the way of encouraging an interest in all those manly exercises and games which tend to the true development of the physical powers. It is indeed lamentable to see to what an extent the mere intellect is cared for, while no regard is paid to the culture of the corporeal powers and faculties. In a lecture recently given before the American Institute of Instruction, Professor S. R. Calthrop thus playfully hits the prevailing feeling and customs, and suggests a remedy: —

"Some time ago I read a tale, which related that a certain gentleman was, once on a time, digging a deep hole in his garden. He had, as I myself had in my younger days, a perfect passion for digging holes, for the mere pleasure of doing it; but the hole which he was now digging was by far the deepest which he had ever attempted. At last he became perfectly fascinated, carried away by his pursuit, and actually had his dinner let down to him by a bucket. Well, he dug on, late and early, when, just as he was plunging in his spade with great energy for a new dig, he penetrated right through, and fell down, down, to the centre of the earth.

"To his astonishment, he landed upon the top of a coach, which was passing at the time, and soon found himself perfectly at home, and began to enter into conversation with the passenger opposite to him, a very gentlemanly-looking man, enveloped entirely in a black cloak. He soon found out that the country into which his lot had fallen was a very strange one. Its peculiarities were thus stated by his gentlemanly fellow-passenger. 'Ours, Sir,' said he, 'is called the country of Skitzland. All the Skitzlanders are born with all their limbs and features perfect; but when they arrive at a certain age, all their limbs and features which have not been used drop off, leaving only the bones behind. It is rather dark this evening, or you would have seen this more plainly. Look forward there at our coachman: he consists simply of a stomach and hands, these being the only things he has ever used. Those two whom you see chatting together are brothers in misfortune; one is a clergyman, the other a lawyer; they have neither of them got any legs at all, though each of them possesses a finely developed understanding; and you cannot help remarking what a massive jaw the lawyer has got. Yonder is Mr. ——, the celebrated millionnaire,—

he is just raising his hat; you see he has lost all the top part of his head, — indeed, he has little of his head left, except the bump of acquisitiveness and the faculty of arithmetical calculation. There are two ladies, members of the fashionable world: their case is very pitiable, they consist of nothing whatever but a pair of eyes and a bundle of nerves. There are two members of the mercantile world: they are munching some sandwiches, you see, but it is merely for the sake of keeping up appearances, as I can assure you, from my own personal knowledge, that they have no digestive organs whatever. As for myself, I am a schoolmaster. I have been a hard student all my life, at school and at college, and moreover I have had a natural sympathy with my fellow-men, and so I am blessed with a brain and heart entire. But see here.' And he lifted up his cloak, and lo! underneath, a skeleton, save just here! 'See, here are the limbs I never used, and therefore they have deserted me. All the solace I now have consists in teaching the young children to avoid a similar doom. I sometimes show them what I have shown you. I labor hard to convince them that most assuredly the same misfortune will befall them which has happened to me and to all the grown-up inhabitants; but even then, I grieve to say, I cannot always succeed. Many believe that they will be lucky enough to escape, and some of the grown-up inhabitants pad themselves, and so cheat the poor children into the belief that they are all right, though all the elder ones know better. You will now perceive the reason why all the gentlemen you see wear such tight pantaloons: they pretend that it is fashionable, but in reality it is in order to prevent their false legs from tumbling out. Surely my case is miserable enough; my only hope consists in the idea of educating the rising generation to do better. No doubt it is easy to persuade them to do so in the country from which you come, but I assure you,' added he, with a heart-felt sigh, 'that it is sometimes very hard to do so here. Nearly all of us, then, have lost something of our bodies. Some have no head, some no legs, some no heart, and so on; the less a man has lost, the higher he ranks in the social scale; and our aristocracy, the governing body, consists of the few individuals who have used all their faculties, and therefore now possess them all.'

"At this moment a dreadful earthquake broke out, and an extempore volcano shot the gentleman who had listened to this interesting narration right up to the crust of the earth again, and, by a strange and fortunate chance, shot him up into the very hole which he had been digging, and he discovered himself lying down at the bottom of the hole, feeling just as if he had awakened from a dream; and, to his surprise, he heard distinctly the voice of his wife crying out from the top, 'Come, come, dear, you 're very late, and supper is getting quite cold!'

"The name of the country of Skitzland, translated into the vulgar tongue, is the planet Earth, and America is one of the portions thereof. If we were to look round in a circuit of a hundred miles, how many of the Skitzland aristocracy should we find, think you? What a dropping off of limbs and features there would be, if the letter of the law of Skitzland were carried out! But it is absolutely certain that this is in effect the law of nature, which does not act, it is true, all in a moment, but which slowly and truly tends to this. The Hindoo ties up an arm for years together, as a penance, thinking thereby he does Brahma service; the limb, with fatal sureness, withers away and rots. The prisoner in solitary confinement has his mind and faculties bound, fettered, and tied, and, by a law as fixed as that which keeps the stars in their places, the said prisoner's mind grows weaker, feebler, less sane, day by day. School-children are confined six long hours in a close school-room, sitting in one unvarying posture, their lungs breathing corrupted air, no single limb moving as it ought to move, not the faintest shadow of attention being paid to heart, lungs, digestive organs, legs, or arms, all these being bound down and tied, as it were; and so, by the stern edict of Heaven, which, when man was placed upon earth, decreed that the faculties unused should weaken and fail, we see around us thousands of unhealthy children whose brains are developed at the expense of their bodies, the ultimate consequence of which will be deterioration of brain as well as body.

"What is the remedy for all this? I have before stated, that, in large, crowded cities, gymnastic training, systematically pursued *as a study*, is the only thing which seems possible to be done, and most assuredly will be beneficial wherever it is introduced. But there is a different method of physical education, which can be pursued either exclusively or in association with gymnastics, which can be followed up either in the country, or in towns, where playgrounds can be obtained. This is the method which I have invariably pursued myself, namely, the systematic pursuit of health and strength by all manner of manly sports and games. I myself learned to play and love these games at school and at college. I have given them now nearly four years' trial in my school, and every day convinces me more and more of their beneficial results."

Drawing. — This branch is deserving of more attention than it has yet received in our schools. An ability to draw will prove of advantage to all classes of people; for all will find occasions on which it will be pleasant, if not positively valuable, to be able to exercise skill in drawing. To the mechanic, this subject is of the utmost importance; and one who is well skilled as a draughtsman will be far more successful than one who is not, other things being equal.

The facilities for imparting instruction in this branch have been greatly increased within a few years, and there are many excellent elementary treatises and pattern-cards within reach of all. I can see no reason why the exercise of drawing may not be introduced into most of our schools. It will give a pleasant variety to school lessons; and minutes, that might otherwise be spent in idleness or mischief, may be usefully employed in copying models. While, therefore, I would insist upon thorough training in the branches alluded to in previous letters, I would certainly encourage pupils to improve some of their leisure minutes in practising on drawing-lessons. But do not imagine, nor allow your pupils to feel, that they can become proficients in the art of drawing by receiving a few hours' instruction. It will be only by patient and persevering study and effort, and by long-continued practice, that one can acquire a desirable degree of skill and readiness. Let this be understood from the beginning, and here, quite as much as in any other branch, insist on care and thoroughness.

History.—Something of history should be taught in our schools. In the study of geography, the teacher will have frequent opportunities for communicating some historical information; and these, if wisely improved, will awaken in the minds of his pupils a desire to know more, and induce them to investigate for themselves. So much history as relates to our own country ought to receive particular attention in our schools; and there would be ample time for it if pupils would be regular in their attendance, and continue at school for a few months longer than they have been wont to do. The adoption of any plan or exercise that will awaken an interest will result in good. I do not intend to give any particular instruction in relation to the study of history, but merely to call your attention to it, and to advise that you give it as much consideration as circumstances will allow.

My eye just meets with a little exercise or game bearing upon this subject, which may be turned to good account. The following I take from the New York Teacher, though the plan described has been previously published.

The teacher or some pupil fixes his mind or thoughts upon some individual, place, or event of historical notoriety, and the other members of the class ask questions to ascertain what person, place, or event is thought of. One having selected, mentally, a subject, the others question him, and receive answers somewhat as follows: —

Question. Is the subject you have in mind an individual, place, or event?

Answer. An individual.

Q. Now living, or dead?

A. Dead.

Q. Male or female?

A. Male.

Q. Did he live in Europe, Asia, Africa, or America?

A. In Europe.

Q. In England, France, Spain, Italy, or Russia?

A. In France.

Q. Within five hundred years, or within a century?

A. Within a century.

Q. Within fifty years?

A. No.

Q. Was he celebrated as a king, statesman, warrior, poet, or philosopher?

A. As near a warrior as anything you have mentioned, and, though not a statesman, he was connected with national affairs.

Q. Was he connected with the French Revolution of 1792?

A. He was.

Q. Was he a Royalist or Republican?

A. Republican.

Q. Did he die in France?

A. He did.

Remark by some of the class. Then it is not Bonaparte.

Q. Did he die a natural death?

A. He did not.

Q. Was he murdered by Charlotte Corday?

A. He was not.

Remark. Then it is not Marat.

Q. Was he Jacobin or Girondist?

A. Jacobin.

Q. Was he a leader of the Jacobin party?

A. Yes.

Q. Is he noted for his cruelty during the "Reign of Terror"?

A. He is.

Q. Robespierre?

A. It is Robespierre.

Game is won by the questioners.

Another pupil has a subject.

Q. An individual, an event, or a substance?

A. An event.

Q. Did it transpire in Europe, Asia, or America?

A. America.

Q. Within fifty years?

A. No.

Q. Within a hundred years?

A. Yes.

Q. Before the American Revolution, or after?

A. Before.

Q. Was the event brought about by the agency of man, or was it a natural event?

A. Effected directly by man.

Q. A disastrous or fortunate event?

A. Disastrous to some, fortunate to others; but we consider it fortunate, because its results have been good.

Q. Was it a national event?

A. Its results were at least national.

Q. Had England any interest in this event?

A. She had.

Q. Did it transpire in the Eastern, Middle, or Southern States?

A. Eastern.

Q. On land, or on water?

A. On water.

Q. Was there any loss of life or property?

A. Of property, but not of life.

Q. Was the property destroyed tea?

A. It was the destruction of the cargo of tea in Boston Harbor.

This game is instructive and amusing in the school, the home circle, or at social gatherings. It exacts an extensive and an accurate knowledge, and strengthens the memory. It also requires considerable skill to ask questions in a connected, chain-like manner, and is therefore an excellent mental discipline. It induces a search into the characters of individuals, and into the cause, nature, and effects of events, thus making pupils more philosophical and more self-reliant.

This exercise might be introduced into history classes one day in a week, in place of recitation, and scholars might prepare for it as for a recitation.

Singing. — Vocal music has already assumed a somewhat exalted position in some schools, and yet in scarcely any have its merits been fully estimated. It is, indeed, less than a score of years since school-room songs were a very great novelty; and we can well remember that those who first favored their introduction were strongly censured by parents and others. It was regarded by many as a monstrous innovation. For children to go to school, term after term, and sit, *aching*, on wretched seats, in still more wretched school-houses, caused no regret, because such penance seemed to be an essential part of school life; but for school-boys and schoolgirls to *sing*, — who ever heard the like? It was a great waste of time; and, moreover, it caused the little ones to be happy, and for a brief time to forget their aches, which, it was thought, would be a perversion of the object of schools. Such was the feeling very generally. But a pleasant change has come "over all the land"; and now the joyous songs of merry pupils may be heard in a large number of our best schools, alike promoting their happiness and cheering them on in the performance of the less agreeable duties of the school-room, and meeting the approval of all kind and intelligent people.

Though we cannot sing,—our school days having been passed all too early for receiving any instruction in singing, — we would strongly advocate the teaching of music in all our schools. It is a good disciplinary exercise, and its indulgence always tends to give an air of cheerfulness to the school-room. But we would have the songs, and the sentiments of the songs, of a truly pure and elevating character. We have no partiality for the practice — now, we feel, quite too common — of having lessons and recitations set to music. This we think a perversion of the object. We fully agree with that veteran of song, Lowell Mason, whose name has become so intimately connected with the music of our land, who says: "Music's highest and best influence is of a moral nature; and the introduction into schools of such songs as tend to mere levity, frolic, or idle mirth, or such as are low, coarse, or vulgar, in thought or in language, or such as contain equivocal or ambiguous expressions, is most deeply to be regretted."

The following remarks on the "Power of Music" I take from the Indiana School Journal. The little incident named is certainly full of interest.

"In looking over an old 'newspaper' printed several years ago, I came across this beautiful piece, which struck me as being true to nature.

"Leaning idly over a fence, a few days since, we noticed a little four-years-old 'lord of creation,' amusing himself, in the grass, by watching the frolicsome flight of birds, which were playing around him. At length a beautiful bobolink perched on a bough of an apple-tree which extended within a few yards of the place where the urchin sat, and maintained his position, apparently unconscious of his close proximity to one whom birds usually consider a dangerous neighbor.

"The boy seemed astonished at his impudence, and, after regarding him steadily for a minute or two, obeying the instinct of his baser part, he picked up a stone lying at his feet, and was preparing to throw it, steadying himself for a good aim. The little arm was drawn backward without alarming the bird, and 'bob' was 'within an ace' of danger, when lo! his throat swelled, and forth came nature's plea: 'a-link, a-link, a-link, bob-a-link, bob-a-link, a-no-sweet, a-no-sweet! I know it, I know it, a-link, a-link, don't throw it, throw it, throw it,' &c. And he did n't. Slowly the little arm fell to its natural position, and the now despised stone dropped. The minstrel charmed the murderer! We heard the songster through, and watched his unharmed flight, as did the boy, with a sorrowful countenance. Anxious to hear an expression of the little fellow's feelings, we approached him and inquired, 'Why did n't you stone him, my boy? you might have killed him and carried him home.'

"The poor little fellow looked up doubtingly, as though he suspected our meaning, and, with an expression half shame and half sorrow, he replied: '*Could n't cos he sung so!*'

"Who will say that 'music hath no charms to soothe the savage breast,' or aver that God hath not made melody to move the purer fountains of our nature, to awaken those sympathies that are kindred to heaven, the angels, and to God himself? Let the sweet tones of music break upon the ears of the dull school-boy, and he will awake with new life and energy. Pour the notes of melody into the ears of the wilful child, and you disarm him; the anger will fall from his heart, and he will become obedient and attentive. Let music be the first to break the silence of the school-room in the morning, and the chords of young hearts that are put in motion will continue to vibrate during the day. Happy will be the time when not only the tones of our school-bells can be heard all over the land, but when the notes of our school-children, in the morning, breaking upon the silent atmosphere along the Atlantic coast in the East, shall reverberate along the Gulf of Mexico, and the echo be heard in California."

Then I would say, give some attention, daily, to vocal music. This may be done without any detriment to other branches. Indeed, I believe it will prove a pleasant auxiliary in all the work of the school-room. If your pupils are sad, or dull, or uneasy, or too playful, call upon them to sing one or two sweet songs, and the result will be highly salutary. All angry and dull feelings will at once be dispelled, and a spirit of cheerfulness will be produced throughout the school. You may safely introduce music, and devote some time to it daily, without any fear of encroaching upon other branches, for it will prove a help, and not an injury. Such, at least, is the belief of

Your sincere friend,

C.

LETTER XIX.

DECLAMATION.—STUDY OF NATURE.—STUDY OF WORDS.—MISCELLANEOUS KNOWLEDGE.

My dear Friend:—

In this letter I purpose to speak of two or three other exercises which should receive occasional attention in school.

Declamation.—In a large number of schools the speaking of pieces receives some attention, but only in a few does it occupy the time and care which its importance demands. If a half-day semi-monthly should be devoted to declamation, and the several performances should be made subjects of faithful criticism, much good would result from the exercise. It is, however, of the utmost importance that whatever is done be well done. Improper positions, disagreeable tones, indistinct enunciation, or bad habits of any kind, should receive prompt attention, and be corrected if possible. While, therefore, I would urge you to require exercises in declamation, I would earnestly advise that you guard against the practice, quite too common, of allowing the repetition of words and sentences to be considered as satisfactory declamations. Lead your pupils to study their pieces with a particular view of ascertaining the writer's ideas, thoughts, and feelings, and then encourage them to give correct and forcible utterance to the same. A mere formal and monotonous style of speaking, performed simply as a required exercise, will be of but little service. Strive to awaken an interest in the subject, which will induce your pupils to engage in it with an earnestness which cannot fail of leading to right study and correct expression and delivery.

The plan, adopted, in some schools, of devoting every alternate Wednesday afternoon to exercises in declamation and composition, is a very good one, and if judiciously managed will do much to awaken a desirable amount of interest both on the part of pupils and their parents. Many of the latter will feel inclined to spend an hour or two in the schoolroom to listen to such exercises as I have alluded to, and an interest once awakened in this way will become expansive and permanent. The introduction of such exercises may increase your labors, but the results will be highly gratifying in themselves, and their influence upon the daily studies of school will be favorable. On the afternoons devoted to these miscellaneous exercises the girls can take part in dialogues, in reading original essays, or in giving select readings.

Political Economy. — In a country like ours, all should have some knowledge of the constitution and of the laws. Much valuable and interesting information on these points may be given in the form of brief and familiar lectures, if it is found inconvenient to make use of a regular text-book, — though the latter is preferable. It would certainly be well if our youth could all be made familiar with the matter contained in such a work as Shepard's Constitutional Text-Book, or some work covering the same ground. Such knowledge would tend to make them intelligent and independent citizens and voters.

Study of Nature.—You may do much to awaken in your pupils a love for the study of Nature. How many "live and move" in the midst of the most beautiful and sublime works of Nature, — works full of instruction, — and yet see nothing, learn nothing. Let it be your aim to lead your pupils to move about with observing eyes and listening ears, — eyes and ears trained to draw from Nature whatever is lovely and instructive. Our Heavenly Father has thrown before us the great book of Nature wide open, and so plain are its great lessons that he "who runs may read," and learn, if he will. Can you not learn and teach a lesson from the following pretty lines, from the pen of S. G. Goodrich, so extensively and favorably known as Peter Parley?

A LESSON FOR TEACHERS.

"I saw a child some four years old
Along a meadow stray;
Alone she went, unchecked, untold,
Her home not far away.

"She gazed around on earth and sky, —
Now paused, and now proceeded;
Hill, valley, wood, — she passed them by
Unmarked, perchance unheeded.

"And now gay groups of roses bright
In circling thickets bound her;
Yet on she went, with footsteps light,
Still gazing all around her.

"And now she paused, and now she stooped,
And plucked a little flower, —
A simple daisy 't was, that drooped
Within a rosy bower.

"The child did kiss the little gem,
And to her bosom pressed it;
And there she placed the fragile stem,
And with soft words caressed it.

"I love to read a lesson true,
From Nature's open book,
And oft I learn a lesson new
From childhood's careless look.

"Children are simple — loving — true;
'T is Heaven that made them so;
And would you teach them, be so too,
And stoop to what they know.

"Begin with simple lessons, — things
On which they love to look:
Flowers, pebbles, insects, birds on wings, —
These are God's spelling-book.

"And children know His A B C,
As bees where flowers are set:
Wouldst thou a skilful teacher be?
Learn, then, this alphabet.

"From leaf to leaf, from page to page,
Guide thou thy pupil's look,
And when he says, with aspect sage,
'Who made this wondrous book?'

"Point thou with reverent gaze to Heaven,
And kneel in earnest prayer,
That lessons thou hast humbly given
May lead thy pupil there."

"In childhood the senses are open to the reception of truth from the outward world. A child sees and hears a thousand things that escape the observation of a man. Train him in the usual mode of education, and he soon loses the habit of attending to outward things, learns to tread upon the insect and to pass by the flowers, to let the birds sing unnoticed, and the pebble glitter untouched. But give him a true education, including in his studies, as a prominent part, the elements of chemistry, botany, and zoölogy, and his eye shall not become dim nor his ear dull of hearing; in manhood his heart will be open to the sweet influence of the flowers, and to the grandeur of the starry heavens; he will read the meaning of each singing-bird, and catch the true expression of the solemn tones of the thunder. When the forest ocean surges under a July breeze, and the clouds sail majestically through the blue sky, they will fill his heart with emotions unknown to one who despises these glorious works of the Most High as being mere matter."*

In cultivating a love for the beautiful in Nature, you will, at the same time, be promoting true mental growth, and developing the better feelings of the heart. A boy who delights in hill and valley, woodland and lake,—one whose heart is made joyous as he beholds the blossoming tree and opening flowers, will not be wholly reckless and wayward. By kindly influences he may be led "through Nature up to Nature's God," and his heart may be made to swell with gratitude towards that great and good Being, who rolled up the mountains and spread out the earth with all its beauty and loveliness.

To one who has been brought to

> "Find tongues in trees, books in the running brooks,
> Sermons in stones, and good in everything,"

there will be a sincere delight in attending to the culture of flowers, which speak so unequivocally of the great goodness of Him who has made the flowers,—

> "To comfort man, to whisper hope,
> Whene'er his faith is dim;
> For whoso careth for the flowers
> Will much more care for him."

Whenever we see a house, with its neat flower-garden and well-trained vines and shrubbery, whether it be in the thriving village or away from the "busy haunts and noisy shops," up among the

* Rev. Thomas Hill.

hills or mountains, we always feel that the indwellers have hearts that feel for others' woes. "God, who careth for the flowers," will not be unmindful of those who appreciate the *beauties*, as well as the *utilities*, of his handiwork. What a bright, joyous, cheerful aspect would the earth wear, if all who dwell thereon would plant and cultivate a few flowers? It would not only tend to strew man's pathway to the tomb with flowers, but also to shed a sweet fragrance around his daily walks and vocations. Then will not teachers do what they can to foster a flower-loving spirit? If they will, they will be amply compensated by the reflex influence in promoting a genial disposition in the hearts of the little ones under their charge. Whenever we see a happy boy or girl gayly tripping along the school-ward path, with a bunch of flowers, whether culled from the garden or road-side, for the teacher's desk, we always feel that in the young heart which prompted the gift the teacher will find a ready and cheerful obedience to his wishes.

We hope the time is not distant, when every teacher will feel it not only a *duty*, but a *privilege*, to cultivate in the hearts of the youth a refined love for music, paintings, and flowers; feeling assured that thereby much will be done to promote both the happiness and true usefulness of their pupils. And, when it shall be deemed an essential part of a school-yard to have a neatly arranged flower-plot, we shall find the love of school increasing, and a growing dislike for coarse and uncourteous acts on the part of the young. Whatever tends to adorn and beautify the place in which children spend much of their time, will leave a pleasing and lasting impression upon their young and tender hearts. In the language of Keats:

> "A thing of beauty is a joy for ever;
> Its loveliness increases; it will never
> Pass into nothingness, but still will keep
> Full of sweet dreams, and health and quiet breathing:
> Therefore, on every morning let 's be wreathing
> A flowery band to bind us to the earth."

And, as another says, "if rightly wreathed, the band will bind us to Heaven no less."

Study of Words. — This may be made highly interesting and instructive, and if you can succeed in awakening a true spirit of investigation, you will at the same time open a way in which your pupils will employ much time that would be otherwise spent in idleness or in a useless manner. But few realize how much valuable information may be gained from an investigation into the origin of words and phrases. Sir James Mackintosh has well said, that, "in a language like ours, where so many words are derived from other languages, there are few modes of instruction more useful or more amusing than that of tracing out the etymology and primary meaning of the words we use. There are cases in which knowledge of more real value may be conveyed from the history of a word, than from the history of a campaign." Let me call your attention to a few cases that occur to me. I will first refer to two or three words still in use, applied to objects quite different in their material or mechanism from the object to which the name was originally given. The article has been materially changed, though the name remains unchanged. Of this class are ink-*horn*, powder-*horn*, &c., so called from the fact that they were composed of *horn*.

A part of a plough, now made of metal, is still called mould-*board*, the name given when it was made of wood, or board.

Our word "window," and the phrase "Open the window," will possess a new interest to pupils when told that formerly windows were constructed so that they opened as doors, — a mode now in use to some extent. They were *wind-doors*, or doors for the admission of air. Hence it was quite appropriate to speak of opening a window, or wind-door, — though it would seem more fitting now to speak of "raising a window."

The word *villain*, or *villein*, as it was formerly spelt, simply meant a servant employed on a villa or farm. A *boor* was a farmer, and a *neighbor* was only a *nigh boor*. A *coward* was one who *cowered* in the presence of an enemy.

Case-knife had its origin in the time when every man carried his own knife in a *case*. The name is still retained, though the *case* is not used.

How often is the word *ringleader* used, and yet how few have the remotest idea of its origin, — and how significant it becomes when we trace it, and learn that it is derived from the practice, which men associating to oppose law have sometimes adopted, of signing their names to articles of agreement, in a "ring," so that no one could tell who signed first, — as such a one would be considered the most guilty. Though the practice is not in use with us, we still use the word as expressive of the leading person in any wrong-doing, always considering the "ringleader" of a party as the most influential, and, in cases of damage or wrong-doing, the most reprehensible.

Our word *candidate* is derived from a Latin word signifying white, — those who were candidates for office in Rome being required to wear a white gown. If all candidates for office in our times should be required to dress in white, our streets would present quite a gala appearance.

The word *windfall* is quite an expressive word with us. By the tenure of some of the estates in England, the felling of trees was prohibited, the timber being reserved for the royal navy. If any trees were prostrated by the wind, they became the property of the occupant of the grounds. Hence a tornado was quite a god-send or "windfall" to tenants of estates. With us the term is used to express any pecuniary fortune received by any one.

The word *blackguard* is said to have originated in the fact that a number of filthy, ragged, and roguish boys attended the Horse Guards at parade in St. James's Park, to black the boots of the soldiers, etc. These, from their constant attendance about the time of Guard meeting, received the appellation of "blackguards,"—a term now applied to a class of persons who are many degrees below a common boot-black.

The word *humbug*, perhaps quite too common with us, is said to be a corruption of Hamburg. "During a period when war prevailed on the Continent, so many false reports and lying bulletins were fabricated at Hamburg, that at length, when any one wished to signify his disbelief of a statement, he would say, 'You had that from Hamburg,' or, 'That is Hamburg,' and, finally, 'That is a *humbug*.'"

The expression "under the rose" had its origin from the fact that confessionals, or the ceilings of the rooms, were ornamented with representations of the rose.

The word *quarantine* is often used by those who comprehend neither its origin nor signification. It is derived from the Italian word *quarantina*, meaning forty. It was customary among the Venetians, by whom the practice was originated, to confine vessels at quarantine forty days, it being generally believed that, if contagion did not spread within that time, there need be no apprehension thereafter. The time for the detention with us varies with circumstances.

The expression "robbing Peter to pay Paul," has been explained as follows: "In the time of Edward VI., much of the lands of St. Peter, at Westminster, were seized by his Majesty's ministers and courtiers; but, to reconcile the people to the robbery, they allowed a portion of the income to be appropriated to the repairs of St. Paul's Church.

"The origin of the phrase, 'Mind your *p*'s and *q*'s,' is said to have been a call of attention, in the old English alehouses, to the *pints* and *quarts* being scored down to the unconscious or reckless beer-bibber."

"Some words," says Trench, in his excellent work on the Study of Words, "having reference to the family and the relations of family life, are not less full of teaching. For example, 'husband' is properly 'house-band,' the *band* and *bond* of the house, who shall bind and hold it together. Thus old Tusser, in his Points of Husbandry: —

'The name of the *husband* what is it to say?
Of wife and of *household* the *band* and the stay.'

So that the very name may put him in mind of his authority, and of that which he ought to be to all the members of the house. And the name 'wife' has its lessons too, although not so deep a one as the equivalent words in some other tongues. It belongs to the same family of words as 'weave,' 'woof,' 'web,' and the German 'weben.' It is a title given to her who is engaged at the web and woof, these having been the most ordinary branches of female industry, of wifely employment, when the language was forming. So that in the word itself is wrapped up a hint of earnest in-door, stay-at-home occupations, as being the fittest for her who bears this name." Again, the author just quoted says: "You will often be able to glean knowledge from the names of things, that will prove both curious and interesting. What a record of invention is presented in the names, which so many articles bear, of the place from which they first came, or the person by whom they were first invented. The *bayonet* tells us that it was first made at Bayonne; *cambrics*, that they came from Cambray; *damasks*, from Damascus; *arras*, from the city of the same name; *cordwain*, or *cordovan*, from Cordova; *currants*, from Corinth; the *guinea*, that it was originally coined of gold brought from the African coast so called; *camlet*, that it is woven, at least in part, of camel's hair. Such has been the manufacturing progress of England* that we now send our calicoes and muslins to India and the East; yet the words give standing witness that we once imported them thence; for *calico* is from Calicut, and *muslin* from Moussul, a city in Asiatic Turkey."

We shall find some words used by ancient writers, but not now in use, which were quite as expressive as those substituted for them. Among these are *deathsman* for *executioner; scatterling* for *vagabond* or *spendthrift; moonling* for *lunatic*, &c. In teaching geography, how much interest you may impart to the lesson by explaining the meaning or origin of certain words or names. For example, if "Alabama" occurs, say that it was an Indian word, signifying "here we rest." It is said that a peaceful tribe of the aborigines, being driven from their home, wandered about until they came

* The author resides in London.

to the banks of a river, where they stopped, exclaiming, "Al-à-ba-ma!" or, "Here we rest."

Azores comes from a word meaning hawk, and is applied to a group of islands on which this bird abounded.

Cape is from the Latin *caput*, meaning the head. A cape is the head of the land.

The name "Lena," signifying *sluggard*, is given to a certain river in Asia which is very sluggish in its flow.

Holland is from "hollow land," a large portion of the country being so low as to render it necessary to construct embankments, or dikes, to prevent the inflowing of the sea.

Ladrones comes from a word meaning *thieves*. So named by Magellan, on account of the thievish propensities of the inhabitants.

Patagonia, from the Spanish *patagon*, meaning large feet. Magellan so called the country from the fact that the natives seemed to have feet of extraordinary size.

Porto Rico means "rich harbor."

Schuylkill, from the Dutch, meaning "hidden creek." The first explorers of the Delaware passed the mouth of the Schuylkill without observing it.

Winnipiseogee, the name of a beautiful lake among the highlands of New Hampshire, is said to have come from an Indian word signifying "the smile of the Great Spirit."

But these cases will suffice to give you an idea of the interest that may be awakened in the study of words. As helps in this particular, I would refer you to Trench on the Study of Words, and to Webster's or Worcester's unabridged Dictionary. From either of these works you may derive a vast amount of interesting and valuable information. If you will keep by you a small blank-book, in which you may record such words and phrases as come under your observation, you may, at the end of a year, have a collection that you will highly prize. If you can induce your pupils to adopt a similar plan, you will do much to awaken in them a spirit of observation and investigation.

MISCELLANEOUS KNOWLEDGE. — Improve every opportunity for imparting general information, and awakening an interest in passing events. Almost every newspaper will furnish you some pertinent topics. If you meet with an account of any event or transaction of importance, make it the subject of a few minutes' conversation, and explain whatever may be necessary. If places are named, have them pointed out on the map, thus both fixing in the mind the event itself and the locality of the same. So far as possible, give a practical turn to all miscellaneous exercises. By exercising a little judgment and care, you may introduce all the exercises named in this letter without interfering with any of the regular and prescribed studies of the school; and their introduction will add to the general interest and progress of the school in other matters.

Your sincere friend,

C.

LETTER XX.

PRIMARY SCHOOLS.

MY DEAR FRIEND:—

I IMAGINE you may express some surprise at the subject of this letter. Perhaps you will exclaim, "What have I to do with primary schools?" If so, I will say, that I hope you may, at some time, become qualified to take charge of one, though I confess that I have doubts on this point. We may differ somewhat in our estimates of these schools. In my opinion, they have never been properly appreciated nor suitably cared for. Lying as they do at the very foundation of a system of education, they are too often regarded as unimportant, though unavoidable, appendages to our common-school system. Teachers of moderate attainments and without experience are often employed in them, merely because their services can be secured at a lower rate of compensation. But, in reality, these schools are of the first consideration, and they should receive the services and influence of the best of teachers. As it is in them that the young receive their earliest school impressions, it must be readily seen that it would be no easy matter to over-estimate their true importance. The influence of wrong discipline, erroneous teaching, or improper example, in these schools, will be felt unfavorably in all our higher schools and seminaries of learning. While I hardly dare hope that you will ever become a model teacher of a primary school, I do hope the few lines I may write on this subject will tend to form in your mind a just estimate of the influence of such a school in our educational system.

We well know that the instructions and influences to which we were exposed in early childhood were those which most strongly and indelibly impressed themselves upon our minds and characters. How many lessons which we then learned, how many sights which we then saw, how many impressions which we then received, seem closely inwoven into our very natures, and to be fresh and forceful in our memories, while many of the lessons and scenes and incidents of a later period are either wholly forgotten, or but dimly and imperfectly remembered! How many there are who pass through life constantly suffering from the influences of the exaggerated or fictitious stories and representations to which they listened in childhood's tender years, — influences which maturer years and riper judgment cannot entirely eradicate, though they may bring a sort of conviction of their falsity! How many superstitious notions and absurd ideas have been so thoroughly inwrought into our early being, that no after-training or culture could remove them!

How many foolish prejudices and senseless antipathies the young have received from persons with whom they have associated, or from the circumstances by which they were surrounded! How many, during the first few years of their existence, have formed and fostered those uncharitable feelings, and those distorted and unseemly habits, which have tended to darken and embitter the whole current of subsequent life!

In view of considerations like these, how essential is it that special care and attention be devoted to the early training of the young! The lessons and teachings, the scenes and the habits, which exert their influences during the first six or eight years of existence, make more lasting impressions than those of any score of years of after life. The little songs and hymns, the maxims and the verses, which lisping children learn by slowly repeating as their mothers dictate, find so secure a lodgment in the mind, that no future lessons can wholly supplant them. A distinguished statesman once said, "Let me make the songs for the youth, and I care not who make the laws." With far more of truth one might say, "Let me have the control of the young during the first four years of their school life, and I care not who has their subsequent management."

But notwithstanding the immense importance of early training, how sadly and how extensively is it neglected or perverted! In how many instances are children not only not taught to go in the way they ought, but are left to go in their own way, or, what is worse, left exposed to such examples and impressions as will most surely lead them in the way in which they ought not to go! How many of those untoward manifestations which are so often made in the community, and of those feelings of insubordination and disorganization which so frequently and so greatly shock good citizens, owe their origin to the neglected or perverted opportunities and privileges of early youth!

If such are ever the tendencies or results of injudicious or wrong early training, or of neglect, it must seem obvious that primary schools should assume a high position in the public estimation. In them the young receive their first and most enduring school impressions. In them they form habits and views which will "grow with their growth, and strengthen with their strength." Most truthfully and expressively has the poet said, —

> "The mind, impressible and soft, with ease
> Imbibes and copies what she hears and sees,
> And through life's labyrinth holds fast the clew
> That first instruction gives her, false or true."

How desirable, then, that these early lessons and influences should be of the right kind, and imparted in the right way! The mind of a child may be easily turned from a correct course by ill-judged and unwise plans, or by the chilling effects of neglect, on the part of those under whose care they pass their early years, — and some trivial circumstance, or some apparently insignificant cause, bearing upon the youthful mind, may give a change or tinge to the whole future life.

It would seem that parents acted less wisely in relation to this subject than in any other concern. The judicious and skilful husbandman does not neglect his young trees and leave them to assume uncomely shapes, or to be dwarfed and choked by rank weeds or from want of proper culture, with the idea that they are soon to be removed to a different situation. He will rather watch them with special interest, and train them with extra care, that they may prove specimens worthy of transplantation. Knowing full well that

"As the twig is bent the tree 's inclined,"

he will labor most assiduously to see that every vine and treelet assumes and retains the right "bent"; and, if he has occasion to employ any one to assist him in their culture and training, he will wisely select some one of known skill and judgment.

The farmer who has a colt to be trained, does not manifest indifference as to whom the task shall be committed; nor does he hazard injury and loss by intrusting the work to incompetent hands, with a view to saving a few dollars and cents; for he well knows that much of the animal's value and usefulness will consist in the manner in which he is "broken" to work and travel;—and yet how passing strange is it that parents are often less wise and less interested in relation to the moulding and training of the immortal minds of their offspring, and that, for a trifling pecuniary saving, they will risk the happiness and usefulness of those whom God has intrusted to their charge!

Those employed to teach in our primary schools should not only be well qualified in a literary point of view, but they should abound in every lovely and desirable trait of character. Decided, kind, affectionate, pleasant, and active, all their movements, actions, and expressions should be such as may be safely and profitably imitated. The teacher of a primary school should be a pattern of every good,— a model worthy of the closest imitation. George B. Emerson, Esq., a distinguished educator, in speaking of a recent visit to schools in Germany, thus strongly and beautifully testifies to the importance of elementary schools, and at the same time gives some valuable hints on teaching the alphabet.

"The most striking and beautiful lesson I heard in Germany was in Dresden, conducted by a man of very high qualifications. It was a lesson in teaching the alphabet. Young ladies and young gentlemen are very apt to think, 'What a drudgery this is! Only think, that, with my qualifications, I should be content to teach the beggarly elements! What a position! O, that I could be in a sphere fitter for my capacities!' That is a great and fundamental mistake which leads any teacher to utter such words. *There is no lesson ever taught in any school so important as the alphabet.* Teaching our crabbed English language is the hardest thing in the world. Our language is the hardest one to read, from the fact that there is not the most remote connection between the words used and the sounds expected. There cannot be a higher office than that of giving the very elements of instruction.

"What was very striking, in connection with the school at Dresden, was, that the teacher had a class of about forty boys, all nearly of the same age, and none of them less than seven years old, coming for the first time to learn the alphabet. Those sensible people, who wish to make as much as possible of their scholars, do not allow their children to be taught the alphabet before they are seven years old. The admirable teacher of these boys began by drawing a fish, and asking the boys to tell what it was. Some said it was a fish, some that it was a picture of a fish; but some that it had no color, and therefore was not a *picture*, but something the teacher drew. So they arrived, after a series of questions, at the conclusion that it was a *drawing* of a fish; not a picture, because that would have color; and not a fish, because that would have life. Then all the class were called on to say, together, 'That is a drawing of a fish.' As that would form a good sentence, they were required to repeat it till they could utter it as well as possible, giving every articulate sound clearly. Then he would ask each one to read the sentence. Then, from a set of large blocks, he selected the letters to spell the word *fish*, and, having shown them to the class, he asked them to select the letters to spell it, then to go to their seats and draw the letters on their slates. Some would succeed well, and some would fail entirely; but to those that failed there was no reproof, though to those that succeeded words of encouragement were given.

"In about ten minutes he called on the boys again, and inquired, 'What is a fish?' and put several questions to lead them to think about a fish, and would converse with them about the facts in its natural history; and at each conclusion he would make them express their conclusion as well as their organs could utter it. That was the striking thing, — the lesson in making sentences, in speaking good German, and in pronouncing correctly.

The first thing to be noticed here is the fact that a gentleman of the highest intelligence, possessed of all knowledge, a beautiful knowledge of natural history, did not think himself degraded in the least degree by teaching the alphabet. Another thing to be noticed was, that those things which, in the old-fashioned schools, were considered unsuitable, they were encouraged to do, — that is, to make pictures. Another thing that was very noticeable, was the thoroughness with which the languages were taught in the gymnasia. The master would have forty boys of just the same age and the same attainments. The little which the teacher attempted to teach at one time was a striking feature of the instruction. A single short sentence of three words was given; but in regard to them he led them to observe everything, and reviewed everything they had become familiar with, and they were kept familiar with it by continual repetition. After they had learned a single sentence, they were to use that in making other sentences. The degree of thoroughness with which this instruction was given almost transcends belief."

I trust the extract just given, together with what I may add, will tend to elevate, in your mind, the primary school, and though you may never become a teacher of such a school, it is very desirable that you should possess right views and a proper estimate of its true importance in the great system of popular education. If you clearly understand the subject, you may do much for the dissemination of correct sentiments.

The Rev. Doctor Lothrop, a member of the School Committee of the city of Boston, thus speaks of primary schools: —

"As parts of a great system of public instruction, it is scarcely possible to attach too much importance to the primary schools. They are the base of the pyramid, and in proportion as the base is enlarged and its foundations strengthened, the superstructure can be reared with ease and rapidity, in graceful proportions, and to a towering height. Under the improvements which are now in operation, and others that will be introduced, it is hoped that the children in the primary schools will be rescued from that waste of time and misdirection of powers hitherto unavoidable, and so instructed and carried forward, as that every child, on attaining the requisite age, shall be competent and qualified, not only to enter the grammar schools, but to improve the privileges and advantages there offered. And in proportion as the children entering the grammar schools come thoroughly qualified and prepared, these schools themselves will be improved, and a large number of pupils pass through them at an age sufficiently early to allow them to enjoy the benefit of the high schools, before the time arrives at which they wish to leave school for some active employment. Thus, by improving the primary, we improve the grammar, extend the advantages of the high schools, and make our whole system of public instruction, of popular education, what it ought to be, *progressive* and not *stationary*."

As you may, at some time, aspire to teach one of these elementary schools, let me, in brief, give you a few hints bearing upon them.

The School-House. — When it is remembered that children are educated and influenced by what they see, as well as by what they hear, it would seem very important to have the surroundings of childhood's days pleasant and attractive. Especially should this be true of the school-house, in which the little ones receive their earliest school impressions. The spot itself should be one of Nature's choicest, — one which will be inviting to the eye. The school-room should be constructed with particular reference to the comfort and convenience of the children. The walls should be covered with maps, paintings, mottoes, and drawings; and if a case could be provided for the reception of such objects of interest as the children, or others, may bring to the school-room, it will prove an additional attraction, and become truly valuable in connection with those pleasant Object Lessons which should occupy so prominent a part of instruction in primary schools. A pleasant school-house and yard will have a very happy influence on the early school days of children.

The Hours of Confinement.—In most of our schools the younger pupils are confined quite too many hours in the day. It is no great pleasure for little four-years-old boys or girls to go to school and sit still, on hard seats, some six hours daily,—and it is extremely unreasonable to require them to do so. For all under the age of seven or eight years, two or three hours daily of school confinement will prove sufficient. Let the remainder of the time, usually allotted to school exercises, or rather to motionless position, be spent upon the playground, and let the teacher watch them there, that she may teach them how to play. How many valuable lessons might be given on the play-ground, by judicious efforts in cultivating those kindly and friendly feelings which ought to prevail in all communities,—lessons in patience, self-denial, forgiveness, sympathy, generosity, &c.

The Exercises of the Primary School.—These

should be made brief and interesting. The blackboard and slate, and simple pieces of apparatus, should be in frequent use. But it will not be necessary that I give any detailed list of suitable exercises. An excellent "Manual for Primary Schools" is soon to be presented to the public,— prepared by one* who has taken a deep and judicious interest in these schools. From an examination of the plan and some of the contents of the book, in manuscript, we are persuaded it will be a work of inestimable value to teachers and schools. This work, and Hooker's "Child's Book of Common Objects," will be so fruitful of hints and information, that I can do no better than refer you to them.

I will close this letter by giving a few plain and simple hints, in the form of rules for teachers and pupils.

RULES AND MAXIMS FOR THE TEACHER.

1. Endeavor to set a good example in all things.

2. Never overlook a fault or let it go unnoticed; but always forgive when you find true sorrow for an error.

3. If possible, get at the truth of every charge, and decide neither in word nor deed until the case is clear. Hasty words and acts often cause teachers sorrow.

---

* John D. Philbrick, Superintendent of Schools in the city of Boston.

4. Never punish when anger influences you or the offender.

5. Prepare yourself for every lesson, and encourage your pupils to ask questions; and if they ask some that you are not able to answer, frankly acknowledge your inability.

6. Take special pains with the dull and backward children. It is the highest merit to be able to interest and teach the dull.

7. Remember that you are laying the *foundations* of knowledge, and therefore aim at thoroughness. Not how *much*, but how *well*.

8. Encourage cleanliness of person; neatness of desk, books, floor, &c.

9. If possible, secure good ventilation. Raise the windows during recess and at noon.

10. Improve every opportunity for imparting moral instruction, and making moral impressions.

11. Daily add to your own stock of knowledge, never forgetting that knowledge is power.

12. Let all your intercourse and dealings with your pupils be characterized by a spirit of love for them, and a desire to do them good.

13. Be yourself taught of Him who took little children in his arms and blessed them.

RULES AND MAXIMS FOR THE CHILDREN.

These may be repeated daily, by the pupils, in concert.

1. We must be gentle and kind to each other.

2. We must love and obey our teachers.
3. We must always act and speak the truth.
4. We must never speak evil of others.
5. We must be honest in all things.
6. We must attend to our lessons and to the words of our teacher.
7. We must use no bad words.
8. We must be neat, and keep our books and desks clean and free from marks.
9. We must never be absent, unless we are sick.
10. We must never be tardy.
11. We must be kind to all.
12. We must always speak pleasantly.
13. We must not get angry.
14. We must love and obey God.
15. We must at all times Do Right.

These maxims and rules will be suggestive to you and to your pupils. It will be well, occasionally, to make one a subject for familiar remarks, — and particularly after your attention, or that of the school, has been called to its violation.

Your sincere friend,

C.

LETTER XXI.

HABITS.

My dear Friend:—

Thus far I have written principally in relation to the daily studies of the school, and to its discipline and general management. These of course are all important, but they by no means cover the whole ground of your labors. You have something more to do, and, consciously or unconsciously, you are daily imparting other lessons, which will prove a benefit or an injury to those under your charge. Influences of some kind you must and will daily impart. See to it that they are of the right kind. Do not for a moment imagine that your pupils have received all that is due from you when you have heard them "say their lessons." By word and example you must give to them many a lesson not given in their text-books. Your constant effort must be, not only to make them proficients in their book-lessons, but also to do what you can to promote correct habits of thought, expression, and action. Your example and your expressed views must be the main agencies in this direction. Be sure that your example is a worthy one, and also that your views are correct in themselves, and clearly understood by your pupils. Consider that, when a few brief years shall have passed away, the boys and girls now under your training will be men and women, — acting their parts in the great drama of life. How those parts shall be acted depends, in a great degree, upon the instructions and impressions they receive from you, — their teacher. Constantly and earnestly, then, try so to train and influence them that they will become men and women in the highest and truest sense, — ever acting well their parts, and diffusing good to all around them. In an important sense teachers reproduce themselves in their pupils, — and what they are, their pupils will become. Aim, therefore, to teach them such lessons as they will most need when they become men, — such as will tend to make them good citizens, agreeable associates, faithful in the discharge of every duty that may devolve upon them.

I wish more particularly, in this letter, to call your attention to a few points to which you should direct attention frequently, as tending to the formation of habits which are alike essential to happiness and usefulness. In many cases your known and clearly expressed views in relation to these habits will be sufficient. Aim, then, not only to have your views so clearly understood that they will be felt, but also be sure to have them fully confirmed by examples of the clearest propriety. Precept without example may accomplish somewhat; precept followed by wrong example will often prove worse than powerless; but precept and example, in harmonious action, will be powerful indeed. How often is the usefulness of one who is eminent for scholarly attainments greatly abridged by the indulgence of some unfortunate or unbecoming habit! In view of this, let me urge you to inculcate, by constant example and precept, attention to the following particulars: —

1. *Regularity.* — It is too true that many pupils in our schools are very irregular in their attendance. Reasons wholly unimportant or quite frivolous draw them from the school-room, and cause them to regard their school duties as of secondary importance. Strive to impress upon their minds the importance of regularity in the performance of their duties. He only is successful as a merchant, mechanic, farmer, or professional man, who applies himself with regularity to the peculiar duties of his calling: he, and he only, can become what he ought to be, as a scholar, who applies himself with undeviating regularity to the duties of the school. Habits of regularity formed here will be felt for good in all subsequent life, — while habits of indifference and irregularity in relation to school duties will manifest themselves for evil in all the business relations of life.

2. *Punctuality.* — The habit of punctuality is as

rare as it is important. In all the arrangements of life, inconvenience, and often loss, are experienced from a want of promptness or punctuality on the part of some. In how many of our churches are the exercises interrupted by the entrance of tardy ones! How often are the operations of some committee delayed by the dilatoriness of some member or members! How much annoyance would be avoided in all business operations, if all were scrupulously punctual! A certain committee, consisting of ten members, were to meet at ten o'clock, and the business was such as to require the presence of all. Nine were promptly on the spot, but the tenth came a half-hour behind the time. As he entered the room, he gave a very indifferent apology for his tardiness, when an honest Quaker who was a member of the committee rebuked him in these words: "Friend, thee may have some right to waste thirty minutes of thine own time, but thee certainly has no right to waste two hundred and seventy minutes of the time of those on the committee with thee." Daily inculcate the importance of exact punctuality in relation to every duty and every engagement. If you can train your pupils to exactness in all their school duties and exercises, you will, at the same time, do much to establish a habit of punctuality. He that is punctual in regard to little things will be so in regard to matters of greater importance.

3. *Neatness.*—Habits of neatness and cleanli-

ness are so essential to our comfort and happiness, that no opportunity for urging attention to them should be allowed to pass unimproved. Do what you can, from time to time, to promote a regard for tidiness of personal appearance and apparel, and care and neatness in the use of books, arrangement of desk, etc. Not only inculcate the importance of having a "place for everything and everything in its place," but also of having all things arranged with a due reference to neatness. Habits of neatness formed in youth will be permanent, but if a lad indulges in careless and slovenly habits during the first twelve or fifteen years of his life it will be almost impossible to eradicate the same. "Good or bad habits formed in youth generally accompany us through life."

4. *Courtesy and Politeness.*—Many a man of high qualifications and rare talents has, in a good degree, been lost to the community on account of a lack of courteousness, or from some forbidding trait of character. True courtesy and politeness, manifested on all occasions and in an unassuming way, will give to him who exhibits them a most desirable influence and power. Let a regard to these be daily encouraged in your school. Make it one of your requirements that all questions shall be properly proposed, and all answers courteously given,—and also that the entire demeanor of your pupils, not only towards their teacher, but also towards each other, and all with whom they may have to do, shall

be in strict accordance with rules of propriety and courtesy. Attention to these particulars in the school-room will be promotive of good order and happiness there, and at the same time tend to establish such habits as will be strong helps to success and usefulness in any department of business. If merchants could realize the difference between a truly courteous boy, and one who is the reverse, the former would always be preferred, and the latter left to seek employment of a different nature. The instances are not uncommon in which a customer is driven from a store by direct rudeness or lack of politeness on the part of some lad there employed.

Let me then urge you, not only to give attention to the cultivation of such habits as I have named, but also to encourage and promote, in every suitable way, the formation of all habits that will tend to make good citizens and agreeable associates. Let your aim be, not only to teach the lessons of the book, but also to form true symmetry of character by duly developing every pleasing and desirable trait, and by checking the growth of every habit which may tend to impair one's usefulness, or to detract from one's influences as a companion or friend.

Your sincere friend,

C.

LETTER XXII.

SCHOOL EXAMINATIONS AND EXHIBITIONS.

MY DEAR FRIEND: —

IN this my last letter for the present, I will endeavor to give you my views on two other points in relation to which you have expressed an interest and a desire to have advice. These are "School Examinations and Exhibitions."

With many teachers and committees there seems to be a partial confounding of these two terms, so that an examination often degenerates into a mere exhibition; but we believe an exhibition in no true sense ever becomes an examination. Considering that the two are quite different in their character and results, and that each has its appropriate place and influence in the great work of education, I will briefly give you a few thoughts on each.

I. EXAMINATIONS. — Many teachers have a serious dread of examinations. I think you have experienced something of this; and yet, if you will calmly view the subject, you will find that the earnest and faithful teacher need have no undue anxiety or trouble on this subject. The true object of an examination is to ascertain the nature and extent of mental discipline that pupils have gained. It is not simply and solely to ask them certain questions to be found in the books they have studied, but to test, in every proper manner, their understanding of the various principles, facts, and thoughts that should have been developed by the studies to which attention has been given during the term.

How, then, ought examinations to be conducted? It has frequently been the case, at public examinations, that teachers have asked all the questions; and, I am sorry to add, some teachers have done the profession injustice, by making special and individual assignment of questions and topics, and drilling their pupils on them preparatory to the day of examination. Says an experienced teacher, "We recollect an amusing anecdote of a class in geography, which the teacher had drilled in his set questions, till they could answer every one *before it was asked;* and he felt confident they would do themselves and him great credit. Indeed, his main reliance was on this class, and when he commenced their examination, it was with a very confident and triumphant air. As the questions passed along down the class, and were answered with the rapidity of thought, the village minister and the doctor and parents began to open their eyes with astonishment at the remarkable proficiency which the boys had made. The teacher was so elated at the result, that he did not observe that one of the boys, whose place was at the foot of the class, was absent; and as he passed to the head again, the question was this: 'In what country do you live?' 'Guinea!' shouted the boy. 'What country?' repeated the teacher, wishing to give the pupil time to recollect himself. 'Guinea!' was again the thundering response; and the lad looked as though he was not to be frowned out of it either. 'You mean, no doubt, that you live in the United States of America,' quietly suggested the teacher. 'No, sir; the boy that lives in the United States of America is at home. He was sick to-day, and could n't come.'" On another occasion, some small boys were undergoing examination in geography. They could readily point out, on the outline map, and give the names, of all the grand divisions, etc. A gentleman present, wishing to test the knowledge of the little fellows, said: "Boys, let me ask you a question. What is Asia?" Here was no response. "Is it *land* or *water*, or what is it?" The boys continued silent. They were not used to such questions as that. They could point out Asia on any map,—they knew it by its shape,—but they seemed to have no more idea of it than though it were an arbitrary character, like A or B.

Some contend that the teacher should ask all the questions; others, that the teacher should be silent, and the examining committee propound the questions. We believe that neither of these is the true course, but that both parties should participate in the exercises. We will suppose a class is called in arithmetic. The teacher says to the examiners: "This class has progressed as far as Proportion. Some of the members, I think, understand all they have passed over; others, who have been irregular in their attendance, or less studious than they ought to have been, may not be so perfect. In our daily recitations some uniformly do well, while others frequently fail. In questioning them to-day, unless they appear better than they usually do, you will find the same diversity." With remarks of this kind the examination may be introduced, and then questions may be asked by both teacher and committee. It need not annoy the teacher if some questions fail to receive correct answers. This is to be expected. Neither teachers, committees, nor pupils should expect to have the exercises of examination-day faultless. The true wish and aim should be to exhibit the correct standing of the scholars, — to ascertain what they do *not* understand, as well as what they *do*.

With classes sufficiently advanced, it will be an excellent plan to have a quarterly examination, in which answers to the several questions shall be written by the pupils. This course has many advantages, which will be obvious to any one. In conducting an oral examination, I would recommend that some subjects or topics should be selected, and that pertinent questions be asked, without any reference to the phraseology of the questions in the text-book. In other words, let it be the aim of both teachers and committees to ascertain whether the scholar has *ideas*, or merely *words*.

II. EXHIBITIONS. — The object of an exhibition is somewhat different from that of an examination; or, rather, the object is twofold: first, to interest and train the pupils in certain drill-exercises, in themselves important; and, secondly, to interest parents and friends, by exhibiting evidence of skill and correct instruction in certain departments. Such exercises may indicate what can be done, with special effort, in a particular direction; they will be beneficial to the pupils, if rightly conducted, and at the same time afford an opportunity for enlisting the interest of parents and citizens. Rightly managed, examinations and exhibitions are productive of much good; but, too often, the good effects of both are lost by the improper manner in which they are conducted. In the exercises of an exhibition, consisting usually of declamation and composition, special care should be taken to avoid such as are in the slightest degree of an immoral tendency. It is believed that many schools would be greatly benefited by giving a public and well-arranged exhibition once a year, only let it be distinctly understood that it is an *exhibition*, and not an *examination;* that it does not indicate the proficiency of the scholars in their usual studies, but is rather designed to show what they can do, with special effort and training, in particular departments. With this understanding, we may welcome school exhibitions as an important means of awakening parental interest, and inciting an ambition in the pupils well to perform their parts. I have sometimes thought that examinations, as they have been conducted, tended to encourage haste rather than thoroughness. If pupils have been able to answer a few questions from different portions of the book, it has been deemed sufficient; and yet they might have done this without having been thoroughly instructed in a single rule. On such occasions, too much importance is attached to the amount passed over, and too little to the manner in which it has been done.

I would again urge you to guard against undue haste in school progress. The whole tendency of our times is in this direction. We live in an age of haste. There is haste in travelling, haste in business, haste in learning, haste in eating, haste in all things. But, nevertheless, it is true that great waste and loss often attend great haste. A train of cars is thrown from the track; lives are lost; limbs are broken; property is destroyed. All was the result of an unpardonable attempt to gain two minutes of time. Alas! how many, in rash efforts to gain a few moments of time, have been, as it were, thrust into eternity!

A few years ago, a noble steamer, with upwards of four hundred human beings, and a rich cargo of merchandise, left Liverpool for New York. The joyous company were borne rapidly onward, and were fast approximating the port for which they had sailed. A dense fog hung over the "face of the mighty deep," rendering navigation perilous; but all were "homeward bound," and "haste" was the watchword. The noble ship was urged onward, and, as it were participating in the general feeling, she almost leaped from billow to billow. All were joyous and delighted at the progress that was making, and the gallant commander was often congratulated upon the speed of his ship and the prospect of a quick passage, when, almost within sight of the longed-for haven, a sudden crash was heard, which sent a thrill and a chill through every heart; and in less than four hours that proud steamer, with her rich cargo and more than three hundred human beings, was in the caverns of the deep. The telegraphic wires immediately communicated the sad intelligence to all parts of our country, sending keen distress and bitter anguish and crushing disappointment to many a bereaved heart. It was called a "*sad accident*"; but it was in reality the consequence of unwarrantable haste, an undue desire to gain a few hours of time, or to be reported under the heading, ☞ THE SHORTEST PASSAGE ON RECORD! Yet the entire blame was not chargeable to the commander, but in part certainly to that state of the public mind which would not be satisfied with anything short of extra speed. And this same spirit and tendency prevail in relation to the education of youth, — an impatient, unreasonable haste. Children are too early pressed into school, unduly urged onward, and prematurely taken from the school and pressed into life's service, with minds but imperfectly disciplined, with intellects but partially cultivated. And yet the fault is not wholly in the teachers, but quite as much in the parents, who influence and control the teachers. As, then, you engage in the great work of instruction, do what you can to disseminate true and wise views, and secure right action; ever discountenancing undue haste; ever regarding Nature's teachings; — "*First the blade, then the ear; after that, the full corn in the ear.*"

But it is quite time that I bring this letter to a close. I might urge upon your consideration the importance of regarding the laws of physical existence, so that the "house you live in" may be kept in a sound and usable condition. I might dwell upon the importance of regularity and system in all your habits and arrangements, and caution you against the too common tendency of overtasking the powers of endurance by giving extraordinary hours either to labor or amusement. I hope, however, that your own good judgment will lead you to consider the whole subject, and to act according to the dictates of true wisdom.

If aught I have written in these letters shall throw any light about your path as a teacher of youth, or shall encourage or stimulate you to greater effort in your noble calling, I shall not regret that I have written. Let me say, in concluding, what I have already, directly or indirectly, said in previous letters, that if you would look for true success as an instructor, you must engage in your labors with a strong desire to do good. Difficulties and perplexities you will often meet with; but if you love your work, and engage in its performance with the right motives, you will surmount all obstacles, and prove an ornament to your profession. Do not forget that the chief fruits of your labors will be in the future, and that they may mature unseen by you, ever perpetuating and extending themselves. While, therefore, your duty is to labor in "the living present," strive earnestly and prayerfully to have the results of your efforts such as will prove a blessing to the future. With an abiding sense of your dependence upon Infinite Wisdom for support and direction, go forth cheerfully to your daily labors, and strive so to act your part, that when, with you, time shall be no more, you may receive from the Great Teacher the soul-cheering plaudit, "WELL DONE."

Your sincere friend.

C.

APPENDIX.

27*

NOTE.

The Author has, from time to time, received letters asking information on points embraced in the following pages. The various rules, regulations, etc., which are given, are not presented as models adapted to the peculiar wants and circumstances of every teacher; but it is believed that they embody the substance of what will be wanted, and each teacher must change or modify according to the condition or wants of his own school. They will, it is hoped, prove valuable as suggestive aids. Many of them are such as have proved satisfactory with teachers of competent judgment and ability.

APPENDIX A.

MANUAL OF SCHOOL DUTIES.

The following excellent hints and rules were prepared by A. Parish, Esq., one of the most accomplished and successful teachers in New England. Mr. Parish is Principal of the Springfield (Mass.) High School, — a position he has occupied for many years. The Manual of School Duties, which we here give, has been well tried by its author, and others, and with uniformly good results. It will be well for the teacher to read these rules monthly, and accompany the same with such remarks as may be deemed pertinent.

TO A PUPIL ON ENTERING THE SCHOOL.

It is taken for granted, that your special object in becoming a member of this school is, to obtain such benefits as it may be able to afford, for the *improvement of the mind*, that you may be more *useful*; — for the *cultivation of your manners*, that you may be better able to render yourself agreeable to those around you; — for the cultivation of your *moral feelings*, that your *own personal happiness* may be increased.

While it is expected that the *teachers* will be faithful in imparting instruction, and in directing the general operations of the school, in the most thorough and agreeable manner, certain duties no less important for the success of the school are to be faithfully and honestly performed *on your part*, as pupils.

The following directions are given, that all may know, at the beginning, what their duties are, as pupils, and on what conditions they are permitted to enjoy the privileges of this school.

GENERAL DIRECTIONS.

I. *Resolve*, on being received as a member of this school, *to comply cheerfully* with all the requirements of the teachers; and faithfully perform every duty assigned you.

II. Always manifest and cultivate a *kind* and *accommodating* disposition towards *schoolmates*, — and *respect* towards *teachers*.

III. At all times let the school-room be regarded as *sacred to study and mental improvement*. Never indulge in *rudeness, childish trifling, loud and boisterous speaking*, or *anything* that would be considered unbecoming in genteel company.

IV. *Resolve*, to lend your influence, in every possible way, *to improve the school*, and *elevate its character*.

DEPORTMENT.

Remark. — It is as much a part of your education to correct bad habits and obtain good ones, — to cultivate good manners, and learn to conduct with propriety on all occasions, — as to be familiar with the studies pursued in school. Read carefully and remember the following particulars.

STILLNESS.

1. On entering the school, pass as quietly as possible to your seat, taking care to close the door gently, and avoid making unnecessary noise with the feet in crossing the room.

2. Take out books, slate, etc. from your desk with care, and lay them down in such a manner as not to be heard. Avoid making a rustling noise with papers, or noisily turning over leaves of books. Never let the marking of a pencil on your slate be heard.

3. Be careful to keep the feet quiet while engaged in study; or, if it be necessary to move them, do it without noise.

4. In passing to and from recitations, observe whether you are moving quietly. Take special care if you wear thick shoes or boots, or if they are made of squeaking leather.

5. Avoid the awkward and annoying habit of making a noise with the lips while studying.

6. *Scuffling*, *striking*, *pushing*, or *rudeness* of any kind, must *never* be practised, in the least, *under any circumstances*, within the school building.

PROMPTNESS.

1. *Be punctually at School.* — Be ready to regard every signal without delay, — to commence study, at once, when "study hours" begin, — to give immediate and undivided attention, when a teacher addresses you, either individually, with the class, or with the whole school.

2. On appearing in the school-room after an absence from one or more exercises, your *first duty* will be to present a *written excuse* specifying the *time* and *cause* of the absence.

NEATNESS.

MOTTO. — "A place for everything, — and everything in its place."

Remark. — The habit of observing neatness and order should be cultivated as a virtue.

1. Let your shoes or boots be cleaned at the door-steps; always use the mat, if wet, muddy, or dirty.

2. Never suffer the floor under your desk, or the aisles around it, to be covered by papers, or anything else dropped on it.

3. Avoid spitting on the floor; it is a vulgar, filthy habit.

4. *Marking* or *writing* on the *desks*, *walls*, or *any part of the building*, or school premises, with pencil, chalk, or other articles, manifests a bad taste, or a vicious disposition to deface and destroy property. None but a vicious, reckless, or thoughtless person will do it.

5. Knives must never be used in cutting anything on a desk.

6. Particular care should be observed to avoid spilling ink anywhere in the school building.

7. Let your books, etc. be always arranged in a neat and convenient order in your desk and upon it.

8. After using brooms, dust-brushes, etc., always return them to their places.

9. Be ambitious to have every part of our school in so neat and orderly a condition, that visitors may be favorably impressed with this trait of our character.

SCHOLARSHIP.

MOTTO. — "Knowledge is power."

Remark. — *Three things* should ever be sought for by the scholar in all his studies and recitations. They are the *index of scholarship*.

I. *Aim at perfection.*

II. *Recite promptly.*

III. *Express your thoughts clearly and fully.*

1. Let the tone of voice be distinctly audible and perfectly uttered. Let your words be chosen with care, so as to express your thoughts precisely.

2. Determine to solve every difficult point in your lesson yourself, (if possible,) rather than receive assistance from another.

3. Scholars are in no case to assist each other about their lessons, in study hours, except by permission, for very special reasons.

RECITATIONS.

1. A scholar must never stay from recitation, *because* he "has *no lesson.*" If you have a good excuse, give it to your teacher, and go and hear the others recite.

2. A scholar must never have *anything* in his hands during recitation, nor during study hours, except what *strictly belongs to the exercise* in which he is engaged.

3. Do not rest satisfied with learning your lesson so as to "*guess* you can say it"; be able to give a clear and full account of it when you recite.

MISCELLANEOUS.

1. *All communications with the scholars are to be avoided* during the *hours of study* and *recitation.* This comprehends whispering, — writing notes, or on the slate, — signs, etc. Every pupil should study *as if there were no one else in the room,* with perfect silence.

2. Ask questions about lessons of teachers to whom you recite; as they are responsible for your improvement; — otherwise one may be overburdened with business which properly belongs to another.

3. No books are to be read in school hours, except such as belong to the studies and exercises of the school.

4. No scholar should go off the school grounds during recess, except with permission.

5. Never meddle with the desk or property of another scholar, without liberty.

6. Caps, bonnets, and all outer garments must be placed on the hook assigned to each pupil, immediately on entering school.

7. Boys must never wear caps or hats in the school-room.

8. Always *be in your own place*, and busy about *your own duties*.

9. Finally. Bear constantly in mind how short may be the time allotted you to enjoy the privileges of school, and how important an influence they may exert on all your future life.

APPENDIX B.

RULES FOR TEACHERS.

The following Rules, with a few slight changes and additions, are taken from the "Teacher and Parent":—

1. From your earliest intercourse with your pupils, inculcate the necessity of *prompt*, *cheerful*, and *exact* obedience.

2. Unite firmness with gentleness; and let your pupils clearly understand that you *mean* exactly what you *say*.

3. Never promise anything, unless you are quite sure you can give, or do, what you promise.

4. Never threaten a definite punishment for an anticipated offence.

5. Study the dispositions of your pupils, and adapt your modes of discipline to the same.

6. Never be late at school.

7. Be courteous in action and expression.

8. Never tell a pupil to do anything, unless you are sure he knows how it is to be done; — or show him how to do it, and then see that he does it.

9. Always punish a pupil for *wilful disobedience;* but never punish unduly, or in anger; and in no case give a blow on the head.

10. Never let your pupils see that they can vex you, or make you lose your self-command.

11. If pupils are under the influence of an angry or petulant spirit, wait till they are calm, and then reason with them on the impropriety of their conduct.

12. Never yield anything to a pupil because he looks angry, or attempts to move you by threats and tears. Deal mercifully, but justly too.

13. A little present punishment, when the occasion arises, is more effectual than the threatening of a greater punishment, should the fault be renewed.

14. Never allow pupils to do, at one time, what you have forbidden, under the like circumstances, at another.

15. Teach the young that the only sure and easy way to *appear* good is to *be* good.

16. Never allow tale-bearing.

17. If a pupil abuses your confidence, make him, for a time, feel the want of it.

18. Never allude to former errors, when real sorrow has been evinced for having committed them.

19. Encourage, in every suitable way, a spirit of diligence, obedience, perseverance, kindness, forbearance, honesty, truthfulness, purity, and courteousness.

20. Never speak in a scolding and fretful manner, but use tones of gentleness. Some teachers defeat their objects by using harsh and boisterous tones.

21. Be consistent in your requirements and uniform in your practice.

22. Set a good example in all things.

23. Constantly aim at thoroughness in teaching.

24. Inculcate habits of neatness.

25. In conduct be what you wish your pupils to become; avoid what you wish them to avoid.

APPENDIX C.

QUESTIONS FOR SELF-EXAMINATION.

THE following are some of the questions prepared for the teachers of Elementary Schools in Prussia. If all teachers would seriously examine themselves by the use of these questions, how much greater would be their interest and success!

1. In commencing the day, have I consecrated myself anew in prayer to my Creator?

2. Have I implored His blessing on the labors of the

day, especially seeking his favor for the children confided to my care?

3. Have I implored aid especially for such of my pupils as have the greatest need of assistance?

4. Have I commenced the day full of strength and confidence in God?

5. Have I sufficiently reflected, before school hours, on what I have to do through the day; and have I suitably prepared myself for my duties?

6. Are my cares and efforts extended equally to all my pupils, or do I manifest more interest in some than I do in others?

7. Has my attention been more particularly directed, and according to their need, to those among them who were weaker or more idle than the rest? Or, consulting only my own taste, have I occupied myself more willingly with the most intelligent, and those most desirous of being instructed?

8. In what manner have I influenced the moral progress of my pupils?

9. With regard to that which is exterior, have I required order, quietness, suitable manners, cleanliness?

10. Have I been guilty of any negligence in these respects from idleness or inattention?

11. Have I not, from disgust, abandoned to their evil propensities some children who resisted all my efforts?

12. Have I not, without confessing it to myself, condemned some among them as incorrigible?

13. And have I not thus neglected one of my most important duties; that of never despairing of the improvement of a single child confided to me?

14. When it has been necessary to censure, punish, or recall to duty by exhortation, have I done it with calmness,

reflection, and in an impressive manner? Or have I yielded to precipitancy, impatience, anger, and want of charity? or, on the other hand, have I been too indulgent?

15. Am I in general *just* with regard to my pupils?

16. Have I not an ill-judged aversion to some, and predilection for others?

17. Do I not yield in general to the influence and disposition of the moment, and am I not thereby unequal, and capricious; sometimes very kind, and sometimes causelessly in a bad humor, or even passionate and violent?

18. When it is necessary to reprove or punish, do I seek always to bear in mind the particular character of the pupil with whom I have to do, in order to guide myself accordingly in my reproof or punishment?

19. Do I always distinguish offences which proceed from levity, indolence, or rooted habits, from those which are the result of evil dispositions?

20. Have I not sometimes unconsciously excited the desire of praise, and promoted vanity or selfishness?

21. Has there not been in my conduct, thoughtlessness, levity, harshness, and want of love, or even pleasure in inflicting pain?

22. Have I sought to obtain over the parents of my pupils the influence which I ought to endeavor to acquire, if I am faithful in my vocation?

23. Have I, to-day, made any progress in knowledge and virtue?

24. Have I labored to improve myself in my vocation, even out of the hours in which are presented to me positive and regular occupation?

APPENDIX D.

RULES FOR SCHOLARS.

RULES TO BE DAILY REPEATED IN CONCERT BY THE CHILDREN IN A PRIMARY SCHOOL.

1st. I must be silent when the bell rings.
2d. I must always mind my teacher.
3d. I must come to school every day.
4th. I must never be tardy.
5th. I must not be idle.
6th. I must not lie.
7th. I must not steal.
8th. I must not swear.
9th. I must not be angry.
10th. I must not strike nor hurt any one in anger.
11th. I must be pleasant and kind to all.
12th. I must forgive all who offend or injure me.
13th. I must be clean in my clothes, my face, and my hands.
14th. I must be decent in all my ways.
15th. I must not destroy my books or my slates.
16th. I must not injure any of the furniture of the school.
17th. I must always try to do right.
18th. I must remember these rules, and try to keep them.

RULES RELATING TO PUPILS.*

1. Every scholar on entering the school grounds shall

* Taken from the published regulations of the public schools of Norwich, Conn.

go directly to his school-room, or to such portions of the grounds as are assigned for recreation; and none may loiter on the walks or steps, or in the halls or anterooms, for conversation or other purposes. And on leaving, they shall pass in a quiet and orderly manner directly from the school grounds and premises.

2. Unexcused tardiness is regarded, and may be punished, as a misdemeanor; also leaving the grounds or school during school hours without permission. And no excuse or request, save in case of sickness or of some sudden necessity, may be entertained by a teacher, unless made by the parent or guardian in person, or in writing, over his or her signature.

3. No pupil is expected to be absent from school, except on account of sickness or some other urgent cause; and an excuse from the parent or guardian of the pupil in person, or by writing over his or her signature, shall be required for all absences. And in all cases, the teacher may require an examination of the pupil in the lessons recited by his class during such absence. In case of such irregularity in attendance as, in the judgment of the teacher, to incapacitate the pupil from advancing with his class, the teacher may transfer such pupil to the next lower class; or the Board may, if necessary, order such pupil to a school of the next lower grade.

4. No scholar is expected to appear at school with unclean and slovenly person, or with garments indecently torn or soiled. Such pupil shall be sent to the wash-room for greater cleanliness, or may be ordered home for decent apparel; and his conduct shall be reckoned as a misdemeanor.

5. No disrespectful, profane, or obscene language shall be uttered in or about the grounds or rooms of any school-

house. The use of such language shall be regarded as a misdemeanor of the highest kind, and shall be punishable by the teacher. All such cases may be referred to the Board, who may suspend such offender, or, in incorrigible cases, expel him from the school. And no scholar suspended or expelled, for this or any other cause, shall be admitted, during such sentence, into any school under the government of the society.

6. Every pupil who shall, either accidentally or otherwise, injure any school property, whether pertaining to the buildings, grounds, or apparatus, or deface or defile them by pictures, marks, writing, or otherwise, shall within one week, or as soon thereafter as the nature of the case admits, make good all such injury or defacement, or be suspended from the school till permission to return be given by the Board. And any wilful injury or defacement shall be punishable as a misdemeanor; and such offender is liable to the action of the civil law.

APPENDIX E.

RULES AND REGULATIONS APPLYING TO TEACHERS AND PUPILS.

OPENING OF SCHOOL.

1. It shall be the duty of the teachers to be present at their respective school-rooms fifteen minutes previously to

the time for opening the school, punctually to observe the school hours, and faithfully to devote themselves to the public service.

MORNING EXERCISES.

2. The morning exercises of all the schools shall commence with the reading of the Scriptures; and it is recommended that the reading be followed with prayer by the teacher.

MORALS AND MANNERS.

3. The teachers shall use every suitable influence to lead their pupils to the formation of correct moral habits, and shall inculcate the importance of good manners.

DISCIPLINE.

4. The teachers shall practise such discipline in their schools as would be exercised by a kind, judicious parent in his family, and shall avoid corporeal punishment in all cases where good order and obedience can be maintained without it.

5. Pupils are expected to render prompt and cheerful obedience to the requirements of their teachers, to conduct towards them with becoming propriety, and to observe a kind and courteous demeanor towards each other. And when a pupil shall be guilty of grossly immoral conduct, or if, after due admonition and effort to reform him, he shall persist in conduct which interrupts the order and progress of the school, he shall at the discretion of the visiting committee be expelled.

6. The teachers shall exercise a special supervision over the conduct of their pupils, while in school, or whenever they come within the school buildings or grounds, and, as

far as practicable, while coming to, and returning from school.

VENTILATION, HEALTH, ETC.

7. The teachers shall carefully preserve neatness in the school-rooms, by having them properly swept and cleaned; and they shall also give vigilant attention to the ventilation and temperature of their rooms.

INJURIES TO SCHOOL BUILDINGS.

8. The teachers shall prescribe such rules for the use of the yards and out-buildings connected with the school-houses, as shall insure their being kept in a neat and proper condition; and in case any pupil shall wilfully deface, defile, or otherwise injure the school buildings, trees, or other property, he may be suspended from school by the district committee.

ATTENDANCE AT SCHOOL.

9. As regularity and punctuality of attendance are indispensable to the success of a school, it is important to maintain the principle that *necessity alone can justify absence;* and sickness, domestic affliction, and necessary absence from town, are regarded as the only rightful causes of non-attendance. In every instance of absence, the teacher shall be authorized to require a written excuse from the parents or guardians of the pupil.

TARDINESS.

10. Tardiness shall be accounted a misdemeanor, and be treated as such, except when it is excused by a written statement from the parents or guardian.

IRREGULARITY.

11. The pupil cannot appreciate too highly the importance of continuing in school until the term has closed; the practice of leaving the school near the close of the term is exceedingly injurious, both to those who leave and those who remain. It is earnestly desired of parents and guardians, that they use their influence effectually to do away with this evil, and all the evils of irregular attendance.

APPENDIX F.

BOOKS FOR TEACHERS.

Every teacher, who would hope to become truly useful and eminent in his profession, should cultivate a habit of reading. Remembering that "knowledge is power," he should be constantly learning. There are but few works of a strictly professional nature. These we shall enumerate first, and then give a list of books which will be found extremely valuable as books of reference. While we do not attempt to give the titles of all the good books now before the public, we do intend to name only such as we know to be valuable.

Theory and Practice of Teaching. By David P. Page, M. A., late Principal of the New York State Normal School.

The History of Education in Europe and America, collected from the most reliable Sources, with an Introduction, by Henry Barnard, LL. D. A work of great worth.

POPULAR EDUCATION. By Ira Mayhew, late Superintendent of Schools, Michigan. 12mo. pp. 467.

AMERICAN EDUCATION, — its Principles and Elements. By Edward D. Mansfield.

AMERICAN INSTITUTIONS, and their Influence. By Alexis de Tocqueville.

SCHOOL AMUSEMENTS; or, How to make the School Interesting. By N. W. Taylor Root.

DAVIES'S LOGIC OF MATHEMATICS. The Logic and Utility of Mathematics, with the best Methods of Instruction, Explained and Illustrated. By Charles Davies, LL. D.

The seven volumes named above are published by A. S. Barnes and Burr, New York, under the title of "School Teachers' Library." We will only say, that any teacher will find the volume first named worth far more to him than the cost of the entire set.

MY SCHOOL AND SCHOOLMASTERS; or, The Story of my Education. By Hugh Miller. Boston: Gould and Lincoln. 1 vol. 12mo. pp. 551.

This is the autobiography of a very remarkable self-educated man. It is an excellent illustration of the acquisition of knowledge and character under difficulties.

THE SCHOOL AND THE SCHOOLMASTER. In Two Parts. Part I. by Alonzo Potter, D. D. Part II. by George B. Emerson, A. M. 12mo. pp. 552.

THE TEACHER. Moral Influences employed in the Instruction and Government of the Young. By Jacob Abbott. 12mo. pp. 352.

The two volumes last named are published by Harper and Brothers, New York, and are worthy a place in every library.

THE FIRESIDE; or, Hints on Home Education. Boston: Crosby, Nichols, & Co. 16mo. pp. 325.

This volume abounds in valuable hints. It should be read by every teacher and parent.

THE LIFE AND CORRESPONDENCE OF THOMAS ARNOLD D. D.,

late Head-Master of Rugby School. By A. P. Stanley, A.M. London and New York. 8vo. pp. 490.

Locke Amsden; or, The Schoolmaster. By D. P. Thompson. Boston: Bazin and Ellsworth. 12mo. pp. 231.

Teaching a Science; the Teacher an Artist. By Rev. Baynard R. Hall, A. M. New York: Charles Scribner. 12mo. pp. 305.

The District School as it was. By Warren Burton. Boston: Phillips, Sampson, & Co.

The Teachers' Institute; or, Familiar Hints to Young Teachers. By William B. Fowle. 12mo. pp. 258.

The Teacher Taught; or, The Principles and Modes of Teaching. By Emerson Davis, D. D. 12mo. pp. 79.

The Teachers' Manual. By Thomas H. Palmer. Boston: Ticknor and Fields. 12mo. pp. 263.

Lectures on School-Keeping. By S. R. Hall. Boston: J. P. Jewett & Co.

Lectures on Education. By Horace Mann. 12mo. pp. 338.

Confessions of a Schoolmaster. By William A. Alcott, M. D. New York: Ivison and Phinney. 12mo. pp. 316.

Normal Schools, and other Institutions, Agencies, and Means designed for the Professional Education of Teachers. By Henry Barnard, LL. D. Hartford: Case, Lockwood, & Co. 8vo. pp. 435.

National Education in Europe: being an Account of the Organization, Administration, Instruction, and Statistics of Public Schools of different Grades in the different States. By Henry Barnard, LL. D. 12mo. pp. 878.

These two volumes by Dr. Barnard contain a vast amount of valuable information.

Educational Biography; or, Memoirs of Teachers, Educators, and Promoters and Benefactors of Education, Literature, and Science. By Henry Barnard, LL. D. Vol. I. New York: F. C. Brownell. 12mo. pp. 524.

This work promises to be one of rare merit and value, and well deserves a place in every teacher's library.

Reference Books.

SCHOOL ARCHITECTURE. By Henry Barnard, LL. D. With many Illustrations. New York: A. S. Barnes and Burr. Large 8vo.

PENNSYLVANIA SCHOOL ARCHITECTURE. A Manual of Directions and Plans for Grading, Locating, Constructing, Heating, Ventilating, and Furnishing Common School-houses. By Thomas H. Burrowes. 8vo. pp. 276.

COUNTRY SCHOOL-HOUSES: containing Elevations, Plans, and Specifications, with Estimates, Directions to Builders, Suggestions as to School Grounds, Furniture, Apparatus, &c., and a Treatise on School-house Architecture. By James Johonnot. New York: Ivison and Phinney.

The three volumes last named contain a vast amount of information on very important subjects. They should be in every school-teacher's library.

MENTAL PHILOSOPHY: including the Intellect, Sensibilities, and Will. By Joseph Haven, late Professor of Intellectual and Moral Philosophy in Amherst College. Boston: Gould and Lincoln. 12mo. pp. 58.

THE ENGLISH POETS. With Critical Notes. By Rev. J. R. Boyd. New York: A. S. Barnes and Burr.

This series of five volumes includes Milton, Young, Thomson, Cowper, and Pollok, — each made interesting and intelligible by judiciously arranged explanatory notes.

WEBSTER'S DICTIONARY, UNABRIDGED. This work, published by G. and C. Merriam, Springfield, Mass., should be in every library. No teacher can afford to be without it. It contains an inexhaustible fund of information.

WORCESTER'S DICTIONARY, UNABRIDGED. This work, published by Hickling, Swan, and Brewer, of Boston, will deserve a place in every library.

LIPPINCOTT'S PRONOUNCING GAZETTEER. A complete Pronouncing Gazetteer or Geographical Dictionary of the World. Philadelphia: J. B. Lippincott & Co. 12mo. pp. 2182.

This is unsurpassed, and indeed has no rival in the department of which it treats.

APPLETON'S CYCLOPÆDIA OF BIOGRAPHY, Foreign and American, embracing a Series of Original Memoirs of the most Distinguished Persons of all Times. With 600 Engravings. One large 8vo. A truly excellent and useful volume.

A BIOGRAPHICAL DICTIONARY: comprising a Summary Account of the Lives of the most Distinguished Persons of all Ages, Nations, and Professions. By John L. Blake, D. D. Philadelphia: H. Cowperthwait & Co. 8vo. pp. 1366.

APPLETON'S NEW AMERICAN CYCLOPÆDIA: a Popular Dictionary of General Knowledge. Edited by George Ripley and Charles A. Dana. New York: D. Appleton & Co.

This work is to be in fifteen volumes, large octavo. Six volumes have already been published, and from these we feel warranted in saying that the work is eminently worthy of public patronage. It will constitute a library of itself, — containing a vast amount of information on subjects in general and of prominent individuals. As a work of reference it will prove invaluable.

THESAURUS OF ENGLISH WORDS AND PHRASES: so arranged and classified as to facilitate the Expression of Ideas and assist in Literary Composition. By Peter Mark Roget. Revised and edited, with a List of Foreign Words defined in English, and other Additions, by Barnas Sears, D. D., President of Brown University. Boston: Gould and Lincoln. 12mo. pp. 510.

CRABB'S ENGLISH SYNONYMES EXPLAINED. With copious Illustrations and Explanations, drawn from the best Writers. New York: Harper and Brothers. 8vo. pp. 535.

ON THE STUDY OF WORDS. By Richard Chenevix Trench, B. D., Professor of Divinity, King's College, London. New York: Redfield. 12mo. pp. 231.

CHAMBERS'S CYCLOPÆDIA OF ENGLISH LITERATURE. Boston: Gould and Lincoln. 2 vols. 8vo. pp. 2400, and more than 300 elegant illustrations.

A selection of the choicest productions of English authors, from the earliest to the present time. A most valuable work.

CYCLOPÆDIA OF AMERICAN LITERATURE: embracing Personal and Critical Notices of Authors, and Selections from their Writings. From the earliest Period to the present Day. With Portraits, Autographs, and other Illustrations. By Evert A. Duyckinck and George L. Duyckinck. New York: Charles Scribner. 2 vols. Royal 8vo. pp. 1500.

The Encyclopædia of all Nations: comprising a complete Physical, Statistical, Civil, and Political Description of the World; exhibiting its various Rivers, Mountains, Lakes, Plains, &c.; the Natural History of each Country, Beasts, Birds, Fishes, Shells, Minerals, Insects, Plants, &c.; and the Productive Industry, Commerce, Political Institutions of all the Empires, Kingdoms, and Republics of the Globe; including the late Discoveries of Drs. Barth, Kane, and Livingstone. Also a General View of Astronomy. By Hugh Murray, F. R. S. E., assisted by Professors Jameson, Wallace, Swainson, and Hooker. Edited by Elbridge Smith, A. M., Principal of the Norwich Free Academy. The whole embellished with Maps, Charts, and over 1,100 Engravings. Norwich: Henry Bill. 2 vols. pp. 1670. Very valuable.

The Grammar of English Grammars. By Goold Brown. New York: W. and S. Wood. Large 8vo. pp. 1028.

This volume should be in the hands of every teacher. It is emphatically the Grammar of Grammars.

History and Chronology. The World's Progress. With Chart. 12mo. pp. 716.

General Literature and the Fine Arts. By George Ripley and Bayard Taylor. 12mo. pp. 647.

The Useful Arts. By Dr. Antisell. 12mo. pp. 690.

Universal Biography. By Parke Godwin. 12mo. pp. 821.

Universal Geography: a Comprehensive Gazetteer of the World. 12mo.

Science: including Natural History, Botany, Geology, Mineralogy, &c. By Samuel St. John.

These six volumes, published by S. A. Rollo & Co., New York, are intended to comprise a comprehensive view of the whole circle of human knowledge; in other words, to form a

General Cyclopædia in a portable shape, for popular reference, for family libraries, for teachers, for school libraries, and for the general reader.

OUTLINES OF UNIVERSAL HISTORY, from the Creation of the World to the Present Time. By George Weber. Boston : Hickling, Swan, and Brewer. 1 vol. Royal 8vo. pp. 559.

In this work we find the principles of historical perspective applied to the annals of the world with wonderful success. Though a vast multitude of objects are introduced to the reader, there is not the least indistinctness or confusion.

MATHEMATICAL DICTIONARY; and Cyclopædia of Mathematical Science. Comprising Definitions of all the Terms employed in Mathematics, — an Analysis of each Branch, and of the Whole, as forming a single Science. By Charles Davies and William G. Peck. New York : A. S. Barnes and Burr. 1 vol. 8vo. pp. 592.

ELEMENTS OF CRITICISM. By Henry Home, of Kames, one of the Lords Commissioners of Justiciary in Scotland. Edited by Rev. James R. Boyd. New York: A. S. Barnes and Burr. 12mo. pp. 486.

BOUVIER'S FAMILIAR ASTRONOMY: illustrated by Celestial Maps and upwards of Two Hundred finely executed Engravings. To which are added, a Treatise on the Globes, and a Comprehensive Astronomical Dictionary. Philadelphia : Childs and Peterson. 8vo. pp. 499.

FAMILIAR SCIENCE; or, The Scientific Explanation of the Principles of Natural and Physical Science, and their practical and familiar Applications to the Employments and Necessities of Common Life. Illustrated by nearly Two Hundred Engravings. By David A. Wells, A. M. Philadelphia: Childs and Peterson. 8vo. pp. 566.

MAURY'S GEOGRAPHY OF THE SEA. This excellent work is published by Harper and Brothers, New York. It is well illustrated with wood-cuts and charts.

THE EARTH AND MAN: Lectures on Comparative Physical Geography, in its Relation to the History of Mankind. By Arnold Guyot. Boston : Gould and Lincoln. 12mo. pp. 334.

THE HAND-BOOK OF HOUSEHOLD SCIENCE. A Popular Account of Heat, Light, Air, Aliment, and Cleansing, in their Scientific Principles and Domestic Applications. By Edward L. Youmans. New York: D. Appleton & Co. 12mo. pp. 470.

THE CHEMISTRY OF COMMON LIFE. By James F. Johnston. Illustrated with numerous Wood Engravings. New York: D. Appleton & Co. 2 vols. 12mo.

TREATISE ON ENGLISH PUNCTUATION. Designed for Letter-Writers, Authors, Printers, Correctors of the Press, and for School Use. With an Appendix, containing Rules on the Use of Capitals, a List of Abbreviations, Hints on Preparing Copy and on Proof-Reading, Specimen of Proof-Sheets, &c. By John Wilson. Boston: Crosby, Nichols, & Co. 16mo.

This is unquestionably the best work of its kind now before the public. Every teacher should own it.

Fowler and Wells, New York, publish some very good books. "How to Write," "How to Talk," etc. will be found exceedingly useful to all classes.

APPENDIX G.

BOOKS FOR SCHOOL LIBRARIES.

MANY school libraries have been established within the last ten years. The usefulness of these will depend greatly upon the character of the books selected to furnish them. The press is teeming with books for the young, but many of the volumes issued are entirely unsuitable, and their circulation will do harm and not good. The following we commend as interesting and instructive books for school or family libraries.

ROLLO'S TRAVELS. By Jacob Abbott. Rollo on the Atlantic; Rollo in Switzerland; Rollo on the Rhine; Rollo in London; Rollo in Paris; Rollo in Geneva, etc. 10 vols. Boston: Brown, Taggard, & Chase.

These are beautiful 16mo vols., each containing about 225 pages, and full of instruction pleasantly expressed. They will be read with pleasure and profit by adults as well as by children.

SEEDTIME AND HARVEST. Tales from the German of Rosalie Koch and Maria Burg. By Trauermantel. With six colored Illustrations. 1 vol. 16mo.

WELL BEGUN IS HALF DONE; AND, THE YOUNG ARTIST. Tales translated from the German. By Trauermantel. With six fine Illustrations, printed in oil colors. 16mo.

A WILL, AND A WAY. Tales from the German of T. Michel and Aug. Moritz. By Trauermantel. With six colored Illustrations. 1 vol. 16mo.

THE AGE OF CHIVALRY. Or, King Arthur and his Knights of the Round Table. By the Author of "The Age of Fable." Illustrated with Engravings. 12mo.

THE LIFE OF WASHINGTON, FOR CHILDREN. By E. Cecil. Illustrated with Engravings. 16mo.

NANNIE'S JEWEL-CASE; OR, TRUE STONES AND FALSE. Tales translated from the German. By Trauermantel. With six fine Illustrations, printed in oil colors. 16mo.

THE BOY OF MOUNT RHIGI. By Miss C. M. Sedgwick, author of "Home," "Live and Let Live." 16mo.

THE JUVENILE LIBRARY. By Mrs. Tuthill, Mary Howitt, and others. In sets of 14 volumes, uniform in size and style, embellished with engravings. Put up in neat boxes. 18mo. The titles are: — I will be a Lady; I will be a Gentleman; A Strike for Freedom; The Boarding-School Girl; Onward, Right Onward; Anything for Sport; Happy Days; Childhood of Mary Leeson; Ellen Stanley; The Boy of Spirit; When are we Happiest? Hurrah for New England; Keeper's Travels; The People of Bleaburn.

The twenty-one volumes last named are very neatly published by Crosby, Nichols, & Co. of Boston. They are at once attractive and instructive.

KNOWLEDGE IS POWER. A View of the Productive Forces of Modern Society and the Results of Labor, Capital, and Skill. By Charles Knight. Boston: Gould and Lincoln. 1 vol. 12mo. pp. 502.

FRANCONIA STORIES. By Jacob Abbott. New York: Harper & Brothers. 10 vols. 16mo. Comprising Malleville, Mary Bell, Ellen Linn, Wallace, Beechnut, Stuyvesant, Agnes, Mary Erskine, Rodolphus, and Caroline.

These are highly interesting stories, each complete in itself, — and imparting intellectual and moral instruction in a manner charming to the young.

ILLUSTRATED HISTORIES. By Jacob Abbott. New York: Harper & Brothers. Comprising 22 vols. 16mo, written in an attractive and interesting style, embracing biographies of the following persons: Cyrus the Great, Darius the Great, Xerxes, Alexander the Great, Romulus, Hannibal, Pyrrhus, Julius Cæsar, Cleopatra, Nero, Hernando Cortes, Alfred the Great, William the Conqueror, Mary Queen of Scots, Queen Elizabeth, Charles I., Charles II., Josephine, Marie Antoinette, Madame Roland, Henry IV., Christopher Columbus. These volumes may be had separately if desired.

MARCO PAUL'S TRAVELS AND VOYAGES, in the Pursuit of Knowledge. By Jacob Abbott. New York: Harper & Brothers. 6 vols. 16mo, each containing about 200 pages; being Marco Paul in New York, on the Erie Canal, in the Forests of Maine, in Vermont, in Boston, and at the Springfield Armory.

These volumes are at once amusing and instructive. They represent Marco Paul as a lad, travelling in the places named, under the guidance of a competent instructor, who, in an entertaining manner, imparts all desired information.

THE AIMWELL STORIES. Boston: Gould & Lincoln. This series is admirably adapted to amuse and instruct the young. There are 6 vols. 16mo. Being, —

I. OSCAR; or, The Boy who had his own Way.
II. CLINTON; a Book for Boys.
III. ELLA; or, Turning over a New Leaf.
IV. WHISTLER; or, the Manly Boy.
V. MARCUS; or, The Boy-tamer.
VI. JESSIE; or, Trying to be Somebody.

THE POOR BOY AND THE MERCHANT PRINCE; or Elements of Success, drawn from the Life and Character of the late Amos Lawrence. By William M. Thayer. Boston: Gould and Lincoln. 16mo. pp. 349. An excellent volume.

COWDERY'S MORAL LESSONS. Philadelphia: Cowperthwait & Co. A book worthy of a place in every school and family.

THE COTTAGE LIBRARY. 10 vols. This juvenile series was prepared by S. G. Goodrich, — widely known as Peter Parley. They are published in New York by Sheldon & Co., and are good books.

AUTOBIOGRAPHY OF BENJAMIN FRANKLIN: with a Narrative of his Public Services. By H. Hastings Weld. New York: Harper & Brothers. 8vo. pp. 549. This is a very interesting book.

MERRIE ENGLAND. By Grace Greenwood.

THE DESERT HOME; or, Adventures of a Lost Family in the Wilderness. With 12 Illustrations.

THE BOY-HUNTERS; or, Adventures in Search of a White Buffalo. With 12 Illustrations.

THE YOUNG VOYAGEURS; or, The Boy-Hunters in the North. With 12 Illustrations.

THE BUSH-BOYS; or, The History and Adventures of a Cape Farmer and his Family, in the Wild Karoos of Southern Africa. With 12 Illustrations.

TANGLEWOOD TALES FOR GIRLS AND BOYS. Being a Second Wonder-Book. By Nathaniel Hawthorne. With fine Plates.

A WONDER-BOOK FOR GIRLS AND BOYS. By Nathaniel Hawthorne. A Series of Six Stories, illustrative of Classical Mythology. Embellished with many beautiful Plates.

TRUE STORIES FROM HISTORY AND BIOGRAPHY. By Nathaniel Hawthorne. Comprising the whole History of Grandfather's Chair, and Biographical Stories of Benjamin West, Sir Isaac Newton, Samuel Johnson, Oliver Cromwell, Benjamin Franklin, and Queen Christina. With Illustrations.

The eight volumes last named are published by Ticknor & Fields, Boston, who also publish many other valuable works for libraries.

Delisser and Proctor of New York publish a very attractive series of books under the title of "The Household Library." The following are the titles: —

I. THE LIFE AND MARTYRDOM OF JOAN OF ARC. By Michelet.
II. THE LIFE OF ROBERT BURNS. By Carlyle.
III. LIFE, TEACHINGS, AND DEATH OF SOCRATES. By Grote.
IV. LIFE OF COLUMBUS. By Lamartine.
V. LIFE OF FREDERICK THE GREAT. By Macaulay.
VI. LIFE OF PETER THE GREAT.
VII. LIFE OF MAHOMET. By Gibbon, with Notes.
VIII. LIFE OF TORQUATO TASSO.
IX. LIFE OF OLIVER CROMWELL.
X. LIFE OF LUTHER. By Chev. Bunsen.
XI. DR. FRANKLIN'S AUTOBIOGRAPHY.

SPARKS'S LIFE OF WASHINGTON, and SPARKS'S LIFE OF FRANKLIN, are good books for school libraries.

ARCTIC EXPLORATIONS. The Second Grinnell Expedition in Search of Sir John Franklin, 1853, '54, and '55. By Elisha Kent Kane. Philadelphia: Childs & Peterson. 2 vols. 8vo.

This exceedingly interesting work is copiously illustrated, containing upwards of three hundred engravings from sketches by the author. It should be in every library of our land, and will be read with great interest by all classes.

SHIP AND SHORE, in Madeira, Lisbon, and the Mediterranean. 1 vol. 12mo.

LAND AND LEE. In the Bosphorus and Ægean; or, Views of Constantinople and Athens. 1 vol. 12mo.

Deck and Port; or, Incidents of a Cruise in the U. States Frigate Congress, to California, with Sketches of Rio Janeiro, Valparaiso, Lima, Honolulu, etc. 1 vol. 12mo.

Three Years in California. Being an Authentic History of California from the Time it came under the United States Flag down to the Present Time. 1 vol. 12mo.

The Sea and the Sailor. With Notes on France, Italy, &c. 1 vol. 12mo.

The five volumes last named were written by the late Rev. W. Colton, and they are at once interesting, instructive, and amusing. They are reliable works. Published by S. A. Rollo, New York.

Harper's Story-Books. A series of Narratives, Dialogues, Biographies, and Tales, for the Instruction and Entertainment of the Young. By Jacob Abbott.

There are some 12 or 15 volumes of these books already published, and they are full of instructive and entertaining reading. Published by Harper & Brothers, New York.

E. O. Libbey & Co., of Boston, have in course of publication a series of books for children, under the general title of "American Biography." Three volumes — "Captain John Smith," "Israel Putnam," and "Benedict Arnold" — have been published. They are well written and beautifully printed, and must be favorite books with the young.

From Poorhouse to Pulpit; or, The Triumphs of the late Dr. John Kitto, from Boyhood to Manhood. By William M. Thayer. Boston: E. O. Libbey & Co. 16mo. pp. 349.

Phillips, Sampson, & Co., Boston, publish a set of the Rollo Books, 14 vols., which are excellent for school libraries. The same firm publish many valuable books for libraries. Among them may be named Hume's and Macaulay's Histories of England; Prescott's Histories; British Essayists, etc.

APPENDIX H.

RULES AND REGULATIONS FOR SCHOOL LIBRARIES.

The following rules and regulations have been adopted for many of the school libraries of Connecticut. If they are not just what may be desired, they may prove valuable in a suggestive point.

"I. The district committee, clerk, and treasurer, shall constitute a Board of Trustees, who shall have a general charge of the Library, appoint a suitable person to act as Librarian, and said Trustees shall, at the annual meeting, make a report to the district respecting the number of volumes and condition of the Library.

"II. 1. The Librarian shall be responsible to the Trustees for all matters connected with the Library, and upon accepting the office, he shall give to the Trustees a receipt, containing the names of all the volumes, and stating the condition of the same, — and upon surrendering his trust, he shall give unto them a satisfactory account of the volumes intrusted to him. If new books are added after he enters upon his duties, he shall give to said Trustees an additional receipt, containing the names and condition of the same. For his services, the Librarian shall receive such compensation as the Trustees may decide to be sufficient.

"2. The Librarian shall keep a book in which he shall record the names of those entitled to receive books, and the number of each book delivered, the time of its delivery, and to whom delivered. He shall also keep a fair catalogue for the use of those who desire to select books.

"III. The Library shall be kept in such place as the Trustees may direct, and at the expense of the district.

"IV. Each book shall be well covered, distinctly numbered, and contain the name or number of the district to which it belongs, and no number shall be changed.

"V. Books may be drawn by the inhabitants of the district, subject to the rules and regulations hereafter named. Minors may draw in their own names, but on the responsibility of their parents or guardians. If the number of applicants for books shall, at any time, exceed the number of volumes ready for delivery, only one volume shall be allowed to a family.

"1. Only one volume shall be taken by one person at a time, and any one having drawn a book must return it before he can be allowed to draw another.

"2. Books may be drawn at such times as the Trustees may decide.

"3. No book shall be retained longer than two weeks at a time, — provided, however, if the same book is not wanted by any other person, it may be taken for an additional two weeks.

"4. The drawer shall be subject to a fine of 10 cents per week for every octavo kept more than two weeks, and 5 cents per week for every smaller work.

"5. If a volume is kept more than four weeks, the person so keeping it shall be notified of his delinquency by the Librarian, and if not returned within a week thereafter, it shall be considered as lost, and the holder be fined accordingly.

"6. If any volume shall be injured or destroyed, it shall be made good by the person in whose name it was drawn;

and if it belongs to a series, the damage to the set shall be paid.

"7. The Librarian shall have a set of these rules posted where they can be seen."

APPENDIX I.

APPARATUS, SCHOOL MOTTOES, RECORDS, ETC.

APPARATUS.

So far as possible, every school should have a supply of apparatus designed for the illustration of certain principles, etc. The use of this will tend greatly to interest and instruct pupils. The "Holbrook School Apparatus" is the only set within our knowledge intended expressly for our common schools. It is certainly a very useful set, and can be had at a very moderate price. It consists of the following articles: —

Orrery.
Tellurian.
Geometrical solids.
Terrestrial Globe.
Numeral Frame.
Magnet.
Text-Book, or Teacher's Guide to Illustration.

This apparatus, with many other valuable articles, is now manufactured and sold extensively by Geo. & C. W. Sherwood, Chicago, and may be made exceedingly useful in the hands of an intelligent teacher.

SCHOOL MOTTOES.

Short and appropriate mottoes learned by children will be remembered and felt during life. It is well for teachers to have them placed upon the school-room walls or upon the blackboard, and occasionally to make one the subject of conversation or remark.

I will try.

I will not be tardy.

Always ready.

Who does the best he can, does well.

I will never be absent.

Excelsior. Higher and higher; but only step by step.

"The pure in heart shall see God."

An error confessed is half redressed.

Speak the truth; act the truth; think the truth.

If we would excel, we must labor.

I can if I will.

I must try to do right.

Only the truly good are truly happy.

I must never violate my conscience.

Thou, God, seest me.

Always speak the truth.

Labor conquers all things.

Dare to do right.

Study first, — amusements afterwards.

By perseverance we overcome difficulties.

We must try to be good and do good.

Learning is better than silver and gold.

He liveth long who liveth well.

We must aim at thoroughness.

Never put off till to-morrow what can and should be done to-day.

I must obey my teacher.
We should be kind to our schoolmates.
"If sinners entice thee, consent thou not."
Better late than never, — but better still, never late.
If we would have friends, we must be friendly.
As we sow, so shall we reap.
A tree is known by its fruits.
We must not whisper in school.
Be slow to promise, quick to perform.
Do as you would be done by.
Diligence will insure success.
Evil communications corrupt good manners.
To err is human; to forgive, divine.
"A good name is better than great riches."
Fear God and keep his commandments.

SCHOOL RECORDS.

Every teacher should keep a careful record of the daily recitations and deportment of his pupils. It would, however, be a very difficult matter to give a formula adapted to the wants of all schools. Each teacher must aim to have one prepared with reference to the peculiar circumstances and classification of his school. In giving the following formulas it is intended merely to give such as may be used in our common schools, — and these even are designed to be suggestive, and not as models. If an account of recitations and deportment is recorded but once daily, form No. 1 will answer. In this case let each pupil be made responsible for his own report; — that is, let each be required to give, when called upon, the number of failures in recitation, and the number of errors in deportment, that he has made during the day. The teacher should also keep a private account, as a check against wrong reports from pupils. In form No. 1, the upper line denotes deportment, and the lower one recitations. At the close of each day, if a pupil has not failed in recitation, he will, when called upon, report "10," — denoting that all his recitations have been correct. If he has failed once, he will report "9," — twice, "8," etc. "10" will also denote satisfactory deportment, — and every deduction from that will denote a degree of deviation. In form No. 2, a record of each recitation is made at the time (say four times daily), and the deportment once daily, — the figure to the right of + indicating the deportment. In this 3 is the highest mark for each; 0 denotes an entire failure or defect, either in recitation or deportment; a *blank* denotes absence. It will prove very serviceable if an abstract from these records is sent to parents weekly or monthly.

No. 1.

Pupils' Names.	Mon.	Tues.	Wedn.	Thurs.	Friday.	Total.
Amos Dean	10 9	10 10	10 10	10 9	10 10	50 48
Moses Brown..........	8 9	9 8	10 10	7 9	9 10	43 46
John Hall.............						
Charles Ames..........	7 6		5 7	6 6		18 19
Mary Mason						
Ellen Stone						
Lucy Somers						
Sarah Lum............						

No. 2.

Pupils' Names.	Monday.	Tuesday.	Wednes.	Thursd.	Friday.	Total.
Frederic Churchill,	3,3,2,3+3	3,3,3,3+3	2,3,3,2+3	3,3,3,3+3	3,3,3,2+3	56+15
Frank Jameson,	3,3,3,2+3	3,3,3,3+3	3,3,3,3+3	2,3,3,3+3	3,2,3,3+3	62+15
George H. Clark,	2,3,2,2+2	2,2,3,3+3	3,1,2,3+2	2,2,1,3+2	2,1,3,2+2	44+11
William Northend,						
Chas. W. Tenney,						
Amos Dilatory,	1,2,1,2+1	2,1,1,2+2	2,1+1	1,2,2,2+2	3,1,2,1+0	29+ 6
Mary Stanley,						
Alice Tuck,						
Clara Nason,						
Ellen Bartlett,						

Note. — In the two forms given, it has been considered sufficient to fill only a few of the blanks, — enough to indicate the plan.

MANUAL EXERCISES.

It will contribute much to the happiness of pupils in primary schools if they are required several times, daily, to go through with certain manual exercises in concert. Such exercises will also be promotive of health. After a little careful practice, they will, with remarkable precision and readiness, assume the position as the teacher calls the number. Let perfect attention and promptness be required. Two sets of these exercises follow, and the teacher can add, change, or extend, as circumstances may render desirable.

Set No. 1.

1. Sit erect.
2. Fold arms.
3. Extend right hand.

4. Extend left hand.
5. Extend both hands in front.
6. Clap three times.
7. Place right hand on head.
8. Place left hand on head.
9. Raise both hands perpendicularly.
10. Clap twice.
11. All rise, — without noise.
12. All face the north.
13. All face the east.
14. All face the south.
15. All face the west.
16. All sit, quietly.
17. All take slates (or books), without noise.

Set No. 2.

1. Hands clasped and resting on edge of the desk.
2. Arms folded and sitting erect.
3. Arms folded behind.
4. Ends of fingers resting on shoulder.
5. Fingers meet on top of the head.
6. Palms of the hands meet above the head, with one clap.
7. Arms folded on the desk, head resting on them.
8. Arms akimbo, hands on the hips, fingers towards each other.
9. Right hand extending, left hand on the hip.
10. Positions reversed.
11. Both hands extended horizontally.
12. From the 11th position, hands brought up perpendicularly, fingers shaking.
13. Soft part of the ends of the fingers tapping on the desk, imitating the sound of rain.

14. Hands twirling one over the other, then brought suddenly to the desk with a noise.
15. Right hand extended, left hand on breast.
16. Positions reversed.
17. Both hands crossed on breast.
18. Arms extended forcibly and carried back.
19. All rise.
20. All sit.
21. Assume a devotional posture, — hands on the face, and head bending upon the desk.
22. Same as 1.

SUBJECTS FOR DISCUSSION.

If teachers would be truly successful, and keep alive a progressive spirit, they should hold occasional meetings of those employed in the same town, county, or State, for the discussion of topics of a common interest. Such meetings will prove highly beneficial to all concerned. The following subjects, and others suggested by them, may be very profitably discussed : —

1. The proper age for attending school.
2. The studies and exercises adapted to primary schools.
3. Requisites for success in a teacher of a primary school.
4. Should the Bible be used as an ordinary reading-book in schools ?
5. Ought the sexes to be educated together ?
6. Should our Common Schools be free ?
7. Should the Lancasterian system of teaching be encouraged ?
8. Some of the means for securing right discipline.

9. Is a resort to corporal punishment ever necessary?
10. If corporal punishment is inflicted, should it be done in the presence of the school?
11. Some of the means for true moral culture.
12. Ought the subject of "manners" to receive the attention of teachers?
13. Should youth be taught only those things which will be of practical use in life?
14. Ought Normal Schools to be supported by the State?
15. Some of the modes of teaching Reading; Spelling; Grammar; Geography; Arithmetic; Composition; Penmanship, etc.
16. To what extent should teachers render assistance to their pupils?
17. What influence and authority should a teacher aim to exercise out of school?
18. Should pupils be allowed to play in the school-room during intermission?
19. Has the teacher any duties relating to the school-house, yard, etc.
20. The evils of absence, and means for preventing the same.
21. The evils of tardiness, and means for preventing the same.
22. Will the possession of knowledge merely make one a successful teacher?
23. What are some of the requisites for success in teaching?
24. Some of the prominent causes of failure in teaching.
25. The best course to pursue in organizing a school.
26. Is it advisable to publish a special code of laws for the government of a school?
27. Should teachers keep a record of attendance, recitation, and deportment?

28. The duties of teachers to the parents of their pupils.
29. The duties of parents to teachers.
30. Object-lessons, — their importance and extent.
31. To what extent should oral teaching be adopted?
32. Should pupils be required to give answers in the precise language of the text-book?
33. *How many branches may a pupil profitably pursue at a time?
34. *Should pupils be required to study out of school hours?
35. What use should be made of the Bible in school?
36. What should be the frequency and length of recesses?
37. What exercises and amusements are best adapted to recesses?
38. Are school prizes or rewards to be commended?
39. Some of the means of interesting and advancing dull pupils.
40. Proper method of conducting recitations.
41. What should be the frequency and length of vacations?
42. How should examinations be conducted?
43. Some of the means of professional improvement.
44. The duties of a teacher to his profession.
45. How shall parental interest and co-operation be secured?
46. Some of the advantages of Teachers' Meetings and Teachers' Institutes.
47. The relation of Common Schools to higher institutions.
48. The true importance of *primary* schools.
49. The difficulties and trials incident to the teacher's vocation.
50. The pleasures and rewards incident to the teacher's work.

* The grade of school will modify this.

51. The rights of pupils.
52. Truancy, — its causes and cure.
53. The duties a teacher owes to the community.
54. The true relation of teachers and committees.
55. Should pupils be required to report their own accounts of deportment and recitations?
56. School exhibitions, — how to be conducted, and of what good.
57. The true aim of the teacher.
58. Which is the more important, — to keep youth from temptation to wrong-doing, or to teach them to withstand temptation when exposed?
59. The true relation of teachers and school committees.
60. Under what circumstances should pupils be expelled from school?
61. What should be the true object of all disciplinary measures?

THE END.

G. & H. M. SHERWOOD'S

PATENT INK WELL FOR SCHOOLS

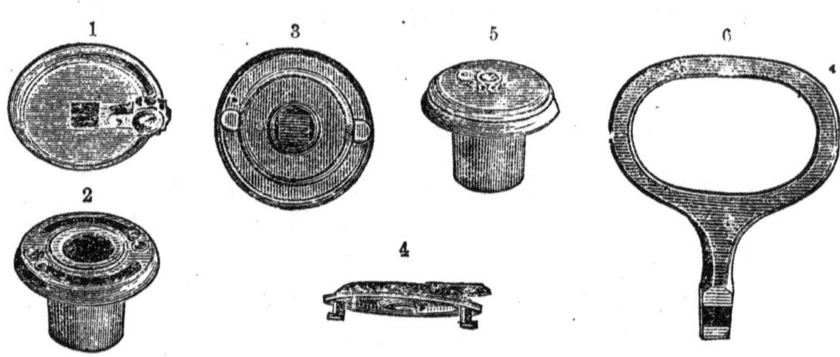

EXPLANATION.—Fig 1 represents a top view of the cover. Fig. 2, a top view of the well without the cover. Fig. 3, a bottom view of the cover. Fig. 4, an edge view of the cover. Fig. 5, a view of well complete. Fig 6, a key to screw on and unscrew cover. The Ink well (Fig. 5) is inserted into the desk through a hole bored for the purpose, so that the flange, (which is of considerably larger diameter than the body,) rests upon the surface of the desk, and is secured in place by screws inserted in countersunk holes. The flange of the well has turned down on its outer edge a lip, which alone rests on the desk, leaving a space within, below the interior part of the flange This space is provided for the purpose of allowing room in which pins or studs projecting downward from the lower side of the cover may freely move The pins have enlarged ends, or heads, (as seen in Fig. 4,) and are first inserted through apertures made large enough to admit them freely in the flange of the well, as represented in cut (Fig 2.) From these apertures extend concentrically in opposite directions, curved slots, just wide enough to allow the necks of the pins to pass freely, (as seen in Fig. 2.) The lower edges of these slots have a slight inclination downward from the apertures, so that as the cover is turned round the heads of the pins become wedged against the inclined surfaces, and draw the cover closely down upon the well on which it is made to fit tightly. The cover is fastened by means of a key, (Fig. 6)

This new Well is simple, and it is confidently believed that, while it contains the combined excellencies of the best wells now in use, it remedies the defects of al l:

1st. By this invention a very convenient, neat and secure fastening for the cover is produced which can only be removed with the key provided for it which is to be kept by the teacher or janitor.

2d. The Well itself, after being fastened by two common screws, never has to be removed—the glass lining only being removed when necessary for cleaning, which can be done by unscrewing the cap with a simple turn of the key.

3d. It will not get out of order, as by its simplicity of arrangement there is no lining to corrode. It cannot burst and spill the ink—and cannot be removed and lost by the pupils.

4th. It can be used in the holes where other wells have been inserted.

5th. It is economical, as the expenditure for each pupil (where double desks are used,) is but twelve and a half cents for his whole school going time.

Price of Ink Well per dozen, $3.50, necessary keys furnished gratis.

Address GEO. & C. W. SHERWOOD, 118 Lake Street, Chicago.

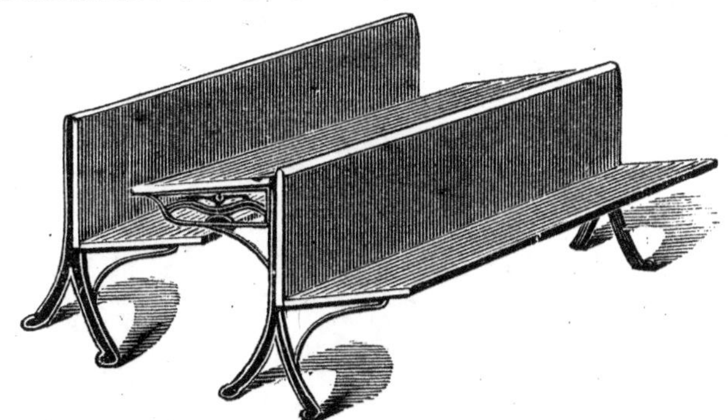

COMBINATION DESK AND SEAT.

Attention is particularly called to this design of Combination Desk and Seat, as being tasteful, convenient, cheap, and durable.

The Stanchions, or end pieces, are iron, to which the wood work is fastened with screws, making the Desk convenient for shipping, as it can readily be put together.

The expense of this Desk is but a trifle more than if made with clumsy wood ends, while it contains the essential requisites of a good Desk and Seat, being convenient to sweep around, and the shape of the end pieces allows the pupil to get in and out of his seat without difficulty. It is durable, and withal tasteful in its appearance.

The standard length of this desk is three feet six inches, for two pupils, and it is made of four different sizes, with seats from 16 to 12 inches high, to accommodate all grades of pupils—size A being the highest, then B, C, and D, graded in regular order. In addition, there is a Back and Seat, made to correspond with the others to place in the rear of the room, or for a recitation seat. The Desk is permanently fastened to the floor by means of screws. In grading where different sizes are required in the same room, the smallest size should be placed in front, and the largest at the back of the room. Care should be taken in ordering, to have all in each row across the room of the same size.

Price, nicely finished, supplied with best Ink Well, screws for fastening, and all complete, boxed and delivered at any depot in the city.

Address,

GEO. & C. W. SHERWOOD,
118 Lake Street, Chicago, Ill.

Samples always on exhibition at our Store.

☞Our Catalogue of School Furniture sent on application.

Speak gently to the little child
So guileless & so free
Who with a trustful loving heart
Puts confidence in thee
Speak not the cold & careless thoughts
Which time has taught thee well
Nor breathe one word whose bitter tone
Distrust might seem to tell -

If on that brow there rests a cloud
However light it be
Speak loving words & let him feel
He has a friend in thee
And do not send him from thy side
Till on his face shall rest
The joyous look & beaming smile
That marks a happy breast.

Oh teach him this - this should thy aim be
To cheer the aching heart
To shine when thickest darkness reigns
Some radiance to impart
To spread a peaceful quiet calm
When dwells the noise of strife
Thus doing good & helping all
To spend thy whole of life

To love

www.ingramcontent.com/pod-product-compliance
Lightning Source LLC
LaVergne TN
LVHW010144110826
845151LV00002B/420

9781425537647